Agrarian Economy of Ancient India

Agrarian Economy of Ancient India

Gian Chand Chauhan

Published by
ATLANTIC
PUBLISHERS & DISTRIBUTORS (P) LTD
7/22, Ansari Road, Darya Ganj,
New Delhi-110002
Phones : +91-11-40775252, 23273880, 23275880, 23280451
Fax : +91-11-23285873
Web : www.atlanticbooks.com
E-mail : orders@atlanticbooks.com

Branch Office
5, Nallathambi Street, Wallajah Road,
Chennai-600002
Phones : +91-44-64611085, 32413319
E-mail : chennai@atlanticbooks.com

ISBN 978-81-269-1804-1

Printed in India at Nice Printing Press, A-33/3A, Site-IV, Industrial Area, Sahibabad, Ghaziabad, U.P.

Prologue

The topic *Agrarian Economy of Ancient India* (From the earliest times to 1200 C.E), appealed to me and I took it up. But it presented difficulties partly because I am not a Sanskritist and partly because the literature of ancient India is a storehouse of human experience and wisdom gathered in course of ages, and religious in nature. It is so vast and scattered that there is scarce material in them on agrarian economy. The chronology of these traditions, literary as well as the epigraphical, are uncertain. Another difficulty in studying the agrarian economy of ancient India lies in the fact that in spite of many common features, Indian agrarian system has regional variations and differentiations. Moreover, it has intimate linkages with other forms of agrarian economy, like pastoralism, land economy, economic thought and feudal economy, etc. In view of paucity of early works on agrarian economy, along with the predominance of official orientation of literary and epigraphical traditions and amorphous nature and regional variations, it is an onerous job to present the agrarian economy of ancient India in its true perspective. The present work is a synthesis and summation of existing knowledge on the agrarian economy of ancient India on the combined bases of archaeological and literary traditions of ancient India.

It was a tremendous task to do full justice to this topic. I do not therefore claim to have drawn a complete and finished portrait and I do not claim this to be pioneer work, and hope that the material that I have been able to lay my hands on, its systematic presentation, and the inferences that it has led me to draw, may form an interesting and attractive book on ancient Indian agrarian economy.

The most fateful change in the human history might have occurred some ten thousand years ago when the transition from hunting—gathering to farming took place. During the preceding 150,000 years, anatomically modern humans had successfully inhabited almost all habitable and accessible regions on the earth and in so doing had learned to subsist, as 'hunter-gatherers', on a great diversity of plant and animal foods. But human population densities remained low throughout these many millennia. However, the most fundamental and far-reaching consequences of the 'agricultural revolution' in the early Holocene period was that it enabled more food to be obtained, and more people supported, per unit area of exploited land. It thus facilitated long-term sedentary settlement and the maintenance of larger and more complex social groups, which in turn enabled urban society to develop.[1]

Credit goes to human beings for the origin of agriculture and its growth, as they continued to practice, evolve and develop the science of producing food in its manifold aspects in all ages and all over the world. V.C. Srivastava rightly holds that the history of agriculture is practically co-terminus with the history of civilization. The story of agriculture, from the earliest stage of incipient farming along with gathering in the Mesolithic period, to biotechnological and genetic farming of the present century is interesting, engrossing and instructive. It is linked with the evolution of man on one hand and associated with the latest scientific and technological culture of recent times on the other.[2]

With the passage of time agrarian affairs like other affairs had undergone a process of evolution which was the result of innumerable contributions by ancient economic thinkers. They played a key-role in the agrarian affairs of the early Indian kings/states. Thus, the early Indian rulers/states themselves took part in a number of economic activities keeping a close watch and control in sectors like trade, treasury, commerce, agriculture, land system and labour problems, etc.

However, ancient Indian economic thought is a field still practically untilled, and economic thought in any age only reflects its time and life. It moves with the variation of economic condition. The economic interpretation of our past economy is one of the first fruits of the study of early Indian economic thought which enabled us to visualize not only the life of our ancestors but also helped us to recognize and interpret even the purpose of their everyday economic activities and affairs. Our knowledge of early economic thought acknowledged the contribution and role of great thinker like Kautilya and established his due position among the economists of the world.

The economic thought of any civilization or age was the reflex of the life of humans of that age or civilization, and the economic life of any people or epoch is again conditioned and programmed very largely by their natural and social environment. The physical background of ancient Indian agrarian economy could hardly have been very different from what it is in the present-day economic scenario.

The origin, antiquity and sources of agriculture and pastoralism in ancient India are very vexed, hazy and controversial. As the issues are associated with prehistoric culture, literary traditions are of no use. Fortunately, archaeological material has recently been retrieved to throw useful light on these problems. "These materials have been reported from sites of Vindhya-Ganga regions of Koldihwa, Mahagara, Kunjhun, Panchoh, Chopani-Mando, Tokwa, Narhan, Chirand, Senuwar, etc. Plant remains, agricultural tools and pots, dental pathology, settlement remains, etc. have been utilized to throw light on the origin and antiquity of cultivation in India."[3] The antiquity of cultivation of plants in the Indian subcontinent may be traced back to seven to six millennium B.C., if not earlier, in our present state of knowledge.

The growing of crops and the rearing of cattle and domestication of animals are indispensable ingredients of agrarian economy and the significant step in a chain of operation which provided foodstuff for ancient man. Thus, the study of the origin of agriculture and pastoralism in ancient India is currently engaging the attention of the scholars, and it continues to baffle the scholars of ancient Indian economic history.

It is stated that the ancient agrarian community came into existence when groups of wandering hunters and gatherers settled down upon the land, i.e. during the agricultural state in the development of human civilization. Man first roamed the forest in search of food, but later learnt to cultivate the land and domesticate the cattle. Food production marked the first revolution in human history, and agriculture led to the growth of permanent settlement of agrarian communities.

The study of the agrarian economy of ancient India is engaging the attention of the present-day scholars of the ancient Indian history. It continues to baffle the scholars. There have been few valuable publications in the past which depict the economic life and agrarian structure in ancient India. Agrarian economic formation has found mention as a chapter or an article in many works. This book is an attempt to make a critical analysis of one of the most critical phases of Indian history with main focus on the agrarian development in ancient India.

The primitive people were not aware of the art of cultivation; they wandered from place to place in search of food and water. But the transition from a wandering life to a settled agricultural life was a long and eventful process. Finally, land not only became the main source of livelihood but also a vital bond of union of all the members living in a particular place. It bound together all the inhabitants who guarded their land zealously from external aggression. This was how the agrarian communities came into existence.

Land was the backbone of agrarian economy in ancient India. It has, however, not been given proper attention by the historians to the extent that it rightfully deserved. At the best it has been assigned the secondary importance in order to understand the agrarian economy of ancient India. As ancient Indian economy was predominantly agrarian in nature and largest segment of society lived in villages and survived on agriculture, needless to say that any study of ancient Indian agrarian economy without having a bearing on this aspect is likely to be misleading and liable to depict a partial or distorted view of the ancient Indian land economy.

The peasants in ancient India were quite conscious of the nature of land and its relation to the production of a specific crop of economic importance. The vast knowledge acquired by experience was handed over from generation to generation. It was very intelligently and ably moulded in the form of maxims, proverbs, etc. which were some sort of guidance to the peasants. Ancient Indian peasants were trained enough for the choice of a particular land for a particular crop and they were conversant with the principles of farming.

Land-grants have been assigned a vital role in the agrarian economy of ancient India. No other single phenomenon has been ascribed so much value in Indian history as that of the land grants. Feudalization, ruralization, regionalization, stagnation and backwardness of ancient Indian society, economy and state are traced back to a single factor—that of the land grants.[4] The importance of the study of land-grants emerges from current understanding of the nature and the manner in which land grants were drafted, which provide us a first-hand information regarding the agrarian economy of ancient India. Lands were donated to *brāhmaṇa*, religious establishments, servants and state officers for various services they provided to the state or king. However, land-grants have been given the blanket characterization of being tax-free donation by the state authority, and private individuals and subordinate rulers. Besides, because of their absolutely tax-free nature, the land-grants have also been taken for granted for their entirely charitable characters, bringing nothing in return to the state.[5] But the careful examination of land charters shows that both these presumptions about the nature of land-grants are incorrect. It is thus observed that the fashion of land donation in ancient India hit the economic interests of the state, and the state controlled economy was transformed into feudal economy, and might have proved suicidal for the state and the kings.

The society was fragmented into groups such as landlord, *brāhmaṇa*, land intermediaries and *sāmanta*. All sections of primary producers used to live in the villages. Hence, there was a lack of circulation of coins, which restricted the growth of money economy. The declining process of money economy gave rise to exchange of services and barter system. From the very dawn of civilization, commercial routes followed by the Buddhist monks played a leading role to harmonize the unevenly distributed economic resources over the earth. Through certain trans-country commercial routes, particular goods tended to flow from places where they were plentiful, to those in which scarcity existed, to balance the surplus production. The main proto-historic commercial routes between early China and India became the great commercial trans-continental link routes. Therefore, it was an attempt made to establish the commercial linkages and interaction between the two ancient cultures of Asia with emphasis on various trans-country routes, through which the Indians and Chinese exchanged their trade goods.

The book traces the origin of agriculture and pastoralism in ancient India. It describes the economic thought as gleaned from Kautilya's *Arthashstra* and land rights prevailing in earlier times. Paradigms of land tenure and settlement of disputes have been discussed in an exclusive chapter. Land measurement, economic dimensions of land grants and feudal economy of early medieval North India have also been included. The book will be useful for students, and teachers of economics and researchers in this field, particularly agrarian economy of ancient India.

Gian Chand Chauhan

NOTES

1. Danial R. Harris, (ed.), *The Origins and Spread of Agriculture and Pastoralism in Eurosia*. London, 1996, p. 9.
2. L. Gopal and V.C. Srivastava (eds.), *History of Agriculture in India*, Vol. I, Part 1. Delhi, 2008, p. 29.
3. *Ibid.*, p. 30.
4. Om Prakash. *Early Indian Land-Grants and State Economy*. Allahabad, 1988, p. 1.
5. *Ibid.*, p. 2.

Contents

Abbreviations

ABORI	Annals of the Bhandarkar Oriental Research Institute, Poona
Āit. Br.	Āitareya Brāhmaṇ
Agni P.	Agni-Pūrāṇa
AHI	Aśoka and His Inscriptions by B.M. Barua
Āpastamba	Āpastamba Dharmasūtra
AŚ	*Arthāśāstra of Kauṭilya*
AV	Atharvaveda
Baudhayāna	Baudhayāna Dharmasūtra
BORI	Bhandarkar Oriental Research Institute
Bhāg. P.	Bhāgavata Pārāṇa
Brāh. P.	Brāhmaṇda Pūrāṇa
Br. S.	Brhaspatismṛti
BRWW	Si-Yu-Ki—Buddhist records of the Western World, Vol. IV, by S. Beal
BSS	Baudhayāna Srautasūtra
Chānd, Up	Chāndogya Upaniṣad
D. Bud.	Dialogues of the Buddha
Gautama	Gautama Dharmaśāṣtra
Gopatha Br.	Gopatha Brāhmaṇa
A.H.I.	(ed.) L. Gopal-&-Śrivastava, History of Agriculture in India, Vol. I, Part-I
Indica	Journal of Haras Institutes of Indian History and Culture, Mumbai
IA	Indian Antiquary, Bombay
IAR	Indian Archaeology: A Review

HIS	Indian Historical Studies, Tiruchirapalli
IF	*Indian Feudalism* by R.S. Sharma
JASB	*Journal of Asiatic Society of Bengal*, Calcutta
Jāt	*Jātakas*
JASM	*Journal of the Asatic Society*, Bombay
JBORS	*Journal of the Bihar and Orissa Research Society*, Patna
JGRI	Journal of the Ganga Nath Jha Research Institute, Allahabad.
JNSI	Journal of the Numismatic Society of India, Allahabad
JOI	Journal of the Oriental Institute, Badodara.
JRAS	Journal of the royal Asiatic Society of Great Britain and Ireland, London
Kama S.	Kāmasūtra of Vātsyāyana
Katya S.	Kātyayanasmṛti
Life	Life of Hiuen-Tsang by S. Beal
Malavikag	Mālavikagnimitra of Kalidasa
Manus	Manusmṛti
Mat. P.	Matsya Pūrāṇa
Mbh	Mahābhārata
Megas	Ancient India as Described by Megasthenes and Arrian, ed. by J.W. McCrindle
MPE	Minor Pillar Edict of Aśoka
MRE	Minor Rock Edict of Aśoka
Nār S.	Nāradasmṛti
R.J.S.S.	Research Journal Social Sciences, P.U. Chandigarh
P.U.L.R.	Panjab University Law Review, P.U. Chandigarh
PE	Pillar Edict of Aśoka
QRHS	The Quartly Review of Historical Studies, Kolkata

Raghu	Raghuvaṁsa of Kalidasa
Rājatar	Rājataraṅgiṇi of Kalhana, trans. By M.A. Stein
Rama	Rāmāyaṇa
RE	Rock Edict of Aśoka
RV	Rgveda
Sak	Śakuntala of Kālidasa
Sāma V.	Sāmaveda
SBB	Sacred Books of the Buddhists
S.B.E.	Sacred Books of the East
SBH	Sacred Books of the Hindus
Śat. Br.	Śatapatha Brāhmaṇa
S.H.C.	Studies in History and Culture, Berhampur
Skanda P.	Skanda Pūrāṇa
ŚP	Śāntiparva
Śūdra	Śūdras in Ancient India by R.S. Sharma
Taitt. Br.	Taiṭṭiriya Brāhmaṇa
Taitt. Sam	Taittiriya Saṁhitā
Vayū. P.	Yayū Pūrāṇa
Vās	Vásiśtha Dharmasūtra
Vik	Vikramvoraṣiya of Kalidasa
Viṣṇū P.	Viṣṇū Pūrāṇa
Viṣṇū S.	Viṣṇusmṛti
Yajñ S.	Yajñavalkyasmṛti

Economic Thought as Gleaned from the Kauṭilya *Arthaśāstra*

1

The economic affairs like other affairs had undergone a process of evolution and were the result of innumerable contributions by ancient economic thinkers. They played a key-role in the economic affairs of the early Indian kings/states. Thus the early Indian ruler/state itself took part in a number of economic activities keeping a close watch and control in sectors like, trade, treasury, commerce, agriculture, industries and labour problems, etc. The role played by various economic thinkers in the process of its evolution had been uneven. Some-thinkers appeared like luminous stars like Kauṭilya and dazzled everything in sight, while others appeared rather dim. However, the economic thought of some early Indian thinkers were not very significant, when they were propounded, but every contribution had its own place and relevance in the origin and of growth of early Indian economic phenomena.

However, Early Indian Economic thought is a field still practically untilled, and economic thought in any age only reflects its time and life, it moves with the variation of economic condition. Our knowledge of early economic thought acknowledged the contribution and role of great thinker like Kauṭilya and obtained for him his due position among the economists of the world.

As human knowledge can be analyzed and categorized into different sciences, economic science in ancient India was also a result of the some process which deals with the economic phenomena of human life. However, it can be interpreted as the set of theories, doctrines, laws and analyses applied to the study and solution of economic dimension and problem. But economic thought was not a given and fixed set of economic theories or tools and mechanisms of analyses. However, in present day economics scenario, economics is a dynamic science, a feature which acquires an account of various reasons. Since human society is a complex phenomenon, a very large number of courses are likely to be at work in most cases. The different scholars could very well differ as to the choice of most relevant courses at work. An economy is a dynamic phenomenon and therefore, economic science is a dynamic one with social change, new economic questions present themselves. And man's thinking is influenced by his social and physical environment. Since, the economic thought developed along two lines. One hand, within the basic framework of a free economy and its institutional set up, there is always a scope for deeper and intensive investigation which provides a basis for further analyses and theorizing. On the other hand, the very dynamism of an economy provides a basis for further investigation. In a closed or feudal economy, there is not much scope for further investigation. But free economy poses new challenges which economic thinkers have to meet.

Thus, it seems that science of economics is change oriented. Over successive time intervals, specific sets of economic ideas, theories, doctrines, tools and techniques acquire recognition and acceptance implying thereby that different contexts. We have different system of economic thought. Therefore, the study of the economic thought of Kauṭilya's automatically becomes the study of various system of economic thought of Ancient India.

The economic thought of any civilization or age was the reflex of the life of human of that age or civilization, and the economic life of any people or epoch is again conditioned and programmed very largely by their natural and social environment. The physical background of ancient Indian economy could hardly have been very different from what it is at present day economic scenario. For example, the dependence of our agriculture on the monsoon and on the water supply will explain not merely the emphasis laid by the government of the present day as the provision of vast schemes of protective irrigation, but they will show, how, in ancient India, the provision of similar works utility was justified as much by economic statesmanship of Kauṭilya that rural bodies or villagers should maintain an efficient system of irrigational tanks and channels of villages. Those who damage lakes, embankment and works of irrigation would be penalized.[1]

The Arthaśāstra a work of substantial importance has been attributed to Kauṭilya, who was not only a thinker of ancient India but also a powerful statesman. He was not only a great political thinker but was a great economist of his times, played dominating role in the formation of the Mauryan Empire that expelled the Macedonian army from India. His role in the field of scholarship is undoubtly laudable, gave detailed analysis of different aspects of early Indian economy. Kauṭilya and his master work *Arthaśāstra* are misunderstood. Historians and economists are of the opinions that in early India kings were self-centred and their concern was the attainment of personal aggrandizement. But it is simply misconception and the misunderstanding of the scholars. We glean from *Arthaśāstra* (hereafter as *AŚ*) various welfare measures of the state for its subjects, it speaks of king's aims:

"In the happiness of his subject lies the king's happiness; in their welfare his welfare. He shall not consider as good only that which pleases him but treat as beneficial to him whatever pleases his subject."[2] For clear comprehension of Kauṭilya's economic thought and apply them judiciously to the present economic scenario, then we have to be aware of the essential characteristics of the core content of the *AŚ*. The *AŚ* speaks of every significant features of early Indian economy, such as, agriculture, mining accomplished by state and private sectors as well as by joint enterprises. Industries and forestry, transport, trade and commerce, taxation, wages, allowance, salaries, social security, replenishment of treasury during emergencies, provision for uniform weights and measurement, fixation of percentage of interest, regularization of marketing of commodities etc.[3] Kauṭilya states that if state passes through a deep economic crisis in that situation king should direct the superintendent of the temples to collect the property, money gold, silvers of the temples and deposit them in the state treasury.[4] The *AŚ* speaks that "a person cannot acquire and maintain wealth, who possessed deep faith in astrology". It is stated that "wealth will pass away from the childish man who constantly consults the stars; for wealth what will the stars do". Men without wealth do not attain their object even with hundreds of efforts; objects are secured through objects, as elephants are through elephants set to catch them.[5] Thus Kauṭilya advised the king not to adopt such religious beliefs which put hurdle in the execution of his important programmes. He should not hesitate to prescribe for the deposition of the wealth and property of temples in the state treasury during the grave economic emergency.

Early Indian literary traditions refer four branches of knowledge such as, philosophy, religion, economic and polity. The term *Vārtā* (economics) is referred in *AŚ* which primarily represents *Vṛṭṭi* or means of livelihood. It is very clearly depicted in *AS* that *Vārtā* deals with agriculture, cattle breeding and trade.[6] But in modern nomenclature, *Vārtā* deals with the economic of agriculture, trade, banking and industry, which shows that consumption, distribution, and taxation, forming a modern economic were left out of the scope of *Vārtā*. It seems that *Artha* and *Artha-Śāstra* were quite distinct,[7] the later never deals with the *artha* in the sense of wealth, which was the subject matter of *Vārtā*. Ancient literary traditions of India fully recognized the significance of economic science where the *Vārtā* was considered as essential for the material interest of the people as were the *Vedas* for their spiritual well-being.[8] K.V.R. Aiyangar rightly argued that the "aim of the ancient Indian conception of wealth was to be its material quality, its appropriability, its being the result acquisition, its not being quite identical with gold, its consumability, and its attractiveness due to scarcity".[9]

Ancient Indian thinkers were aware of the significance of wealth in the scheme of life for the gaining the ends of human life, and were fully conscious of depressing influence of poverty. Wealth however, was regarded as an end in itself, but as a means to an end. Contrary to common notions, they condemned asceticism and held those seeking to embrace the ascetic order without discharging their duties liable to punishment,[10] both ancient and modern economists, give predominance to rural economies, because agriculture has been the occupation of the pupils throughout ages. Along with cattle breeding and doing farming agriculture contributed the most important part of *Vārtā*, which a king was enjoined to study. The *AŚ* speaks that concerted efforts of the state are essential to attain growth with stability in the field of state agricultural production. It is further stated that for enriching the state treasury, abundance of harvest was considered absolutely essential. Thus the attainment of maximum agricultural production was considered as basic requirement for the welfare of the subject and strengthening the state. Farmers were under an obligation to cultivate their fields. It was punishable offence for a farmer, or a tenant, to neglect or abandon his field at the time of sowing or for the farmer to take away the land from tenant; only when circumstances were such that cultivation was impossible was this obligation lifted.[11] Thus it seems that development of land was the principal factor in the success of agriculture. The state and the people were enjoined to strive for the prosperity of agriculture. The interests of the peasantry were guarded against distraction or nuisance by banning the intrusion of non-productive classes such as actors, dancers, singers, drummers, buffoons and wandering minstrels into village."[12] The state officers and servants were to live outside the limits of the village apparently to save peasantry from oppression. The *AŚ* prescribes that army men should not enter into villages except in emergency they were not to oppress peasants or have any dealings with them. It was further depicted that the army was to be used for no other purpose than fighting.[13] The economic interest of the farmers were safeguarded by fixing fair prices with a view to lowering agricultural prices.[14] A. Dasgupta rightly argues that "The Mauryan state attached considerable significance to the landholding, settlement and cultivation of land."[15] The *AŚ* prescribes that the state should bear in mind the settlement of the agricultural region, which had settled before, or which had not been settled before, by bringing in people from foreign lands or by shifting the overflow of population from his own country.[16] It is prescribed by Kauṭilya that in newly settled villages, agricultural operations were carried through after preparing the waste land. He states that such land worth of cultivation should be settled permanently, and economic burden should not be put on peasants, who cultivated waste land, but they should be provided with cattle and seeds to colonise waste land. It was also kept in mind that local markets were to be founded for the sale of agricultural produces and variation of fertility was to be considered while fixing the taxes on peasantry.[17] The productivity of piece of land was dependent not merely on its soil, irrigability and cultivability, but on its quality of extension, size, situation and accessibility. The *AŚ* speaks of certain penalties if some body abstract agricultural operation. If a person forcibly occupied the land of other, he was to be punished like a thief. Encroachment and destruction of boundaries were considered serious offences, encroachers and guilty were fined 24 *pāṇas*. If the person encroaches land of other during the time of sowing seeds was to be punished with 12 *Pāṇas*.[18] Kauṭilya refers certain penalties for harming pastures, which were considered beneficial for the development of agricultural economy. Extremely stringent punishment has been prescribed for setting fire to pastures. Such person if found guilty, was to be thrown into fire.[19] It seems that Kauṭilya prescribed such hard punishment only in order to check completely the deliberate burning of pastures. However, it must be admitted that prescription of such stringent punishment lacked humanitarian touch. The damage of crops of peasant by the cattle, the owner of the cattle was punished by imposing fine double the amount of loss incurred. If an owner of the cattle deliberately left them to stray, he was to be punished with a fine of 24 *pāṇas*.[20]

However, we notice certain incentives prescribed by Kauṭilya to peasants, who played very vital role in agricultural economy by producing food products not only for their family members but also for those who live is urban areas. The land tenures provided incentives to peasant for better participation in agricultural operation. Prepared land was allotted for lifetime to the peasants. The *AŚ* reveals that "unprepared lands shall not be taken away from those who are preparing them for cultivation".[21] The peasant should be provided relief by the state during the famine and other calamities, and they should be provided seeds and provision.[22] The *AŚ* further speaks of exemption from the payment of grain tax for year together, when they had contributed to improvement of infrastructure, such as the construction of new tanks, lakes, roads, etc., repairing neglected or ruined works of similar nature, taxes were remitted for years, for extending or restoring water sources, over-grown with weeds.[23] The *AŚ* prescribes proper arrangement for weight and measures for market places so that peasants could obtain reasonable price of their surplus yield. The peasants were duly helped by the state to utilize maximum irrigation facilities in order to raise production. The *AŚ* depicted the seasonal agricultural operations extremely essential, it is argued that peasants while engaged in agricultural works would not be arrested.[24] The peasants were given loans in forms of cash or kind. The rate of interest on such loans was at one *pāṇa* and a quarter per hundred, i.e. 15% per annum for non-commercial purpose. The rate of interest was higher if related to trade. Those who were engaged in overseas-trade had to pay at the rate of 20% which was highest. The Kauṭilya's theory of Interest in the field of agriculture varied between five times and one-third of the value of the quantity of pledged.[25] The *AŚ* tells us that interest on grain was not to exceed in season of good harvest, more than half when valued in terms of money. Interest as stocks was one half of the profit and it had to be regularly paid. If it was allowed to accumulate intentionally, the amount payable was to be equal to twice the share or its principal.[26] His theory of rate of interest reflects the welfare of the state. He states that, "the welfare of the state depends on the nature of the transactions. They should be properly scrutinized.[27] Thus the payment of interest when due only have been inforced through the power of law or else as Kauṭilya had so shrewdly observed. The welfare of the state would have been disturbed resulting in economic disturbance. This implied that public welfare depended largely on the economic dealing between debtors and creditors.

The *AŚ* has prescribed reasonable relief to debtors, who, due to circumstances over which they had no control, were unable to pay interest over period during which the disability on inability least, he argued that for non-accumulation of debts were minority of the debtors, illness, stay in the teacher's house (to complete education), engaged in a sacrifice lasting for a considered period and bankrupting or extreme physical infirmity and widow, etc.[28] Thus Kauṭilya reminded money-lender and state agencies of their social responsibilities by giving certain exemptions and relief's on the ground of their educational or socio-religious preoccupation which shows that Kauṭilya concern sociological values and mechanism to check the hardship of such categorizes of people living thereon. The land-system which has been referred in the *AŚ* time and again is debatable, and has been debated by the scholars since remotest time. The question of land ownership is still undecided, but the difference of opinion among the scholars reflects a difference on how ownership is to be defined, but it can be surmised that the actual position might have changed over the period of time. The *AŚ* recommended tax free land-grants to *Brāhmaṇa* priests, state official such as, superintendents, accountants, *gōpas*, *Sthānikas*, veterinary surgeon, physicians, horses trainers, and messengers,[29] might be in lieu of cash salary for their services, but they had no right to alienate it by sale or mortgage. Thus, the Mauryan State indicates the scarcity of coins and certain ingredient of feudal economy?

The Mauryan state took keen interest for the development of forests, of which it was the sole owner. The *AŚ* refers that it was the duty of the state to protect, develop, promote and maintain forest, emphasized the need of afforestation,[30] keeping in mind the enormous benefit of forest for mankind. Kauṭilya laid the duty of the superintendent of forest. The superintendent of forest shall collect timbers and other products of forest by employing those who guard productive forest, fixes adequate fines, which cause any damage to productive forest. It was further prescribed that state should establish productive forests, one for each important products, as well as factories for manufacturing goods made from the forest produce to enhance economy of the state.[31]

The great advance in agriculture in early India and the full knowledge of the minute details of agricultural pursuits possessed by ancient economist are seen in *Arthaśāstra* such as the concept of irrigation by rain, rivers, tanks, reservoirs. The numbers of villages were held jointly and severally liable for keeping, water, channels, and tanks in efficient repair, which ensured project maintenance of irrigational works. Any damage of such works of public utility was to be urgently rectified even from resources of temples. Special facilities were to be given to those who constructed tanks, dams, wells out of piety, so that the state might receive co-operation from individuals in providing irrigation works.[32]

Land revenue was the main source of income and formed an important ingredient of the Mauryan economic system. The *AŚ* refers one-sixth of state share as land revenue from the peasants. But during economic emergency,[33] the *AŚ* prescribes one-third or one-fourth as state share. Generally a large portion of the revenue was collected in kind, and the proper keeping and periodical/renewal of the collected stock was prescribed. Kauṭilya insists on a full and flowing treasury for the state by appropriating a large portion of the state revenue for the creation of a reserve fund or treasury, which was not to be touched except on occasion of a grave calamity.[34] Thus policy of Kauṭilya on economics is quite understandable when one considers the unstable political condition of the time demanding constant preparedness for war because of constant danger from neighbouring state. Thus, in early India, when state load was unknown, the only mean available for the state to tide over an economic crisis was the possession of a well-stocked treasury and granary. The *AŚ* depicted different sources of revenue differently at the different place. Two important categories were body of income and sources of income, each subdivided under seven heads.[35] For irrigated agriculture, a water rate was an even more important source of state revenue than the land tax.

This was payable whenever water for irrigations works was used by the peasants, even if the works belong to the peasant himself.[36] There was a graduated schedule of the rate to be changed, depending on the nature of the irrigation works used. If the works were such that the water was set in motion by land, the rate payable was one-fifth of the produce, if set in motion by shoulders, the rate was one-fourth, the latter rate also applied to lift-irrigation, water being lifted from tanks, wells, rivers and lakes while the rate increased to one-third when water was set flowing in channels by a mechanical device.[37] In all cases the water rate was addition to the normal land tax of one-sixth.[38] This means that a peasant utilizing mechanical irrigation which used flowing water were liable to pay half of his produce as tax. The *AŚ* presented certain exemption from water tax for limited period five years for newly built tanks and embankments, four years for ruined or abandoned tanks or renovated embankment, three years for those that one cleared after having become overgrown with weed.[37]

Now the question arises whether there were any limits to the state levying exorbitant taxes. Kauṭilya has considered the point, and he was of the view, that the threat of disaffection among the subject and their possible migration to another state appears to have worked as a deterrent on kings' taxing their subject beyond their means. The *AŚ* prescribes partial or total exemption of taxation, it is noticed that on humanitarian grounds certain classes of people like learned *Brāhmaṇas,* the dumbs, the deaf, the blind, student studying in a *Gūrūkula*, and hermits were exempted from paying taxes; infants, those far advanced in age, women newly confined or destitute, poor widows, and people otherwise helpless were also tax free.[39] Kauṭilya, prescribed special efforts by the state to enrich the treasury during economic crises, emergencies, besides benevolences, forcible loans and donations, emergency taxes, arbitrary enhancement of normal rates, and fraudulent and forcible collection under several pretexts, which are exhaustively dealt with by Kauṭilya, who prescribes to the sale of divine images and the entire property of the religious shrines was to be confiscated. The dramatists, singers, dancer, prostitutes had to pay 50% their income as compulsory payments to the state.[40] Thus certain undesirable methods to enrich the state treasury during economic crises was the practice of the Mauryan times. But state officials, drawing high amount as salary, were left unaffected during economic crises.

The development of mineral resources was the important state activity and special attention for the exploitation of mines was paid, and considered mining as the important source of state income. The mining during the Mauryan times was directly connected with various kinds of industrial production. The *AŚ* speaks of the opulence of industrial production contributed significantly in enriching the treasury. All mines belonged to the Mauryan state were put under the supervision of the superintendent of mines who must be an expert in *Sulbaśāstra* geology, and *dhatuśāstra,* metallurgy.[41] The digging of new mines and the renewal of old discarded ones was an important duty of the superintendent of mines. Kauṭilya states that those mines are the best which yield rich ores, are easily accessible and capable of being operated at a small cost. Diamond and gold mines were highly preferred.[42] But Kauṭilya was in favour of a large mine, even if it yields products of small economic value, as the ground that products of small economic value command continuous sale, but the product of high economic value have a limited sale and demand particularly among the common people.[43] Although all mines belonged to the state, but not all of them were to be worked directly by the state. The mines with high operating cost were leased out, on for a fixed rent.[44] Kauṭilya prescribes that all salt mines should be leased out for a share on hire.[45] Thus credit goes to Kauṭilya for providing new dimension to the exploitation of mines and setting up separate department for operating mine and manufacture of metals.

The early Indian economy was an agricultural economy; the fertile Indo-Gangetic plains provided ample scope for the greater industrial enterprise in the form of agriculture. But other industrials or agricultural products and natural wealth of the land also developed during Mauryan times. Sugar industry was the most important industry of early India. Kauṭilya suggests that the lands that are frequently overflown by water for long are suitable for growing sugar cane, and the forming of sugar-cane possessed the risk of facing flood or flood like situation, comparatively the cost of production of growing sugar-cane was much greater. The *AŚ* prescribes that the special efforts and expenditure were required for transporting and crushing reaped sugar-cane.[46] Thus the sugar production was considered most at difficult and worst in agricultural production system.

Another industrial activity of the Mauryan state which was given considerable attention was textiles. The Artisans of the Mauryan state had attained a high degree of proficiency in spinning and weaving fine textiles. The Mauryan economy was partly pastoral and partly agricultural. As such tending of cattle and shearing off goats and sheep hair constituted important occupation, resulting in the weaving of woolen clothes. Textile industries during the Mauryan were not state monopoly, but Kauṭilya refers to private production. However, the Mauryan state was expected to engage in production of textile on an extensive scale, and to maintain strict state control and supervision of that part of industry which was in private hand.[47] The *AŚ* refers to the *Sūtradhyakṣa* who was suppose to get yarn spun from wool, bark-fibre cotton, hemp and flax by woman, especially those without support, women from respectable families should be allowed to spin in their homes. The officers in change was directed to look after the manufacture of ropes, thongs and straps, useful for carts, chariots, etc., used in the army.[48] The *AŚ* prescribes that those women who do not stir out of their Houses, those whose husbands are gone abroad and those who are cripple or girls may, when obliged to work for subsistence, be provided with work in due courtesy through the medium of maidservant while making construction in a new fort, places were allotted to artisans in a corners of a fort, guild of artisans and cooperation of workmen resided within the fort. It was on the sweet will of the artisans to allow others of their profession to reside in the locality.[49] Thus besides giving protection to the workers and artisans, state also kept a strict watch over their mal-practices and mischiefs. Ratio of raw material and finished goods were fixed. Adulterations in commodities were properly supervised and monetary and corporal punishment was suggested to anti-social workers.[50] We notice plethora of reference to various guilds and corporations in *AŚ*. Kauṭilya states that the guilds of artisans as well as those who carry on any co-operative work shall divide their earning either equally or as agreed upon among themselves,[51] certain artisans working independently with their own capital and in their own work-shop. Whereas the artisans working in guild system, guaranteed the customer against loss, damage, etc., caused by artisans.[52] Even there were master artisans, employing a number of artisans to do work for the customers, and earning a profit, the delay in delivery and failure to carry out the customers instructions were offence punishable by the state. During the Mauryan times guild had become very rich and powerful and some of them maintained troops of their own. The *AŚ* refers to the danger of provoking these corporations and advocates several methods of exploiting them in the king's name.[53] The potential danger to the state from the unrestrained power to these guilds seems to underlie the severe regulation restricting their activities. Another important responsibility of the Mauryan state was to arrange for storage of a wide variety of goods. The construction of the stores is described at length. The part of the stores was made up of goods produced by state and enterprise, the rest was received by the state in kind. The store provided a convenient means of creating buffer stocks and preventing a wide fluctuation in rice, the director of the trade being expected to buy when there was a slut and sell when there was scarcity.[54]

The media of exchange was also an important ingredient of the Mauryan state. Throughout the Mauryan times, money has been an important media of exchange. It has on the one hand relieved the commercial and economic fields from the defects of barter system while on the other guaranteed a great impetus to payments for goods or carrying other kinds of business obligations. The *AŚ* refers to several types of coins, such as gold, silver and copper coins. The coinage was a state monopoly, and the special official under the Mint Master received bullion from the public to be struck into coins on payment of seignior age changes.[55]

Trade was one of the most significant economic activities in early Indian state. The Mauryan state received a large part of its income from trade and was having monopoly over the manufacturing of a large variety of goods. The *AŚ* tells us that it was made obligatory for traders to get licence, while, foreign traders were required to get passport in addition. Kauṭilya classified trade into two distant categories— *Svabhūmija*, indigenously produced or *parabhūmija*, produced in foreign lands. Indigenous good belonging to the state were sold in one place, presumably, the capital city, where all state stores were located. Imported goods were to be sold in a number of centres. In both the interests of the customers were to be kept in mind while fixing the selling price. The *AŚ* prescribes that a large profit must be avoided if it was harmful to the subjects, especially in the case of commodities constantly in demand.[56] The *AŚ* refers two factors to be considered in fixing value of price were (a) the cost of production as determining the supply; and (b) the demand for article as determined by its utility.[57] Whole scale price for goods were fixed by the superintendent of commerce, as they passed the custom house. A margin of profit was allowed to retailers. The public, consumers and customers were protected by the state, which employed an army of spies and market inspectors against unauthorized price and fraudulent transactions. Goods had to be sold at fixed market places, and the dealer had to specify particulars as to quality, quantity, and price, which were scrutinized and recorded in official book.[58] The superintendent of commerce not only prevented or minimized the chances of deceit, or of undue advantage being taken by the seller over the buyer, but also ensuring that the prices were not exorbitant or unconscionable, and that the material, its style, quantity, or measure precisely corresponded to the terms of the bargain.[59] Normally state goods were sold by the state officials but the help of private traders was sought. In that case, traders were required to pay a fee, to make up for the loss of profit which the state would have earned by sale through its officials.[60] The involvement of private traders in selling state goods indicates the ingredients of the privatization of trade even during the Mauryan period, which is considered the feature of present day economic trends and ideas.

The economic advantages of both inland and foreign trade were duly recognized. The organization of castes and guild led not only to localization of industry, but also to the creation of special local market for the sale of product. The freedom of the market was implied in the rule prohibiting the king from going into the market with his retinue. The existence of grade of middle men, between retail traders and the powerful magnates who were able to create 'corners' and to manipulate the market in their own interest was not only implied but provided against.[61] The officer in charge of trade was to arrange for the export of state goods to foreign lands. When undertaking such a venture, he was to taken to consideration all relevant factors such as costs of transport, duties prevailing prices in different places and so on to determine the profitable. He could also investigate the possibility of bartering state goods for those from foreign lands.[62] The general principle of export-import trade was to ensure profit. Should there be no profit, he should see it there is any advantage in taking out goods or in bringing goods in exchange for goods, and along river routes he should ascertain condition of trade before hand and should proceed to where there is profit, avoiding places where no profit can be had.[63] They had to secure new market for the surplus products of the country. Rest houses and store-houses were to be provided for traders, for whose protection proper police escorts were also recommended. River boats and ocean going ship were to be pressed into services. The *AŚ* prescribes that the state administration must grant it security against thieves, forest tribes, wild forest folk, etc., and undertook to make good losses in transit.[64] The *AŚ* further prescribes to encourage import, suitable-rebates to foreign traders, if current rate did not leave a proper margin of profit for them.[65] To encourage, promote, and facilitate trade, both inland and foreign, state were enjoined to improve and increase the means of communication and transports. Thus Kauṭilya refers several trading facilities which were afforded to encourage foreign trade. Foreign merchant could sue in Indian court, and were protected from being harassed by suits against them in local courts.

Kauṭilya accepted that in spite of all precautions; it was impossisble to eradicate corruption from amongst the state employees who participated in financial transaction. He states that "just as it is not possible not to teste honey or poison placed on the surface of the tongue, even so it is not possible for one dealing with the money of the state not to taste the money in however small a quantity".[66] The *AŚ* depicted that, just as fish moving under water cannot possibly be found out either as drinking or not drinking water, so the state employee carrying out state work cannot be found out while taking money for themselves. Kauṭilya prescribes the transfer of state employee from one work to another work or one place to another place, so they could not misappropriate government money,[67] thus it is very clear that the problem of corruption among the state employee is as old as early Indian state and not the practice of modern time only. It seems to be a universal practice from ancient to present time, which is not accepted fact in our modern administrative system. But *AŚ* also prescribes certain incentives to those employees who enhance the state revenue instead of eating it up, and loyally devoted to the state services, should be made permanent in state services.[68] Even *AŚ* refers forty ways of embezzlement of revenue of the state by its officials. All possible efforts were suggested by Kauṭilya to minimize the practices of corruption among the government employees.

The *AŚ* prescribes and discusses the principles on which salaries of the various state/government officers and employees should be determined.[69] The amount of salaries paid to different grades of employees during the Mauryan times reflected some basic aspects of an economy. Monthly salary was prescribed by Kauṭilya in terms of *Pāṇa*, which were legal tender as well as medium of exchange. A *Pāṇa* contained silver equal to three-fourth of *Tōlā* (10 gm).[70] The silver content of a *Pāṇa* in the present time will be approximately of the value of rupee fifty. The salaries were fixed on a cash basis but could be paid in kind or as a mixture of the two; a formula is given for converting a part of salary into a mixture of mostly grain and a little cash. An official could, in lieu of a part of his salary, be allotted land to be formed by him for his own benefit but such land could neither be sold nor mortgaged and could be used only as long as he held the office.[71] The paying state officers through land grants is the indication of the presence of the ingredients of feudal economy. The principles of salary fixation as depicted in *Arthaśāstra* is as follows:

The total salary bill of the state shall be determined in accordance with the capacity (to pay) of the city and the countrysides and shall be (about) one quarter of the revenue of the state. The salary scales shall be such as to enable the accomplishment of state activities (by attaching the right type of people), shall be adequate for meeting the bodily needs of state servants and shall not be in contradiction to the principle of *dharma* and *Artha*. If the (amount of the actual cash in the) Treasury is inadequate salary may be paid (partly) in forest produce, cattle or land, supplemented by a little money.[72] However, in the case of the settlement of virgin lands, all salaries shall be paid in cash; no land shall be allotted (as a part of the salary) until the affairs of the (new) village are fully stabilized.[73] The *AŚ* further states that salary of any individual employee, permanent or temporary, shall be fixed in accordance's with the principles of salary fixations, taking into account each one's level of knowledge and expertise in the work allotted.[74] The *AŚ* refers to special provision for the honorarium for teachers and learned men as minimum 500 *pāṇas* and a maximum of 1000 *pāṇas* (for each occasion). Traveling allowances are prescribed for middle grade officers as 10 *pāṇas* per *yojaña*, upto 10 *yojañas* – 20 *pāṇas* per *yojaña*, between 10 to 100 *yojañas*, if any government officer dies during his duty. His sons and wives shall be entitled to his salary and food allowances. Minor children and old or sick relatives shall be (suitably) assisted economically.[75] Table of the different grades of the state officers and employees is as follows:[76]

SALARIES

Grade	Annual Salary (in *pāṇas*)	Position	Remarks
A. The Higher Grades			
1.	48,000	Palace Officiating Priest King's guru Pūrohiṭa Crown Prince King's mother The Queen Civil Service Councillors Armed forces Chief of Defence	This is enough to prevent them from succumbing to the temptations (of the enemy) or rising up in revolt.
2.	24,000	Palace *Prasastr* (?) The Chancellor The Treasurer	Enough to make them efficient in their work.
3.	12,000	Palace Princes, (other than the Crown Prince) Queens (other than the seniormost) Civil Service Ministers Governor General of the City Head of manufacturing establishment Provincial Governors Governors of frontier regions Armed forces City Commandant	
4.	8,000	Civil Service Magistrates Armed forces Chief commanders of Infantry Horses Elephants Chariots	Enough to enable them to carry their men with them.

(Contd...)

Grade	Annual Salary (in *pāṇas*)	Position	Remarks
5.	4,000	<u>Civil Service</u> Chief Elephant Forester Chief Superintendent of Productive Forests <u>Armed forces</u> Divisional Commanders of Infantry Horses Elephants Chariots	
B. The Middle Grades			
6.	3,000	<u>Palace</u> Grade 1 courtesan	
7.	2,000	<u>Palace</u> Grade II courtesan King's charioteer King's physician Elephant trainer Horse trainer Chief Engineer Animal breeders <u>Armed forces</u> Camp superintendent	
8.	1,000	<u>Palace</u> Grade III courtesan Soothsayer Reader of omens Astrologer Narrator of *Puranas* Storytellers Court poet Bard/Praise singers Deputy *purohitas* <u>Civil Service</u> Heads of Departments <u>Secret Service</u> Intelligence officer; Agents under the cover of monks, householders, merchants and ascetics	
9.	500	<u>Palace</u> Instrumental musicians and instrument makers	

(*Contd...*)

Grade	Annual Salary (in *pāṇas*)	Position	Remarks
		Civil Service Accountants, clerks and similar subordinates Secret Service: Village level secret agents disguised as wandering nuns. Armed forces Commandos and other specialist soldiers	
10.	250	Palace Minstrels, actors, etc. Civil Service Occasional secret agents (minimum)	Secret agents pay to be increased according to work done.
C. The Lower Grades			
11.	120	Palace Artisans, sculptors	
12.	60	Palace Servants in charge of animals and birds Labour foremen Valets [of the King] Bodyguards of the King Mahout of the Kings elephant *Manavaka* Miners (?) King's servants not elsewhere specified.	

Economic thought of Kauṭilya attracted the attention of scholars all over the world. Probably no early human civilizations practically witnessed the economic system prevailed as envisaged in the *Arthaśāstra* of Kauṭilaya. But it is also true that *AŚ* does not discuss wholly impossible utopias; the economic thought was often pedantic, but usually more or less feasible. However, it is not likely that any state conducted its affairs wholly on textbook lines, and the prescriptions of the experts were/are not always put into practice. The so-called state controlled economy of the Mauryan kings was confined to the middle Gangetic plains, which did not last during the later Mauryan times and post-Mauryan periods, where land seems to have been newly in possession of individual farmers and peasants. The controlled cultivation was replaced by individual cultivation. But we must bear in mind that Kauṭilya had little interest in ethical issues, unlike the Buddhist. However, Kauṭilya categorises three types of goals such as spiritual goals, material well-being and sensual pleasure, but he advocated that material well-being alone is supreme, spiritual goals and sensual pleasure depend on material well-being. Thus, he states, it is wealth not stars, that leads to achievement of any kind.

Bernhard Breloer is of the view that the Mauryan economy was a planned economy and points out that Kauṭilyan economic planning was necessitated by the very circumstances and factors presented in early India occasioned by climate and nature.[77] He further argues that there is no trace of such a planned economy in European theories until recent time.[78] His extensive work on Kauṭilyan planned economy can be negated from the stand point of modern economics. Kauṭilya presented virtually as an anticipator of economic planning. This is a serious proposition and eminently opens to challenge and negation. Breloer had been trained in Marxist tradition and ideology, and influenced by Russian and Marxist ethos and ideas. Thus it is inevitable that he would want to compare and trace the idea of Russian planned economy model with that of early Indian Economy of the Mauryan times. The economic planning was indeed in one sense such a simple, elementary and human category that almost every individual even of the most primitive times may be said to be an economic planner in so far as he makes provisions for the future. Similarly every state that make a yearly budget is also used to planning out the future ahead.[79] In a more limited sense economic planning implies his intervention of the state in the private economy of its citizen, even modern state also control and interfere in the private economy through certain laws. This is almost an eternal as well as a universal fact of economic history from the remotest times. The regulation of prices, wages, and interest, the prescription as to the kind of foodgrains to grow, the control of commerce by tolls, excise and customs, the redistribution of national wealth and income by taxation and currency, manipulations, and of course, the promotion of public health *Vidyās*, *Kalās*, arts and services, etc., have been the regular features of state activities in the East and the West.[80] Breloer used a common place category economic planning without distinguishing its old and new contents. But we must bear in mind that modern economic planning has to be distinguished from the kind of planning visualized in *Arthaśāstra*. The modern concept of economic planning or for the development, the state prepares a plan which may spread over a certains number of years, lays down priorities in the matter of development, allocates resources in men and capital in accordance with the priorities and watches over the progress of the plan in the various field from year to year, but *Arthaśāstra* does not prescribed these things.

How for does the picture of economic thought gleans from the *Arthaśāstra* conform to actual conditions? This is indisputable that some sort of control over economic activities was necessary in the interest of the state revenue. But we cannot state in precision that Kauṭilya was directly associated with the economic policy of the Mauryan state. As a matter of fact, the economic thought depicted in *AŚ* might not be the innovation of Kauṭilya, that might be derived from earlier traditions. The *Arthaśāstra of Kauṭilya* prescribed the model of mixed economy, in which private and public sectors played their important role. It prescribed for the adoption of standardized weight and measures for the entire economy. Kauṭilya was aware of the fact that regularized marketing and provision of cheap credit were basic requirement for the rapid and stable economy. Some of the features of the Kauṭilyan economy are adopted by states of modern world. The state had monopoly in the production of served goods and participated with private entrepreneurs in the exploration of mines. Fixed rates of interest and profit were prescribed. Traders were compelled to use standard weight and measures, the implication of a comprehensive programme of social security measures. Utmost care was taken to promote economy and the welfare of the people which was the main agenda of the Mauryan state.

Thus it can be surmised from the analytical survey of *Arthaśāstra* that some of the Kauṭilya's economic thought keep relevance in the present day economic scenario.

The *Arthaśāstra of Kauṭilya* emphasized to pay proper attention for aforestation. He advocated the adoption of monoculture of some valuable trees species to enrich the forest reserve of the country. The *AŚ* prescribed for the proper maintenance of recreational forest. Wildlife protection was given due importance, chief credit and marketing was prescribed in order to accelerate the tempo of economic growth. Kauṭilya suggest the maximum irrigation facility in farming to attain growth with stability, and was in favour of regularized marketing system in the field of agricultural production. Kauṭilya paid supreme importance to the maintenance of rich treasury, which favourably affected entire activities of the state. In his opinion the augmentation of the treasury depends mainly on abundance of harvest, opulence of industrial production, prosperity of trade and commerce as well as on good economic management. The *AŚ* prescribed that the dependants of deceased employees of the state, must provided maintenances for those economic security measures adopted by the state keep relevance in the present time.

It was suggested that state must run a diversified economic activity, efficiently, prudently and profitably. The kings were advised to be ever active in the management of economic policy because the root of wealth was economic activity and inactivity brings material distress. Without any active state economic policy, both current prosperity and future gains are destroyed. Thus state should be active in managing the economy because source of material wealth is economic activity. Without it natural well-being is not possible. And kings were advised to maintain a diversified economy, within the limits of the technology available at that time. It is very clearly depicted in *AŚ* that *artha* has a much wider significance than merely 'wealth'. The material well-being of an individual was a part of it. As *Arthaśāstra* in its concluding part depicted that the source of the livelihood of human being is wealth which is both the territory of the state and its inhabitants who may follow a variety of profession. Thus it is the sacred duty of government of a state/nation to maintain the material well-being of the nation and its people.

REFERENCES

1. R. Shamasastry (ed. and trans.) *Kauṭilya Arthaśāstra*, Mysore, edition, 1929 and 1960-61 (hereafter R. Shamasastry *AŚ*, pp. 47, 227. R.P. Kangle, *The Kauṭilya Arthaśāstra*, 3 Pts. Rep. Delhi, 1986 (hereafter as Kangle *AS*) II.I, IV.10, L.N. Rangarajan, *Kauṭilya The Arthaśāstra*, Delhi, 1992. (hereafter as L.N. Rangarajan *AŚ*).
2. R.P. Kangle, *AŚ*, IV.3, V. 2. 37-38, R. Shamasastry, *AŚ*, p. 38. T. Ganapati Sastri, *The Arthaśāstra of Kauṭilya*, Pts. Trivandrum, 1924-25. (hereafter as T. Ganapati Sastri *AS*) Devadatta Sastri, Hindi Tr. *Kauṭilya Arthaśāstra*, Allahabad, 1957 (hereafter Devaddutta Sastri, *AŚ*).
3. L.N. Rangarajan, *AŚ*, pp. 14, 16, 81, 89-95, 242-93. R.P. Kangle, II.12, 16, 17, 19, IV. 2, III, 14, V. 2, 3.
4. R.P. Kangle, *AŚ*, V. 2.37-38.
5. R. Shamasastry, *AŚ*, pp. 378-79, L.N. Rangarajan, *AŚ*, p. 637, R.P. Kangle, IX, 4. 26-27.
6. R.P. Kangle, *AŚ*, I.2, 4.
7. *Ibid.* I.4, XV.1. Vidyabhaskar Vedratna and Udayveer Sastri, (tr.) *Kauṭilya Arthaśāstra*, 1.4, XV.1 (hereafter Vidyabhaskar *AŚ*).
8. *The Cultural Heritage of India*, published by The Ramakrishna Mission, Vol. II, Calcutta, 1962, pp. 655-56 (herafter as *CHI*).
9. K.V.R. Aiyangar, *Aspects of Ancient Indian Economic Thought,* Varanasi, 1934, pp. 23-26.
10. CHI, *op.cit.* p. 656.
11. R.P. Kangle, *AŚ*, I.5, III. 10.8.
12. *Ibid.* I.1.
13. *Ibid.*
14. *Ibid.* IV. 2.
15. Ajit Dasgupta, *A History of Economic Thought*, London, 1993, p. 29 (hereafter as Ajit Dasgupta).
16. R.P. Kangle, *AŚ*, II. 1.1.
17. *Ibid.* II. 4.3, II. 24, R. Shamasastri, *AŚ*, pp. 116-17.
18. R. Shamasastri, *AŚ*, pp. 192-94, *AAIC, op.cit.*, p. 71, R.P. Kangle. *AŚ*, II. 10.1, IV. 10.
19. *Ibid.* IV. 9.
20. *Ibid.*, III. 10, K.N. Jha and L.K. Jha, *Chanakya the Pioneer Economist*, Delhi, 1997, p. 63 (hereafter K.N. Jha and L.K. Jha).
21. R.P. Kangle, *AŚ*, II.1.

22. *Ibid.* IV.3.
23. L.N. Rangarajan, *AŚ*, pp. 81-82, 265-69. R.P. Kangle, *AŚ*, III.9.
24. K.N. Jha and L.K. Jha, *op.cit.* p. 56, *AŚ* III. 11.
25. R.P. Kangle, *AŚ*, XI. 1, 2, 5. Nagarajan, *Foundation of Hindu Economic State*, Nagpur, 1997, p. 205.
26. G.C. Chauhan, "The Kauṭilyan Theory of Rate of Interest: An Ingredient of Welfare State", in *ABORI*, LXXXIX, 2008, pp. 35-37.
27. Vidyabhaskar, *AŚ*, III. 5, R.N. Saletore, *Early Indian Economy*, 2nd Ed. Bombay, 1993, p. 668.
28. R.P. Kangle, *AŚ*. III. 11.
29. *Ibid.* II.1. G.C. Chauhan, *Origin and Growth of Feudalism in Early India*, (*From the Mauryas to 650 A.D.*), Delhi, 2004.
30. R.P. Kangle, *AŚ*, II. 1-2, L.N. Rangarajan, *op.cit.* PR 44, 27, 83, 88 181, 623.
31. *Ibid.* II. 17, 25.
32. *Ibid.* II. 1-2, 24, VII, 11, VIII. 4, L.N. Rangarajan, *AŚ, op.cit.*, pp. 78, 237-40.
33. *Ibid.* II.6, 15.
34. *CH1*, *op.cit.*, p. 665.
35. R.P. Kangle, *AŚ*, II.6. two categories such as *ayasarira* (body of income and *Ayamakha*, Sources of income).
36. Ajit Dasgupta, *op.cit.*, p. 34.
37. R.P. Kangle, II. 24.
38. *Ibid.* II. 9.
39. R.P. Kangle, *AŚ*. II, 1. 7-18, III. 9-33.
40. *Ibid.* V. 2, L.N. Rangarajan, *op.cit.*, pp. 14-16, 55, 265-69.
41. *Ibid.* II. 12.1, II. 12.7.
42. *Ibid.* VII.12, Ajit Dasgupta, *op.cit.*, p. 30.
43. *Ibid.*VII. 12. 14-16.
44. *Ibid.* II. 2.22.
45. *Ibid.* II 12.28.
46. *Ibid.* II. 14-15.
47. *Ibid.* II. 23, Ajit Dasgupta, *op.cit.*, p. 32.
48. *Ibid.* II. 23.11, 18-19.
49. *Ibid.* II 4, 38.
50. *Ibid.* II. 14-15.
51. *Ibid.* II, 4-6, L.N. Rangarajan, *AŚ, op.cit.*, pp. 95, 181, 252.
52. *Ibid.* IV. 1. 5-7.
53. *Ibid.* XI. 1.
54. *Ibid.* II. 5, 1-6, Ajit Dasgupta, *op.cit.* p. 33.
55. *Ibid.* II. 12-14.

56. *Ibid.* II. 16, 4-6.
57. *Ibid.*
58. CHI, *op.cit.*, p. 661.
59. R.P. Kangle, II. 16, 11, 21, IV. 2. L.N. Rangarajan, *op.cit.*, pp. 16, 77, 91-93, 242-48.
60. *Ibid.* II. 16. 8-16.
61. *Ibid.* IV. 2.
62. *Ibid.* II. 16.
63. *Ibid.* II. 16. 16-25. L.N. Rangaranjan, *op.cit.* pp. 83, 182, 242, 307, 326-48.
64. *Ibid.* II. 21, 22, 28, 34, IV. 13.
65. *Ibid.* II. 16.
66. *Ibid.* II. 9.32.
67. *Ibid.* II 9. 33-34.
68. *Ibid.* II. 9.36.
69. *Ibid.* II. 8.20.
70. *Ibid.* V. 3, L.N. Rangarajan, *op.cit.* pp. 289-93. K.N. Jha and L.K. Jha, *op.cit.*, p. 224.
71. L.N. Rangarajan, *op.cit.*, p. 179, R.P. Kangle, *AŚ*, II. 2.7.
72. Kishor Thanawala, "Kauṭilya's *Arthaśāstra*: A Neglected work in the History of Economic Thought", in B.B. Price, (ed). *Ancient Economic Thought*, Vol. I, New York, 1997, pp. 43-57. R.P. Kangle, *AŚ*, V. 3. 1-2.
73. *Ibid.* V. 3.52.
74. *Ibid.* V. 4.33.
75. *Ibid.* V. 3, 18-21, 28-30.
76. L.N. Rangarajan, *op.cit.* pp. 289-92. R.P. Kangle, the *Kauṭilya Arthaśāstra*, Part III, Delhi, Rep. 1986, pp. 208-210.
77. B.K. Sarkar, "Kautilya, Economic Planning and Climatology", in *Indian Historical Quarterly*, Vol, XX, Calcutta, 1935, pp. 329, 356.
78. B. Breloer quoted by R.P. Kangle in *The Kauṭilya Arthaśāstra*, Part II, rep. Delhi, 1986, p. 191.
79. B.K. Sarkar, *Loc. cit.*, p. 343.
80. *Ibid.*

2

Writing on Economy of Early Medieval Northern India: A Brief Critique

The study of the economic formation of early India is currently engaging the attention of the present day scholars of the ancient Indian history. It continues to baffle the scholars. There have been few valuable publications in past which depict the economic life and agrarian structure in ancient India. Economic formation has found mentioned as a chapter or an article in many works dealing with the economic formation in Indian history. This is an attempt to make a critical analysis of one of the most critical phase of Indian history with main focus on the economic development in Early Medieval Northern India. It is usually asserted that the people of early medieval North India fell easy prey because of the cultivators and villagers of early North-India, were so heavily exploited that they passively accepted any conquest expecting it to bring a change for better. However, the credit goes to U.N. Ghoshal[1] (1929-30), who for the first time ventured to explore the myth of agrarian relation in India, with a limited sources handled critically. The author's information is extensive. But with the coming of Archaeology, a flood of information has comes out, which reveal that the agrarian structure and its characters were undergoing change. The condition and situation was not alike throughout ancient Indian history. But Ghoshal does not give any credence to the foreign accounts which indicate the prevalence of royal ownership of land in ancient India. He discusses the growth of agriculture and land revenue system in Indian history. The growth of agriculture and trade led to the formation of wealthy land-owing classes and rich trading communities. However, the introduction of iron for the purpose of agricultural production might have strengthened the economic condition of landowners. With the increasing emphasis on agriculture more labourers were needed for cultivation of land. This might be a motivating factor to employ slave for agricultural production.

D.D. Kosambi[2] (1956), surveys the course of Indian history right from the earliest time to till the British Conquest, and throws much light on feudal system in Indian history. But he does not show any procroste an adherence to slavery in Indian history. He is of the opinion that slaves in ancient India were specially house slaves and completely denied the slave mode of production, but his theory is questioned by D.R. Chanana[3] (1960). However, Kosambi's attempt to distinguish two processes in development of feudalism in ancient India history, which is "feudalism from above", and "feudalism from below". When the kings began to transfer their administrative rights to their subordinates chiefs who thus came into direct relation with peasantry a process he calls, "feudalism from above". It reached an advanced stage of development during Gupta and post Gupta's periods, "a class of landowner developed within the village between the state and the peasantry, gradually to wield armed power on the local population"—a process he terms, "feudalism from below". A direct influence of Marxist ideology is also seen in the writing of Kosambi's, generally his works give an idea of changes in early Indian society and economy. B.P. Mazumdar,[4] (1960) tries to explain why northern India succumbed to the Turkish invaders. He produced his work in the years after independence when nationalism ceased to remain a source of inspirations, and free India's problems attracted the attention of scholar. Mazumdar made an attempt to understand the early medieval Northern Indian economic life from a fresh angle. P. Niyogi,[5] (1962) discussed in detail about land, land measurement, trade and commerce, crafts currency, state income and expenditure. Her study throws much light on the general pattern of the economic system, which spread over a vast area, was resulted in the study of Economic History of ancient India. However, her work does not cover all aspects of economic life of the people in early medieval India. Moreover the learned scholars has left out the discussion of a most important topic like peasant condition and economic impact on social institutions, does not notice any evidence to prove that the cultivators and peasants were prosperous. B.N. Ganguli's[6] (1964), work is simply a collection of articles seeks to lay stress on those aspects of the economic history which have been received scholarly attention, some changes have been introduced to the original. The edited articles have been presented in the first all India seminars on Indian Economic History, in Delhi School of Economics. We notice that only general idea of changes in Ancient Indian Economy have been depicted in these articles. L. Gopal's[7] (1965, 1980), discusses the various approaches and techniques to the agriculture in ancient and early medieval Indian agricultural history. He suggests the private ownership in agricultural land and further states that the state had proprietary right over certain fields; received revenue from the peasants as the wages for the protection is afforded to the people. He assumed that agricultural land generally belonged to him who cultivated it. His statement seems to be contradictory. He throws much light particularly on the emergence of feudalism in Indian society and equate feudalism with the *Sāmanta* system prevalent in early medieval India. Gopal works contain very useful economic data, often drawn from literary and epigraphic traditions, and prepare the ground for a detailed analytical study of the limited chronological segments of the early economic history of Northern India. R.S. Sharma[8] (1965, 1966), deals with the origin and growth of feudalism in ancient Indian history, discussed the feudal polity and economy during Palas, Prathiharas, Rashtrakutas and Delhi Sulatan. He covers a period of about nine centuries, and mainly dealing with the political and economic aspect of feudalism, his work is the first attempt to cover the entire period. He presents a lot of information coming from his analytical publications, such as, his work shows that the critical characteristics of a feudal formation are found in the social structure of early medieval India, and dominated by a class of landlords who claim and collect rent from the peasants on the ground that they were owners of the land. He further argues that a class of subject peasantry and every peasant family constitutes the smallest unit of production and other meeting its needs of subsistence pays the reminder to the landlords. The peasants actually possessed the land but were compelled to pay rent in kind, cash or labour to the landlords, but the rent and labour services were collected by he donors not with the object of promoting production or the economic growth of the country but only for their own consumption. They paid not because of expectations of turn but because of custom, coercion, legal sanction and ideological influences. The socio-economic formation that we have in early medieval times is the concomitant of a predominantly agricultural economy in which local needs were satisfied locally and in which the scope for the functioning of the market system was extremely limited.

D.C. Sircar's[9] (1966, 1969), works are well-arranged, well-balanced and comprehensive review of land system, which cover almost ancient and Medieval India, not inclined to accept feudalism in Ancient Indian History. He is of the view that landlordism has been confused with feudalism. He further argues that in the feudal system of Europe, the king was regarded as the holder of all the land of the kingdom, much of the land being let out by him to the Barnos or tenants in chief, who in return for the land, agreed to perform certain services for the king and were under the obligation of making some payments and supplied on occasions. But majority of the charters discovered all over the country record grants of land to Gods and *Brāhmaṇas* without stipulating any obligation of the donees to the donors. The donees were exempted from all kind of obligations including the supply of unpaid labour. Sircar's exercise is based on the wrong assumption that the pattern of land granted till recent time, continued to be the same. He mentions that "early Indian rulers sometimes granted *Jagir* for the maintenance of their officers and dependants". But he qualifies this point by adding that those were not under the feudal type of obligation but he does not care to mention their nature. B.N.S. Yadava,[10] (1973) work is a valuable contribution to this subject, his total rejection of the loss of king or state control over donated land may be especially true in early India when land grant were less and religious in nature, but one cannot entirely rule out the loss of the state control over donated land from eight century A.D., onwards. The author is inclined to accept the loss of revenue to the state during his period of study. Yadava's has repeatedly referred to the Western Europe for making a comparison and added great details to Sharma's work studying northern India in the early medieval period. But we cannot compare Indian model with that of western, because, we have to keep in mind socio-culture and economic variations of the regions. B. Chattopadhyay[11] (1987), has prepared an anthology on a particular theme, (the papers presented in I.H.C., proceeding), contributors have thrown much light on the changing status of early Indian Economic History, and peep into any noticeable change in perceptions regarding early Indian Economy in these form. This collection of the articles have conveyed hardly any historigraphical sense, the new source material has been used resulting in the broadening of the scope of early Indian-economic history and more significantly economic history has gone beyond narrow frontiers by relating itself to areas which are general historical relevance certain changes had however to be carried out. S.M. Devi[12] (1987), tried to systematized the economic condition of early medieval Northern India dealing with the different aspects of economy, such as, agriculture, irrigation, domestication of animals, trade and commerce, guilds, money and banking including exchanges. Her work is valuable contribution to the history of economic theories of ancient India, but, the archaeological sources are rarely utilized. She has discussed various aspects of Economic life of the people, such as, agricultural caste, division of soil for the purpose of raising crops of different varieties, methods employed in cultivation, agricultural tools, manures, irrigation facilities, and agricultural seasons for sowing and harvesting, different kinds of crops produced, their value in respect of industry. Antiquity of agriculture, various localities of agricultural goods and danger to the agricultural products has also been discussed. She further made an attempt to show the different kinds of ownership that existed in Northern India, discussed in detail regarding the various industries, moneylending and banking, their nature, rates and types of interest, position of money-lender and plight of the debtors and persons taking loans. She gives the detailed description of trade and commerce in Northern India, land and water routes, important centres of trade, danger faced by the merchant, export and import and barter system. The plight of poor subjected peasant, forced labour and the feudal culture has been discussed. D.N. Jha,[13] (ed) (1987) work is a simply the collection of articles seeks to lay stress on various aspects of feudal social formation which have received scholarly attention. These collected articles give us the idea of Indian feudalism which is at the centre of controversy in Indian historiography. These articles by and large, give us the idea of Marxist perception of early Indian history. Jha introduced some changes to the original without interfering with the style of the individual contributor. D.N. Jha argues that the growth of feudal property in India came to be linked with the condemning of the communal right in land, as is evident from the later grants which refer to the transfer of communal resources (i.e. pastures, forest, water resources, fitness, etc.) to the donors. The economic essence of Indian feudalism, like that of European, it has been argued, lay in the rise of landed intermediaries leading to the inserfment of the peasantry through restriction on peasant mobility and freedom, increasing obligation to perform forced labour, mounting tax burdens and evils of sub-infeudalism. It has been argued that if the similarity in the forms and exploitation of the peasantry in Western Europe and India were present and the manorial structure is accepted as a valid basis for comparison between development in two regions, it may be pointed out on the basis of epigraphic and literary evidence that the peasants and the artisans were at that time attached to the soil more or less in the same way as serfs were in medieval Europe. I am of the view that most of the scholars of ancient Indian History, had been trained in Western Tradition and institutions, it is but natural that they would like to compare Indian economic model with that of West.

Land grant was an important adjunct of economic structure in Early Medieval India history. Om Parkash[14] (1988), work indicates that land grants were not uniformly a drain on state resources; instead, they enriched the state in various ways. On the one hand, the size of the secular award found cutting across all requirements of hierarchy and peerage, and on the other hand, the awards were seem to be wholly without obligation of any kind for prospective service to be contractually discharged by the beneficiary in lieu of the grant. He further argues that the secular land grants were determined by the material gain they brought to the state, and it is not unlikely that many of his work embodies the result of an investigation into the relationship of early medieval Indian land-grants and state-economy. His inquiry originated from the perception of the questionable nature of the most of popular explanation offered for the phenomenon of the innumerable land grants of early India. He has noted that there is hardly any valid ground to infer the existence of a landed aristocracy of chiefs and officials from these grants. It is also not possible to the prevalence of a salary prove fief system on their basis. It has been argued that the land grants also appear to have a linkage with the state policy of imperial expansion. Om Parkash argues that the land grants not only contributed the king's share to the royal treasury but some of them also brought their prides to the king but he ignores large numbers of land grants which had been donated to donors in early India which were absolutely tax-free. He further argues that early Indian land grants were not a drain on state economy. The possibility of generating a landed aristocracy of nobles and officials is, therefore, ruled out. There is again a total absence of any condition of prospective service imposed on the recipients of secular grants. The contractual bond of protection and service between the lord and the vassal which, in one form or the other, almost necessarily characterizes feudal formation is absolutely missing. He rejects the concept of features of feudal system and his self-framed concept of the total missing of feudalism throughout the length and breadth of ancient India.

V.K. Thakur,[15] (1989) work throws much light on the problems of the methodology of the study of economy in Indian history. Dipping deep into the well of his knowledge, V.K. Thakur has brought to our notice not only the problem of the study of Indian economy, but also discussed critically the recent writing on Indian feudalism and economy. To a certain extent he sums up and makes readily available the extensive research on Indian feudalism and economic life which has gone on for many years in India. Each writer is a leading specialist in his own sphere with his own evaluations of specific historical problems whom's work on feudalism and economy he discussed. He argues that the meaning scope and applicability of the term "feudalism" in the Indian context has been confused because of its non-discriminate use in mutually contradictory situations and widely separated chronological sequences such usage's are completely devoid of any conceptual rigour, and view feudalism and its linguistic variants as so many people words lacking any precise body of contents. This has not only given contradictory meaning to the word; but has also led to a reckless use of terms, like "feudatory", "feudal", "feudal lord",. "feudatory state", "feudatory families", etc. As a consequence the word "feudalism" by now, has acquired divergent meanings as between Marxist and non-Marxist historians. The study of feudalism in the Indian context is, however, seriously hampered by the limitations of the available source material. The literary works, however suffer from serious limitations and their nature is such that they do not provide us with clear and categorical references to the contemporary socio-economic patterns. He further argues that the proper use of literary sources becomes all the more important because of the nature of archaeological repository and tools of analysis in India. Historical archaeology is, in fact lagging far behind in respect of the material relevant to the study of the various socio-economic problems.

Johns Deyell,[16] (1990) work is a response to challenge of defining and exploring alternative avenues of economic research. It is concerned with money as an indicator of economic activity. Its major premise is that past economic system can usefully be defined by the pattern of production, exchange and dispersion of their money. He demonstrates that a thorough investigation of the recovered coin hoards permits a fairly coherent reconstruction of the monetary system of early medieval North India. He argues that during five centuries from A.D. 750 to 1250, a few superficially uniform coin types comprised monetary system startling in their complexity and diversity. This was an era of base metal alloy coinage, when the precious metals were not used in form of money, but there was some regional variation in these effects, the relative precious metal contents of coins were not uniform from country to country. In the Ganga basin, the high price of silver was evident as early as the eighth century, but that of gold not until the eleventh century. The silver shortage was not indicated in the North West until the eleventh century. The gold and the silver resources of North India were insufficient to support such a scale of coinage issues; only a copper was available in significant quantities. On the basis of his own analysis, he has stated that there was no shortage of currency in early medieval northern India history but on the other hand he admits the constant debasement of metal content and further argued that the circulation of *daramah* was limited to the zone of Pratihara. A. Dasgupta's,[17] contribution to the Indian economic life in early India, evolution of economic life from very beginning. Only general survey of economic life has been given with a view to showing the progress at each step in Indian economic history. Gupta discusses in his analytical work the Indian economic thought in general, such as, Buddhist economic thought, and some details Buddhist attitudes to economic activity. He further argues the principal economic ideas contained in Kauṭilya's *Arthaśāstra*, laid by the Kauṭilya in respect of taxation and price polity. He devoted full chapter on economic thought in pre-muslim and during period, from the early part of the thirteenth century upto the eighteenth century A.D. Nothing new is noticeable in his work regarding ancient Indian economic formation. From above brief analyses we notice that the scholars of ancient Indian economic history have opened up new lines of inquiry and imply that, the concept of early medieval economic structure far from being a historiographical cliche needs further refinement and sophistication.

B.P. Sahu[18] (1997), highlights the growth and changing contours of historiography with regards to the agrarian history of early medieval India. As such it incorporates some significant early writings as well as contributions which represent research still very much in progress. The pattern of regional socio-economic transformation in the context of wider historical developments comes through in many of these essays. The introduction analysed historiographical trends and focuses on problems and issues, and flowing from it the areas and nature of controversies as well as on related themes. The articles included here deal with aspects of rural settlement, the concept of village community, the problems of the ownership of land, agrarian charges, the structure of rural society and rural unrest. B.P. Sahu has been careful to draw his material from a wide range of publications, representing varieties of source material and approach. The broad area of agrarian history includes various sub-themes, and although historical writings so far available are very much unevenly distributed between the themes. G.C. Chauhan[19] (2003), work is a comprehensive study of Agrarian formation and feudal economy based on literary and epigraphic sources, located between eighth century and eleventh century A.D. It poses new questions on ticklish issues like the structure of feudalism, the nature of peasantry, the impact of land grants in early medieval northern India. Considering the emphasis of present work, the title is slightly inappropriate. The critique of the entire range of literature is the strength of this work. Chauhan presents a deteriorating grim scenario about the agricultural and economic condition of the historical period spanning from eighth century to tenth century A.D. It also traces the causal complexities which forced the peasants to accept their fate passively and without a murmur. While the book provides a fascinating debate on some of the vexatious issues involving land economy, the sheen is somewhat lost due to poor editing and type setting.

The agrarian and economic life of Indian society saw the long and gradual process of feudalization. We notice two ways of development on one hand there were changes in the position of agricultural commune on the other hand, the nature of the feudal estates and the right of the feudal lord over the population change. Feudal agrarian relation differed from area to area because agricultural and landless labourers, manual servants, artisan, etc., were dependent on agriculture and were remunerated mostly in the common lands of the village though their status was not better than that of semi-serfs. One question is still lingering in the mind of scholars whether artisan and peasants were attached to the soil or not? What extent they were attached to the soil? Some Inscriptions indicate that the regular supply of the necessary articles from the artisan, such as, oil men making gifts of a fixed measure of oil per oilman to a temple. It shows that artisan was forcibly attached to the temples or to cater for its economic needs?

The social agrarian aspect of feudal system in early India was intimately connected with the transformation of *Śūrdas*. It seems that in older settled regions *Śūrdas* were provided with land, and in remote parts the tribal peasantry was annexed to the *Brāhmanical* system through land grants. It cannot be assumed that the burden of heavily increased taxes was to put on the villagers. Many charters clearly indicate transfer of artisans and traders to the beneficiaries. The charters clearly show that the peasants, villagers and other inhabitants of the donated villages carry out the orders of the beneficiaries. Thus, if the piece of land or village is transferred, the peasants are automatically transferred. From the eighth century A.D. onwards sub-infeudation has become to common phenomena in Indian history, which gave the rise to graded types landlords, different from the actual tiller of land, this to deteriorate the economic condition of the peasants. Some charters record that the donees were authorized to enjoy the land, to get it enjoyed get it cultivated. Thus with the increase in the number of intermediaries, and peasants seem to be forced to pay additional taxes.

Our ancient Indian villages had a distinctive design which reflected closely the basic values of Indian civilization. This design had crystallized more or less during the classical phase of Indian history. Many changes were introduced into Indian society and economy. There were limits beyond which might not interchange their economic roles in the village. Member of specialist groups might become agriculturists, but not *vice versa*. It was not for just anyone in the village to become a priest, a barber, a washerman, or a carpenter, or a potter. To some extent this was true also of the differentiated role within agriculture. *Brāhmaṇ* no matter how poor, could not themselves till the land, low caste, no matter how enterprising could not become substantial landlord or priest, and it would be quite misleading to view all their members as peasants?

REFERENCES

1. U.N. Ghoshal, *The Agrarian System in Ancient India, Calcutta*, 1929-30, pp. 56-77, he suggests that the land grants refer to the payments in kind and in cash (called *dhanyahiraryadeya*), land grants mentions the usual list of privileges assigned to the donees, further, distinguishes the item of *dharya* from that of *bhāga bhōgakāra*, both of which terms usually connote payment in kind (p. 56). He further suggests that the terms refers to *Udrañga* and *Uparikara* which prove the existence of state owned lands cultivated by tenants in the villages. He argues that Chendella land-grants are concerned with endowments in favour of *Brāhmaṇas* and Temples. Their status is sufficiently indicated by a clause in one of the documents which expressly states that the donees are not to be obstructed with regard to the gift, sale on mortgage of the land. Another record describes a family of *kayasthas* high offices under the down mentions that three of them received villages from different kings. These belonged to the class of assignments granted to officials for service. *Contribution to the History of Hindu Revenue System*, Calcutta, 1940, pp. 32-45. He has suggested that *halikā-kara* might have been a tax on plough but his argument cannot be accepted because if there was the tax on cultivator or on tiller of the land, and tax on plough does not seem a separate tax on *hala* or plough.
2. D.D. Kosambi, *An Introduction to the Study of Indian History*, Bombay, 1956, pp. 298-310." Early Stages of Caste System in Northern India", *JBBRAS* XXII, 1946, pp. 33-48, "The Basis of Ancient Indian History", *JAOS*, IXXV, 1955.
3. D.R. Chanana, *Slavery in Ancient India*, Delhi, 1960, pp. 107-10. He notices elements of slave society in early historical India, neither postulates the existence of a large scale chattel slavery in Indian antiquity. His work shows that the slaves in early India were used for agriçultural as well as industrial

production, which indicates that there was slave mode of production in early Indian history.

4. B.P. Mazumdar, *Socio-Economic History of Northern India, 1030-1194* A.D., Calcutta, 1960, pp. 9-15. "Collective Land-Grants in Early Medieval Inscription (606-1206 A.D.) *JAS*, Vol.X, Nos. 1-4, 1963, pp. 7-17. "Industries and Internal Trade in Early Medieval North India", XLV-XLVI, Pts. 1-IV, 1979, pp. 230-55.

5. Pushpa Niyogi, *Contribution to the Economic History of Northern India from the Tenth to the Twelfth Century A.D.*, Calcutta, 1962, pp. 280-85. She is of the views that "North Indian temples had large area of land under their direct control. She further argues that *Brāhmaṇas* and temples received donations of land from time to time. Somanath Temples was endowed with more than 10,000 villages. The temples in some cases had, large areas of land under its possessions thus giving the organization of status of a landlord. The king of Kashmir Kolasa confiscated the villages which formed the endowment of the Avantiskamin and other temple. It indicates that some temple in North India had vast landed property.

6. B.N. Ganguli (ed.), *Reading in Indian-Economic History*, Delhi, 1964, pp. 9-18.

7. L. Gopal, *Economic Life of Northern India*, 700-1200 A.D., Delhi, 1965, pp. 225-52. It is an interesting and significant source of information covering a large range of literary and archaeological sources. At the same time it is neatly ordered and lucidity and concisely presented. His work throws particular light on the emergence of Feudalism in Indian History. L. Gopal, *Aspects of the History of Agriculture in Ancient India, Varanasi, 1980*, pp. 48-78. L. Gopal, "Ownership of Agricultural Land in Ancient India", in B.P. Sahu (ed), *Land System and Rural Society in Early India*, Delhi, 1997, pp. 95-110.

8. R.S. Sharma, *Indian Feudalism* (300-1200 A.D.), Delhi, 1965, pp. 210-13. He rightly notices following broad developments in early medieval economy, (a) a group of individual ownership of land at the cost of royal and communal ownership, (b) subjection of peasantry through sub-infeudation, eviction and imposition of non-customary taxes and forced labour, (c) conversion of income from trade and craft into benefices and, (d) the existence of a self-sufficient economy bustressed by lesser use of coins and comparative absence of trade. All these may be regarded as features of feudal economy in early northern India. *Light of Early Indian Society and Economic*, Bombay, 1966, pp. 90-101. *Land Revenue in Indian Historical Studies*, Delhi, 1971, pp. 60-75. *Urban Decay in India, 400-1000 AD*, Delhi, 1987, pp. 178-85.

9. D.C. Sircar (ed.), *Land System and Feudalism in Ancient India*, Calcutta, 1966, p. 95. D.C. Sircar is not inclined to accept feudalism in Ancient India. He is of the view that landlordism has been confused with feudalism. In the feudal system of Europe, the king was regarded as the holder of all land of the

kingdom, much of the land being let out by him to the barons or tenants in chief who in return for the land, agreed to perform certain services for the king and were under the obligation of making some payments and supplies on occasions. When a tenant died, it was usual for his successor to pay a fine to the overlord before he could succeed to his estate. He argues that the Sūdra peasants cannot be equated with the unfree serf of Medieval Europe. *Landlordism and Tenancy in Ancient and Medieval India as Epigraphical Records*, University of Lucknow, 1969, pp. 32-35. Sircar states that the state's eagerness to get the uncultivated field cultivated and keep land under cultivation in its own interest is easily intelligible so that the tenant who cultivated the field and paid taxes regularly is scarcely expected to be dispossessed of the plot of land allotted to him for life at the formation of village. This is because it was not possible for the state to cultivate all freshly acquired or reclaimed land. Not only that on the tenant's death, it would be quite normal for his son and grandson to get a lease of the same plot of land for the period of their lives successively.

10. B.N.S. Yadava, *Society and Culture in Northern India in the Twelfth Century AD*, Allahabad, 1973, pp. 164-66. He refers the *Skanda Purana* in support of his argument which leaves little doubt that hundred of people were compelled to do forced labor, and this was evidently meant for production. "Problem of Interaction between Socio-Economic Classes in Early Medieval Complex." *IHR*, Vol. I, No. 2, 1979.
11. B. Chattopadhyaya (ed.), *Essay in Ancient Indian Economic History*, Delhi, 1987, introduction, pp. XV-XVIII. The *hal* may be equated with one of the types of *visti* tax and treated as an equivalent of *hari* system. It denotes the employment of all bullock teams under the field of a landlord for cultivating his land without any payment. The practice gained wide currency throughout northern India and has continued even to this day. The landlords used to call upon all their lands to plough their day, that is, for one day. *The Making of Early Medieval India*, Delhi, 1994, An introduction, pp. 1-35. *Studying Early India Anechaeology, Tents and Historical Issues*, Delhi, 2003, pp. 248-49. *State and Economy in Northern India, Fourth Century to Twelfth Century* in Romila Thapar (ed), *Recent Perspectives of Early Indian History*, 2nd Ed. Bombay, 1998, pp. 334-39.
12. S.M. Deve, *Economic Condition of Ancient India*, (from 750 A.D. to 1200 A.D.), Delhi, 1987, pp. 1-73.
13. D.N. Jha (ed.), *Feudal Social Formation in Early India*, Delhi; 1987, p. 6. It has been argued that the Kaliage is characterized among other things, by *Varṇasamkāra*, i.e. Intermixture of *Varna* or social order, which implies that the *Vaiśyas* and *Śūdras* (peasants antisans and labourers) either refused to pay taxes and refused to supply the necessary labour for economic production. *Economy and Society in Early India Issues and Paradigms*,1992, pp. 1-25. *Studies in Early India Economic History*, Delhi, 1980, pp. 25-35.
14. Om Parkash, *Early Indian Land-Grants and State Economy*, Allahabad, 1988, pp. 2-3, 282-84. According to his religious grants were also converted into sources of state revenue by granting only partial exemptions implying thereby that the unenumerated taxes were to be realized from the donee.

Another methods adopted was to grant total exemption for a limited period only to the agrahara and brahmedeya grants in particular.

15. V.K. Thakur, *Historiography of Indian Feudalism; Towards a Model of Early Medieval Indian Economy, 600-1000* C.A.D., Patna, 1989, pp. XVII-XVIII. The archaeology of the rural settlement of India is a desideratum, while material pertaining to urban archaeology is scanty. The limitation of the source also acts as a restraint to typological studies, because if fails to respond to questions pertaining to the change taking place in the society. Notwith standing this constraint, a typological study is pertinent for a proper understanding of the complex of Indian Feudalism. Aoushman (eds.), Peasants in India History, Vol. 1, Patna, 1996, p. 121.
16. Johns Deyell, *Living without Silver: The Monetary History of Early Medieval, North India*, Delhi, 1990 pp. 6-7, 65. In the Indus Valley under Arab Governors and Amirs, both copper and silver currencies were issued.
17. Ajit Dassgupta, *A History of Indian Economic Thought*, London, 1993, 43-55.
18. B.P. Sahu (ed.), *Land System and Rural Society in Early India*, Delhi, 1997, pp. 102-21. The investigation shows that the peasant was the proprietor of land in every sense of the term The king, as the universal sovereign of every thing in his state, had, no doubt, some claim over the land. He received revenue from he peasant as the ways for protection he afforded to the land, but this in no way amounted to a proprietary right over the land. But the question was not entirely free from discussion even in ancient times, and supporters could be found for the not much favoured view of state ownership of land.
19. G.C. Chauhan, *Economic History of Early Medieval Northern India*, Delhi, 2003, pp. 28-35, 66-78, 101-04. G.C. Chauhan, *Origin and Growth of Feudalism in Early India*, Delhi, 2004, pp. 134-39.

Origin of Agriculture and Pastoralism in Ancient India

3

The culture of the soil is called as agriculture but it seems to be very narrow interpretation and definition. The growing of crops and domestication of animals are indispensable ingredients of agriculture and the significant step in a chain of operation which provided foodstuffs for ancient men. Thus it can be simply defined that the agriculture is the service and practice of farming and rearing of livestock.

The study of the origin of agriculture and pastoralism in ancient India is currently engaging the attention of the scholars, which continues to baffle the scholars of ancient Indian economic history. There have been couples of valuable publications in the past which present the agrarian life of the people in their respective works dealing with the agriculture and its different aspects. However, credit goes to Radharaman Gangopadhyay, who for the first time ventured to explore the possibility of agricultural formation in ancient India, with a limited sources to which he has frankly admitted in his work, *Some Materials for the Study of Agriculture and Agriculturists in Ancient India*, Serampore, 1932, is a simple survey of ancient Indian agrarians history and life of Agriculturists on the basis of literary traditions of early India. A glorification of early Indian peasants and villagers can be seen from his work, which indicates happy and contended life of peasants and villagers in ancient India. He advocates the theory of private ownership of land, where king had no property on the agricultural land and king got only in return of his good governance, he was entitled to charge portion of the gross produce as tax; and the tax was somewhat similar to our modern income tax. He does not give any credence to the foreign and epigraphical sources, which indicates—the prevalence of royal ownership of land in ancient India. He regarded the ancient period of Indian history as of the prosperity and general contentment. This patriotic bias often resulted in an exaggeration of the notion of happy and contented peasantry and villagers and concept of 'Village self-sufficient economy', they had abundant produce and every village had usually a sufficient stock which could give at least a partial relief if famine broke out.[1] This author, however, brought to light certain important facets such as question of the ownership of agricultural land, famine, cattle and cattle rearing and the life of an agriculturist, etc. A.K. Yegna Narayan Aiyer,[2] *Agriculture and Allied Arts in Vedic India*, Bangalore, 1949, is a brief monograph which simply give the brief description of agriculture in *Vedic* period and relied upon the *Rg-Veda Samhita*, by H.H. Wilson in English and Tamil translations of three other Vedas by A.M.R. Jambunathan. He does not throw any significant light on any aspects of agriculture during *Vedic* period, it was simply non-academic work. D. Raghavan (ed.), *Agriculture in Ancient India*,[3] Delhi, 1964, is based on literary traditions texts, divided into fourteen chapters such as Land-division. Irrigation and drainage, tillage and tillage-implements, manures and manuring, cultivations of crops, sequences of cropping, protection of crops from diseases and pests, sowing of seeds, Agricultural Metrology, livestocks in agriculture, Cows and Bulls, Tending of cattle, protection of cattle and use of animals food, medical treatments of cattle. His work is simply a piece of narratology on ancient Indian agricultural life of the people. Author does not give us any idea of the element of charge and continuity. However useful compendium of agriculture or agrarian data, it does not tackle some of the basic question relevant to the understanding of historical processes. It just provides general information of agriculture and animal husbandry on the basis of literary traditions without telling us why and how sendentary agriculture developed in Ancient India.

M.S. Randhawa, *A History of Agriculture in India*,[4] Vol. I, Delhi, 1980. His work is a History of the origin and development of man in which agriculture, in its widest sense, has played a role which is inseparable from human life. He goes back to geologic time to trace the birth of the Indian subcontinent. His work deals with the account of soil, climate, vegetation and agriculture regions in India. This comprehensive work on agriculture of Randhawa refers Hunters and the gathers, discovery of agriculture and domestication of animals. His presentation is a history of agriculture and man's civilization which go hand in hand.

In spite of Randhawa's encyclopedic, laudable factual attempt, there remain many academic issues unanswered. Moreover, many epigraphical evidences have accumulated on the origin, antiquity, diffusion and formation of agriculture in India, after his work. In addition to this, some technical texts of agriculture also had been made available now. Some popular literary traditions have also been ransacked. In addition to these advantages, there are many critical researches on the different aspects of agriculture of ancient India. Thus, it is the first time that synthetic picture of agriculture in ancient India is presented on the basis of archaeological and literary traditions.

L. Gopal, *Aspect of History of Agriculture in Ancient India*, Varanasi, 1980,[5] presents different aspects of agriculture in ancient India and advocated the theory of private or individual right over agricultural land, he has utilized the two inscriptions of Kangra, which record the donation by private individual to a religious shrine. He also admits that the king had proprietary right over certains fields, received revenue from the peasants as the wages for the protection was afforded to the peasants and assumed that agricultural land generally belonged to him who cultivated it. But his statement seems to be self-contradictory.

Another work on agriculture is produced by N.M. Kansara, *Agriculture and Animal Husbandry in the Vedas*,[6] Delhi, 1995, wholly based on the *Vedic* traditions, discusses different aspects of agriculture and animal husbandry in *Vedic* India. This book is a compilation of useful and details of agriculture and pastrolism during *Vedic* period which often float within a thin fluid of unwarranted pre-conceptions, insupportable assumptions, vague and sweeping generalization.

Another encyclopedic work on agriculture is *History of Agriculture in India*,[7] Vol. V, Part I, Delhi, 2009 (eds.) by L. Gopal and V.C. Srivastava, deals with the origin and growth of agriculture in ancient India. This works is the collection of many critical researches on the different aspects of agriculture in ancient India through its history till 1200 A.D. This comprehensive book is a synthesis and summation of the existing knowledge on the history of agriculture in ancient India on the combined basis of archaeological and literary traditions against the backdrop of Asian history in general. Besides summing up the existing knowledge, it opens new avenues for further research on many debated issues in the history of agriculture in ancient India.[8] All facts of the agriculture in ancient India have been enlightened and addressed in this volume.

However, our knowledge of agriculture is largely based upon information gained in the ancient past by farmers and villagers or farming communities by purely empirical means. Local practice is dependent upon very careful marshalling of facts over very long period of time and the development of system which suits soil, climate or location. The climate had played very vital role in the origin of agriculture and pastoralism, flora and fauna, throughout the geological record altered the ecological landscape, which ultimately led to formal adaptation.[9] It is argued that human adaptation and migration in response to severe climatic changes are known from the paleo records.[10] The archaeological finding from Yana River, Siberia, tells us that humans adapted to harsh, frigid climate of the Arctic during the late Pleistocene about 27,000 year ago. Likewise, they adapted to arid conditions in the Thar and Sahara Deserts in the late Holocene. Although some human societies have adapted to rapid climate changes in the past.[11] However, the civilizational collapse took place on this earth under the persistent influence of climate change. The rise and fall of human civilizations are noticed due to abrupt climatic changes in Asia which might have brought drastic change in the patterns of vegetation. Thus these changes in flora and fauna resulted into the domestication of certain animals and plants and gave birth to the process of reciprocity, by which animals and plants species depended on humans for their survival, while provided humans with a large number of benefits in turn and became interdependent. This process of interdependence resulted into the expansion of human civilization and increase in their population during Holocene. Domestication of plants and animals had played very decisive and vital role in the origin of agriculture which ultimately evolved and developed ancient human societies. The change in climate and environment, coupled with the slowly changing ways of living that resulted, stimulated human to make the further changes during Holocene. The outstanding development of the ancient human societies was man's realization that food could be obtained by planting. Agriculture enabled human to settle down or made them sedentary, and this was the first step on the road to civilization. Agriculture also enabled human to have a regular food supply. The most significant change took place in human society about ten thousands years ago, when the transition from foraging to farming began, and during preceding periods anatomically modern humans had successfully colonized almost all habitable and accessible areas of the earth and in so doing had learned to subsist, as "hunter-gatherers", on a great diversity of plants and animals food. The most significant and far reaching impacts of the 'agricultural' revolution in the early Holocene was that it enabled more food to be obtained, and more people supported, per unit area of exploited land. It thus facilitated long-term sedentary settlement and maintenance of larger and more complex social groups, which in turn enabled urban society to develop.[12] Harris is of the opinion that the transition to agriculture was not an unmixed blessing. But by reducing the range of wild foods exploited and increasing dependence on a much smaller repertoire of "domesticated" plants and animals it ushered in nutrition, which coupled with greater disease transmission in more crowded permanent settlement, probably caused, an over-all deliberation in human health.[13] As the village settled, life gradually developed the need for different occupations. As life in ancient society became more complex, new needs arose. Not all men tended the fields, hunted, or were warriors. Some grew skilled in producing the artifacts or objects necessary in a more settled community,[14] they were the forerunners of artisans.

The origin of agriculture can be properly understood only in the light of the evolution of life and the material culture of human race. Man is a part of an unbroken stream of life. That stream in the dawn of life on this earth manifested itself in the form of single microscopic cells. Hundreds of millions of years later, after transformation through the forms of creatures emerged fully mammalian. The four-footed man like creature finally grew into a hominid and it got transformed into a man. This primitive man learned how to control fire and use it for certain purposes. He fabricated stone tools for hunting wild animals and skinning them, domesticated dog, who became his best friend in hunting. This process of domestication of animals and plants were of prime importance for the origin of agriculture in ancient societies. The notion of sedentary and classified societies came into being. As early hominids were hunters and gatherers who relied on naturally occurring vegetation, fruits, nuts, etc. But hunters and gatherers did not establish permanent settlements, kept moving in response to change in the season and climate for thousands of years. Even, subsistence by hunting and gathering is still practiced by ancient tribes throughout the world. Moreover, these tribes are totally marginalized in all senses—geographically, politically and socially. The conditions which they live are different from those of early human but certainly they carry the certain ingredients of ancient hunters and gatherers.

A couple of questions are still lingering in the minds of historian and archaeologists regarding the origin of agriculture on the earth: Why did primitive hunters and gatherers adopted agriculture? Why did they abandon their primitive lifestyle and adopted agriculture is not very clear? It is assumed that these primitive human adopted agriculture because lesser energy was required for agricultural practices to obtain the same calories of food energy than required for hunting and food gathering.[15] Even the external pressure from environmental change and intrinsic dynancies of human population can be held responsible for adaptation of agriculture by primitive hunters and gatherers.[16] But this hypothesis is rightly negated and questioned by Anil K. Gupta, "the early Holocene climate conditions were more conducive with enough rain and river water available throughout the Asian African region that might have caused the origination and expansion of agriculture and not the environmental pressure".[17] Thus favourable climate conditions with enough rains brought significant change in the ecology leading to the exuberance of vegetation and diversification of plant community. It can be argued that the increased greenery and diverse vegetation during early Holocene enhanced man's awareness and sensitiveness towards nature. Human became more curious to learn about the traits and usefulness of plants and vegetation for their subsistence. The availability of stone and metal tools helpful in clearing fields and crops harvesting may have also helped the domestication of wild plants and beginning of agriculture in the early Holocene.[18] Although human beings were able to domesticate plants and cattle and to practice agriculture, but both archaeological and genetic evidence from crop plants indicates that certain regions of the ancient Indian sub-continent were centres of domestications of cattle and agricultures but certain other regions of Indian subcontinent originated agriculture when they came into contact with people one of the centres. Thus the origin of agriculture in India can be linked to the availability of wild plants and cattle that were useful for domestication. It is admitted fact that the fertile crescent of South Western Asia and the Indian sub continent offered many varieties of wild plants and animals which were ideal for domestication. Abounding hunting and food gathering by primitive human being and adopting agriculture and cattle rearing was one of the first forces in the development of agrarian civilization. The settled agrarian communities at one place now care for the crop, instead of unsedentary lives of hunters and gatherers. As these primitive hunters and gatherers settled in small agricultural communities, they began to accumulate possession and adopted more socialized habits.[19] Gradually, as more productive methods of agriculture were developed, and as knowledge spread, the increasing complexity of human relations led to the formation of great states of the ancient world. The close connection between agriculture and civilization is illustrated by the fact that the early man's most important food crops, probably originated in the regions that were occupied by early man.

The traces of domestication of plants, cattle and agriculture were found in Mehrgarh by 8000 B.C.[20] where the transformation from hunting and gathering to settled agriculture and domestication of cattle's took place, which presents the oldest evidence regarding the origin of agriculture and domestication of cattle in Indus system.[21] Mehrgarh also provided an important evidence for the change from hunting-gathering to a subsistence economy. The cultivation of crops like wheat and barley along with the fruits took place at Mehrgarh,[22] the increase in the rainfall in the Indian subcontinent must have created conditions favourable for the expansion of agriculture throughout the Indus Basin and other areas as well. Thus, the early Holocene interval (10,000-7,000 B.C.) was marked by a subsistence economy, based on cultivation of wheat and barley and settled civilization.[23] The Agro-pastoralism in India included planting of crops in rows, storing grain in granaries and agricultural communities became widespread in Kashmir by 5th millennium B.C., as cotton was cultivated in the region by 5th millennium B.C. to 4th millennium B.C.[24]

One of the succeeding stages of human evolution is termed as Neolithic. This stage was marked by the breeding of animals and cultivation of selected wild grasses. The evidence of Neolithic culture have been found in north-western India, Kashmir, the Vindhyan regions, middle Ganga valley, south-eastern India, north-eastern India and Southern India. The Neolithic culture of these regions are characterized by sedentary settlement, cultivation of cereal plants domestication of selected animals, ground stone industries including a microlithic component, hand-made pottery, etc.[25] The indications of agricultural life and activity along the Ganga river were found even before the coming of the Aryan which linked its inhabitants with Harappan civilization. From Bithur and Pariar on the upper Ganges we come to finds of herpoons, which reveal a riparian culture which was confined to the Ganges doabs.[26] The Neolithic people of Middle Ganges valley cultivated wheat, barley, rice, field pea, moong, etc. The rice appears to be the staple food of the Neolithic people and its cultivation goes back to the late 6th and the 5th millennium B.C. in the Sarayupar region of the middle Ganges valley.[27] The certain sites of middle Ganges valley demonstrates that the agriculture was firmly established by the end of 3rd millennium B.C.

As far the origin of agriculture in the Vindhyan Neolithic culture was concerned nothing can be said in precision whether the people had started cultivating land with plough or they were simply digging with hoe like implements to sow seeds. The agricultural practice in the Vindhyan Neolithic culture might have been in an experimental stage where hunting continued along with agriculture and domestication of animals and the antiquity of the farming in the Vindhyas region may be pushed back to 7th Millennium B.C.[28] Thus, this Vindhyan Neolithic phase with rice cultivation seems to be indigenous, where the cultivation of rice was initiated. J.N. Pal rightly stated that there is no direct stratigraphic evidence to demonstrate the transformation of farming culture from the hunting gathering cultures, but it is clear from the comparative study of the cultural contents of both the cultures of northern Vindhyas that several feature of the neolithic culture have their source in the Mesolithic culture of the area.[29] The wild rice found in the form of husk embedded in burnt clay lump at Chopani Mando in the Belan Valley indicates the presence of rice in wild form in the area which was cultivated in the Neolithic period.

In order to understand the Harappan agricultural system, it is essential to study the peasant culture as revealed in the excavation at Mehrgarh and Koldihwa. Both Baluchistan and Ganga valley can be considered as centres for the two important food crops, such as wheat and rice. The early peasants of Mehrgarh cultivated emmer and two-row barley, thereby indicating that the north-western boundaries of Harappan civilization were occupied by peasants as early as the 6th Millennium B.C., and later on rice was cultivated beyond the eastern boundary of the Harappan civilization.[30] The Mehrgarh peasants selected free-threshing wheat and six-row barley where a clear transition from hunting to herding can be seen.[31]

The continued and regular supply of food-grain and food product sustained the Harappan civilization for thousands of years indicates that the people of Harappan civilization had domesticated cattle, and carried on agriculture. The Sumerians developed the plough about 2900 B.C., possibly, the Harappan peasants learnt the use of the plough from them. All primitive ploughs were made of wood, and wood is a perishable material. We did not find an actual wooden plough from a Harappan site. However, a terracotta model of a plough has been discovered from Mohenjo-daro. But, apart from the terracotta plough toy, there is indirect evidence of the existence of the plough in the Harappan times; it was discovered from Kalibangan in western Rajasthan. To the South-east of the pre-Harappan settlement a ploughed field was discovered by B.B. Lal and B.K. Thapar. This is perhaps, the earliest ploughed field so far excavated anywhere in the world. It showed a grid of furrows with one set more closely spaced running east-west and other widely spaced, running north-south.[32] But Lambrick did not agree with B.K. Thapar and negated his theory of plough cultivation. He is of the view that wheat and barley, the principal food-grain on the flood plains were cultivated without ploughing, manuring or producing additional water.[33] The Neolithic peasants were not aware of the plough, as they used to dig pits with a pointed wooden stick, at the top of which a stone ring for weight was fixed. This method continued for some time even after metal came into use,[34] but digging of pits with wooden stick is debatable and questionable issue? But it can be surmised on the basis of study of Mehrgarh excavations in Baluchistan and Koldihwa in U.P. The seven cultural phases have been distinguished at Mehrgarh which is situated on the river Bolan. The first phase 600 B.C. is Aceramic Neolithic culture while the seventh phase about 4000 B.C. represents the Chalcolithic Culture and observed that cotton, lentils and cereals including rice and wheat, were cultivated by the Neolithic peasants by 4000 B.C. and continued to be cultivated by the Harappan peasants at Lothal, Rangpur and Alamgirpur.

The nature of Harappan civilization's agrarian system is still largely a conjectured, debatable and conjecture question due to the paucity of information. But it seems that agrarian systems of Harappan people might have been highly productive. After all, it was so they were capable of generating surpluses sufficient to support urban residents who were not primarily engaged in agricultural activities. But it is clear that the peasants of Harappan times might have used the fertile alluvial soil left by rivers often the flood season, and continues supply of foodstuff to urban areas of Harappan civilization which definitely sustained Harappan urbanization for thousands of years.

The absence of any evidence regarding the irrigation during Harappan civilization could have been destroyed by repeated disastrous floods. The Harappan civilization appears to contradict the hydraulic despostism hypothesis of the origin of state. According to this hypothesis such big cities could not have arisen without irrigation system capable of generating huge agricultural surpluses. To build this system, a despotic, centralized state emerged that was capable of suppressing slaves, the social status of thousands of people harnessing their labour as slaves. It is very difficult to accept this hypothesis which is known about the Harappan civilization. We do not get any idea of kings, slaves, or forced mobilization of labour. It is assumed that intensive agricultural production requires dams and canals. This assumption is easily refuted and negated. Throughout Asia, rice farmers produce significant agricultural surpluses, which result not from slavery but rather the accumulated labour of many generations of people instead of building canals, the people of this civilization may have built water diversion schemes, which—like terrace agriculture—can be elaborated by generation of small scale labour investments. In addition to this, Harappan peasants practiced rainfall harvesting as powerful technology that was brought to fruition by ancient civilization of India but nearly forgotten in twentyfirst century. But we must keep in mind the agriculturist of this ancient civilization, like all farming communities of South Asia, built their lives around the monsoon, a weather patterns in which the bulk of a year's rainfall occurs in a four-month period. At recently discovered sites of this civilization in western India, archaeologists discovered a series of massive reservoirs, hewn from solid rock and designed to collect rainfall that would have been capable of meeting the urban needs during the dry season.

The *Vedic* farmers attached great importance to agriculture as can be very well understood by the references made to it in several hymns. The *Rgvedic* hymn thus run as: "May the oxen draw happily; man labour happily; the plough furrow happily; Auspicious *Sītā* (furrow), be present, we glorify thee: that thou mayest be propitious to us, that thou mayest yield as abundant fruit. May the ploughshares break upon land happily; may the ploughman so happy with the oxen; may Parjanya water the earth with sweet showers happily."[35] However, the Vedic term used to denote agriculture is *kṛṣi* which literally means the act of ploughing, the produce being called *śasya*. Similarly *Yajurveda* considered agriculture as the best of all the professions, since it was the very basis of life, happiness and prosperity. Same source enjoins to practice agriculture so as to reap good crops.[36] The *Ṛgveda* informs us that agriculture was the best profession and suggests that farmer should not play with dice but adopt agriculture, so that he would earn wealth, happiness, cattle and happy married life.[37] The same source informs us that a peasant is bound to obtain immense wealth and propose crops.[38] In *Ṛgvedic* times the cutting of crops was done with sickle, "may the sickles go close to the crop to cut it".[39] Thus, agriculture was considered as the real source of wealth, prosperity and happy married life.[40] we notice plethora of reference in *Ṛgveda*, which touch upon various aspects of agriculture. The *Atharvaveda*,[41] also, is a veritable treasure of agricultural knowledge developed during *Vedic* period. By the end of the *Ṛgvedic* period the Aryan reached the Ganga doab and gradually the pace of migration decreased, and a pastoral people began to exchange their nomadic life for an economic based on agriculture.[42] Since, Vedic traditions or literary sources are associated primarily with religious ideology and nature, do not throw any direct light on the aspect of agriculture and the material life of the people. That is why we do not find any direct references to the material aspects of the life of the farmers based on agriculture. The problem is further accentuated by the Marxist historian to prove the Marxian philosophy of economic determinism with theories of class struggle, change in made of production, etc. It is a pity that no archaeological culture, including P.G.W. can be conclusively identified with the *Vedic* culture. The information in the *Vedic* traditions may be fragmentary and incomplete and, therefore, misleading, because there were many versions of the *Ṛgveda* which are not available to us. Even the Vedic Index of Keith and MacDonell, on which most of the historians depend, does not contain full information in many cases.[43]

There are some assumptions which require further scrutiny. For example, it is a very common assumption that the *Vedic* society was wholly rural, and assumed that *Vedic* society was predominantly pastured and agriculture played a secondary role, though it developed as a primary occupation in the later *Vedic* age. But the theory of the predominance of pastoralism is based upon the desire of the Marxist historians to locate the change in economic life in different periods of Indian history with a view to illustrating the historical development of Indian history in accordance with Marxian prophesy.[44] But the theory of the predominance of pastoralism has been negated and refuted by many historians.[45]

The Agro-pastoral dichotomy of Harappan and *Vedic* times is still undecided and debatable issue. The relationship of Harappan culture with the *Vedic* culture is another question which is yet to be decided permanently. The theory of the Aryan invasion of India is still baffling the scholars and still stands unsolved. G.C. Pande argues that the plethora of reference to cattle in *Vedic* traditions confused historians who assumed that the *Vedic* society reflects the predominance of pastorialism.[46] The *Vedic* seers used to live in hermitages outside the village so that they neither traded nor cultivated lands. They lived on the lands of cattle tended by their disciples and the produce of the forest, therefore, life in the hermitages ought not to be confused with the life of pastoralists in *ghośas* or of tribes in pallis.[47]

The *Vedic* traditions tell us about the ritualistic association of agriculture and certain sacred hymns which were recited at the time of the ploughing the field and harvesting of crops, with reference to the certain agrarian deities.[48] Thus the references to agricultural deities in *Vedic* traditions questioned the theory that agriculture was little known in *Ṛgvedic* time and it was a retrograde step. With the passage of time the role of agrarian deities got changed. For example, Indra the war deity was associated with agriculture and cattle and the protector of the fields.[49]

But the cattle rearing and tending are the basic ingredients of an agrarian society all over the ancient world, and it remain as basic ingredient as long as agrarian society would survive on the earth, agriculturist and pastoralists cannot be separated from each other. Thus we can surmise that agriculture and pastoralism were compatible and interdependent in Ancient India.

II

Pastoralism: Pastoralism is the branch of agriculture concerned with the rearing of cattle. Pastoralism is found in many variations throughout the world. Composition of herds, management, practices, social organization and all other aspects of pastoralism vary between areas and between social groups. Many traditional practices have also had to adapt to the changing circumstances of the modern world. But Bates and Lees argue that pastoralism followed mixed farming like rainfall dependent agriculture with animal's husbandry. Their model indicates that it was the introduction of irrigation to farming which resulted in the selective pressures for specialization.[50]

The increased productivity of irrigation in agriculture ultimately resulted in population growth and pressure on resources, which lead to greater land and greater labour requirements for intensive farming. Marginal areas of land were often all that was left for animals rearing to acquire enough for age, large distance had to be covered by herds. This resulted in higher labour requirement for animal tending. As a result of the increasing requirement of both intensive agriculture and pastoralism, the two practices diverged and specialization took place. Both developed alongside each other, with continuing interaction. But T.E. Levy, and Hole propounded the thesis that pastoralism was derived from hunting and gathering.[51] It seems that hunters of wild goats and sheep already had knowledge of herd dynamics and the ecological needs of the herd animals. These groups were already mobile, and followed the wild herds on their seasonal round. The process of domestication began before the first wild goat or sheep was tamed as a result of the selective pressure of hunters' prey-choice acting upon the herds. In this way, wild herds were selected to become manageable for the proto-pastoralist nomadic hunters and gatherers groups.

Domestication of wild animals were necessary for the evolution of agriculture. As a result the agricultural practices enabled people to establish permanent settlements and expand urban based societies. Domestication of cattle transformed the profession of the early human from hunting and gathering to selective hunting, herding and settled agriculture. The rearing of cattle had become a prime importance for agriculture in ancient societies. Without agriculture, the complex, technically innovative societies and large human population that exist today could not have evolved, which ultimately allowed people to become sedentary. The rearing of cattle is believed to have begun in the tropical and subtropical regions in the early half of the Holocene. Tropics provide enough moisture for the growth of vegetation that provided food to both human and animals. Some of the earliest evidences for the domestication of sheep and goats goes back to, 10,000 years ago, whereas the water buffalo was domesticated in India 4,500 years ago.[52] A.K. Gupta raised a couple of questions regarding the domestication of animals and agricultural expansion. Why did hunting and gathering people turn to agriculture and domestication of animals? And what was the spatial pattern of agricultural origin and expansion?[53] The cause for the people to abandon a hunting and gathering life style and take up agriculture is not very clear. But MacDonald is of the view that more energy was required for hunting and gathering, than to agriculture practices to obtain the same calories of food energy,[54] the external pressure from environmental changes and intrinsic dynamics of human population growth were the main factors which forced hunters and gatherers to turn to agriculture. But, Anil K. Gupta negated this thesis and argues that the early Holocene climatic conditions were more conducive with enough rain and river water available throughout the Asian-African region that might have caused the origination and expansion of agriculture and not the environmental pressure. He thereby suggests that it was amelioration during the early Holocene and not the environmental pressure that triggered the domestication of cattle throughout the tropics and subtropics.[55] Thus, favourable climate conditions with enough rain brought significant change in the ecology, leading to the exuberance of vegetation and diversification of the plants community which ultimately sustained pastoral economy and the lifestyle of hunting-gathering society in ancient India.

We can see a clear indication of transition from hunting to herding. In the lower levels of the Neolithic culture, the found remains are characterized by bone of hunted animals such as wild cattle, onagers, gazelle, wild goat and even elephant. These faunal remains thereby suggest a Savanna type of vegetation in Mehrgarh region of Baluchistan 8,000 years ago.[56] It seems that by the end of the Neolithic phase, the faunal remains included mostly domesticated cattle, such as Zebra and water buffalo were common in Mehrgarh after 5000 B.C. Even in Iranian Neolithic culture, goats and cattle were dependent on the same soil sources as man, opened more fields to meet the needs of the cattle. The ancient man found enormous opportunity to open more fields and increased in cattle wealth during 6th millennium B.C. in the riverine plains of the Indus and Sarasvati.[57]

The Harappan seals and clay toys depict plethora of domesticated cattle whose actual remains in the form of bones have been recovered from excavation. The influence from the faunal remains is that the climate was more humid. It provided an environment for the domesticated animals included humped bull, Indian buffalos, goats, sheep, pig, and humped Indian camel, etc. Hundreds of terracotta figures of cattle of both humped and humpless variety have been found in all major Harappan settlements, including Harappa, Mohenjo-daro, Lothal, Rana Gundai, and Kalibangan. The large number of seals from Lothal have the image of the urus bull along with the images/figure of a cow with udders and genital organs are prominently shown, whereas no image of cow was found at Harappa and Mohenjo-daro.[58] But wild goats were considered to be sacred by the Harappan people, their figures are beautifully carved on seals, the offering of goat in sacrifices is obvious from an engraining of a goat like animals being led by a man to a deity. The presence of bovine bones in the sacrificial alters at Lothal and Kalibangar and among the grave goods of burials at both the places suggest that the cattle were offered to gods in sacrifices as also to the human after death.[59] It seems that the domestication of cattle was the closely linked with agriculture during Harapan civilization. The development of animals' husbandry without crop-raising was impossible. This fact is proved from archaeological excavation which shows that pastoralism and agriculture occur together.

Certain cattle such as buffalo, boars, etc., possibly came as crop-robbers to the field to the peasants of the river civilization of the Sind and the Punjab in early Harappan phase. They were captured by the farmers and ended up as domesticated beasts in their pens,[60] it is proved that domesticated cattle provided men with food in the shape of meat and milk and power. Their power value was probably more important than their food value and the degree of development of an ancient civilization was closely related to the relative efficiency of the domesticated animals available in the country concerned. The Red Indian of North America and the aborigines of Australia had no other animals available to them than the dog, and hence they remained in a primitive hunting stage for centuries when other had gone far ahead. The Indian of Mexico, Central America, Peru and Bolivia domesticated the Ilama and Alpaca for transport and developed a much higher type of civilization,[61] however there were no draught animals in America, and their agriculture was ploughless. They were dependent upon the use of spades and digging sticks for the cultivation of crops. But Bullocks, Elephants, Buffalo, Camels were more efficient than Ilamas and Alpacs that are very huge Harappan civilization was for ahead of the Meso-American civilization.

Thus, it can be surmised that the relation between human and animals in India has been very friendly and complementary scene the cattle domestication, which can be realized from the fact that many Indian sages turned wild animals as their pets. In fact, all ancient civilizations throughout the ancient world were nature worshippers. An excellent example of human animals' relation in India history is where certain animals are considered as the vehicles of deities.

The early *Vedic* Aryans were primarily pastoral when they settled themselves in the Punjab, they cut the jungle, built their villages, grazed their cattle in the jungle. The villages were maintained on pay or a share of produce. Cowherds, who were entrusted with the working of taking the cattle to the pasture ground,[62] a number of hymns in *Ṛgveda* are addressed to Indra for gifts of cattle particularly the cow.

"May we escape poverty by means of cattle",[63] the cow which gave abundant milk and which could be milked with ease are prayed for thus: "These white kine giving milk like well."[64] I invoke the milk cow that is easily milked, that the handy milker may milk her,[65] the quality of the some cows which let down thin milk merely on the sight of their calf has been well observed and referred to thus: "As a cow having a copious stream of milk yields it coming into the presence of the calf."[66] As cows were the principal wealth of the Aryan, they were often stolen, and expeditions were organized for their recovery with prayers to Indra: "Recover thou our cattle, Indra; bring them back, the drum sounds repeatedly as a signal, our leaders mounted on their steeds, assemble, may our warriors be victorious."[67]

Pastoralism in Vedic period deals with the production of domestic animals and livestock, and it embraces all the phases of breeding, feeding and management. The cattle were so intimately associated with the science and practice of agriculture in *Vedic* civilization which cannot be separated from each other. The *Ṛgveda* categorized animals into three groups such as flying, wild beast and domesticated, [68] certain cattle such as cowbull, bullock, horse, sheep and goat were considered popular beasts. The stud bull was left to roam among the cows for procreation. The Zoomarhism of Indra becomes evident from the Ṛgvedic hymn which says: "may this sprinkling be sprinkled in the cows. Which were the semens of the bull? O Indra, be it the same is in thy manly fluid."[69]

In *Vedic* time cattle tending was one of the items of *Vrātā* (trade) and it was entrusted to a certain section of the people who thoroughly understood the business. Cattle rearing has been depicted as, most important and universal occupation. Thus agriculture and cattle farming flourished simultaneously during *Vedic* age.[70] The Pastoral Aryan were always in search of new pastures. The herdsmen were entrusted with the task of taking the cattle to the pastures and forest for grazing and bring them back in the evening safely. A hymn in *Ṛgveda* speaks that *Agni* looks upon the people of world as a herdsman watches his cattle.[71] The Seer Gattuma Visvamitr praises Indra as a good herdsman who nourishes the cows and feeds them with grass and guard them.[72]

It is well established that the *Vedic* seers used to live in hermitages outside the village. Needless to say that the Aryan seers neither traded nor formed, they lived on the herds of cattle tended by their disciples and the produce of the forest. Meat seems to be principal items of their food. The sage Bharadwaja prayed to Indra to grant him and his worshippers' food with cow as the principal item.[73] Agni is called "eater of ox and cow".[74] Bulls were sacrificed to Indra as well.[75] There was even an appointed place for the slaughter of bull and cows.[76] But horse was sacrificed and eaten up very rarely.[77] The cow, ox, however, was gradually "acquired a special sanctity, as is shown by the term *aghnya*"[78] (not to be killed). It shows that there was a school of thinkers who valued the economic and agricultural importance of cow and ox and set their face against the fashion of killing such useful animals for the sake of food.

The *Vedic* people's feeling for cow and ox are very beautifully and naturally portrayed in the hymn of *Ṛgveda*. Come back, go not elsewhere, abounding in wealth, sprinkle us; *Agni* and *Soma*, you who clothe again, bestow upon us riches. Bring them back again, render them obedient.... I nourish you gods, who are everywhere present, with curds, with butter, with milk, may all these deities who are entitled to worship rewards us with riches. Comeback (Ye Cow).[79]

The eager solicitude for the welfare of their cattle will be evident from the following verse: "May Pushan (God of cattle) follow near of cattle, may pushan keep our horse safe: May Pushan gather gear for us. Follow the cattle of him who pours libations out and worship thus."

And who sing songs of praise. Let none be lost, none injured, none sink in a pit and break a limb. Return with these safe and sound.[80] However, the principal cattle domesticated during *Vedic* phase were the cow, the buffalo, the horse, camel, ass, sheep and goat, ox and cow were considered indispensable for agricultural and pastoral production, besides milk products, cow was also used for food and as a standard of value in purchasing goods and became the medium of exchange in barter economy of *Vedic* period.[81] Thus cattle might be exchanged with sedentary agricultural people for obtaining copper and other metals and also agricultural products. Buffalo was well-known to *Vedic* people; it was used for both milk and food purposes.[82] The introduction of horse by the Aryans made themselves more mobile and enabled them to take better care of their cattle.[83] Later on camel came to be domesticated together with cow and horse, they gave rise to pastoral economy, but migratory habits and preoccupation with cattle raising were serious handicaps in the development of agricultural economy and trade. The cattle formed the principal property of the Aryans. It was quite natural therefore, that the *Vedic* peoples were so anxious for the safe keeping "going and returning" of their cattle. Indeed, they formed into *gōtras* and *gōṣthis* for the protection of their cattle against wild beasts and robbers. The literal meaning of *gōtra* and *gōṣtha* are respectively common cow-stall and common pasture land. The number of *Vedic* families entered into a mutual understanding to erect a strong common enclosure for the protection of their cattle. Those families who held a common cow-stall belonged to the same *gōtra* (lineage), and a number of *gōtras* who used a common pasture land, like-wise belonged to the same *gōṣthi* or lineage.[84]

Thus it can be surmised that Harappan *Vedic* society appears to be less agrarian and more non-agrarian pastoralism was a primitive economic activity which involved the care of herds of domesticated cattle in Harappan *Vedic* periods. In its primitive forms it was either practiced as the main mode of subsistence or combined with Agriculture pastoralism and agriculture during Harappan-Vedic times were interconnected and interdependent. Men and cattle herds lived a symbiotic community; the human component of this community took the forms of a settled village life composed either entirely of pastoralists or of some specialized pastoralists living among farmers. However, the pastoral settlement was found primarily in those cultures given over wholly or in significant degree to pastoralism.

REFERENCES

1. Radharaman Gangopadhyay, *Some Materials for the Study of Agriculture and Agriculturists in Ancient India*, Serampore, 1932, pp. 135-41.
2. R.A.K. Yegna Narayana Aiyer, *Agriculture and Allied Arts in Vedic India*, Bangalore, 1949, pp. 1-49.
3. D. Raghavan (ed.), *Agriculture in Ancient India*, Delhi, 1964.
4. M.S. Randhawa, *A History of Agriculture in India*, Vol. I, Delhi, 1980.
5. L. Gopal, *Aspect of the History of Agriculture in Ancient India*, Varanasi, 1980.
6. N.M. Kansara, *Agriculture and Animal Husbandry in the Vedas*, Delhi, 1995.

7. L. Gopal and V.C. Srivastava (eds.), *History of Agriculture in India*, Vol. V, Part-I, Delhi, 2009.
8. Lallanji Gopal and V.C. Srivastava (eds.), *H.A.I.*, pp. 2002-04.
9. Anil K. Gupta, "Origin of Agriculture and Domestication of Plants and Animals Linked to early Holocene Climate Amelioration", in *Current Science*, Vol. 87, No. I, 10 July, 2004, p. 54 (Hereafter as Anil K. Gupta origin of Agriculture).
10. D.N. Pandey, A.K. Gupta and D.M. Anderson, "Rainwater Harvesting as an Adoption to Climate Change", in *Current Science*", Vol. 85, 2003, pp. 46-59.
11. Anil K. Gupta, *Origin of Agriculture, Loc.cit.* p. 45.
12. David R. Harris (ed.), *The Origin and Spread of Agriculture, op.cit.*, p. IX.
13. *Ibid.*
14. C.J.H. Hayes-s-James H. Hanscom, *Ancient Civilization*, Vol. I, London, p. 39.
15. G.M. MacDonald, *Biogeography: Space, Time and Life*, New York, 2003, pp. 578-20.
16. B. Allchin and R. Allchin; *Origin of a Civilization the Prehistoric and Early Archaeology of South Asia*, Delhi, 1997, pp. 287-90.
17. Anil K. Gupta, *Origin of Agriculture, Loc.cit.*, pp. 55-56.
18. *Ibid.*
19. G.C. Chauhan, *Economic History of Early Medieval Northern India*, Delhi, 2003, p. 84.
20. Zaheer Baber, *The Science Empire: Scientific Knowledge, Civilization and Colonial Rule in India*, New York, 1996, p. 19.
21. Anil K. Gupta, *Origin of Agriculture, Loc.cit.*, p. 57.
22. L. Costantini, The Beginning of Agriculture of the Kachi Plain: The Evidence of Mehrgarh, B. Alleber (ed.) *In South Asian Archaeology*, Cambridge, 1984, pp. 29-33.
23. Anil K. Gupta, *Origin of Agriculture, Loc.cit.*, p. 58.
24. David R. Harris, *The Origin of Agriculture, op.cit.* p. 385; Burton Steen, *A History of India*, Blackwell, 1998, p. 47.
25. Purushottam Singh, *Origin of Agriculture in Middle Ganga Plain*, in L. Gopal and V.C. Srivastava (eds.), *H.A.I. op.cit.* pp. 6-7.
26. Steven G. Darian, "The Economic History of the Ganges to the End of Guptas Times", in *Journal of the Economic and Social History of The Orient*, Vol. XIII, Leiden, 1970, p. 62.
27. *H.A.I. op.cit.*, p. 6.
28. V.D. Misra, "*Beginnings of Agriculture in the Vindhyas*", in *H.A.I. op.cit.*, pp. 25-26.
29. J.N. Pal, "*Recent Excavations at Tokwa: Fresh Light on the Early Forming Culture of the Vindhyas*" in *H.A.I., op.cit.* p. 65.

30. S.R. Rao, "Agriculture in the Indus Civilization" in *H.A.I., op.cit.*, p. 177.
31. R.H. Meadow, "Early Animal Domestication in South Asia, a First Report of the Found Remain from Mehrgarh, Pakistan", in H. Hartal (ed.), *South Asian Archaeology*, Berlin, 1981, pp. 143-79.
32. M.S. Randhawa, *A History of Agriculture, op.cit.,* p. 156. B.K. Thapar, Kalibangan, *A Harappan Metropolis Beyond the Indus Valley Expedition*, Vol. 17, Pennsylvania University, 1975, pp. 19-32.
33. Lambrick, "The Indus Flood and the Indus Civilization", in *Geographical Journal*, 1967, Vol. 133, pp. 483-94.
34. S.R. Rao, in L. Gopal and V.C. Srivastava (eds.), *H.A.I., op.cit.*, p. 180.
35. *R.V. IV.* 57. 4-8.
36. *Y.V. IX.* 22.
37. *R.V. X.* 34.13.
38. *R.V. VII.* 93.2.
39. *R.V. X* 101.3.
40. *R.V. III.* 31.15.
41. *Atharva Veda*, III.17.
42. K.M. Panikkar, *Geographic Factors in Indian History*, Bombay, 1955, p. 91. Sir Mantiover Wheeler, *Early India and Pakistan*, New York, 1959, p. 123.
43. V.C. Srivastava, "Agriculture in Vedic Age: A Review" in L. Gopal and V.C. Srivastava (eds.), *H.A.I. op.cit.*, p. 203.
44. *Ibid.*, p. 204.
45. G.C. Pande, *Foundations of Indian Culture*, Vol. II, *Dimensions of Ancient Indian Social History*, Delhi, rep. 1995, p. 70.
46. *Ibid.*, p. 72.
47. *AŚ*, IV. I.4.
48. *R.V.* IV. 57.
49. *Ibid.* II. 13.6-7, II. 14.11.
50. Lees, S. and Bates, D., "The Origin of Specialized Nomedic Pastoralism: A Systematic Model", *American Antiquity*, Vol. 39, 1974, p. 2.
51. T.E. Levy and Hole, "Emergence of Specialized Pastoralism in the Levant", *World Archeology*, Vol. 15, (1), pp. 15-17.
52. G.M. MacDonald, *Biogeography, Space, Time and Life*, *op.cit.*, p. 578. B. Allichin & R. Allichin; *Origin of a Civilization, op.cit.*, p. 287.
53. Anil K. Gupta, *Origin of Agriculture and Domestication of Animals, op.cit.*, p. 55.
54. G.M. MacDonald, *op.cit.*, p. 357.
55. Anil K. Gupta, *Origin of Agriculture and Domestication of Animals*, *op.cit.*, pp. 55-56.
56. S.R. Rao, "Agriculture in the Indus Civilization", in L. Gopal and V.C. Srivastava (eds.), *History of Agriculture, op.cit.*, pp. 177-78.

57. *Ibid.*
58. S.R. Rao, *Lothal and the Indus Civilization, op.cit.* p. 50.
59. S.R. Rao, "Agriculture in the Indus Civilization", in L. Gopal and V.C. Srivastava (eds.), *History of Agriculture, op.cit.*, p. 197.
60. M.S. Randhawa, *History of Agriculture*, Vol.I, *op.cit.*, p. 183.
61. *Ibid.*
62. *R.V. X.*10,
63. *Ibid.* X. 4.2-10; VII. 6.4.22.
64. *Ibid.* VIII.7.10.3.
65. *Ibid.* I.22.8.26.
66. *Ibid.* IX. 4.2.1.
67. *Ibid.* VI. 47.31.
68. I. 116-18.
69. *Ibid.* VI. 28.8.
70. N.M. Kansara, *Agriculture and Animal, op.cit.*, pp. 126-28.
71. *R.V. VII.* 13.3, VI 53-58.
72. *Ibid.* III. 45.3.
73. *Ibid.* VI. 39.1.
74. *Ibid.* VIII. 43.11.
75. *Ibid.*, X.27.2; X, 86. 13-14.
76. *Ibid*, X. 89.14.
77. *Ibid.* I. 162.3, 10-13.
78. *Mecdonell and Keeth—Vedic Index*, London, 1912, Delhi Rep. 1995, II, p. 146.
79. *R.V.* X.19.
80. *Ibid.*, VI. 54. 5-7.
81. *Ibid*, I. 126. 1-4; I. 186.4 V. 30.12-15; VIII.1.33; VIII. 4.20-27, VIII, 5.37; VIII, 5.47, R.S. Sharma, *Perspectives in Social and Economic History of Early India*, 2nd Rev. ed. Delhi, 1995, p. 154.
82. *R.V. IV.* 21.8; V 29. 7-8, VI 5.37, V, 298, VI 17.11, VIII 35.8, IX. 33.1, X. 102.
83. *Ibid* I.3.10; II.41.48; VI 61.3-4; VII 90.3; X 75.8; X 101.7.
84. A.C. Dass, *Rgvedic Culture*, Calcutta, 1925 p. 121. R.R. Gangopadhyay, *Agriculture, op.cit.*, p. 80.

4

Land-Rights as Gleaned from Early Indian Literary and Epigraphical Traditions

Land was the backbone of agrarian economy in ancient India. It has, however, not been given proper attention by the historian to the extent that it rightfully deserved. At the best it has been assigned the secondary importance in order to understand the agrarian economy of ancient India. As ancient India was predominantly an agrarian economy and largest segment of society lived in villages and survived on agriculture, needless to say that any study of ancient India agrarian economy without having a bearing on this aspect is likely to be misleading and liable to depicts a partial or distorted view of the ancient Indian economic reality.

It is stated that the ancient agrarian community came into existence when group of wandering hunters gatherers settled down upon the land, i.e. during the agricultural state in the development of human civilization. As man first roamed the forest in search of food, but later learnt to cultivate the land and domesticate the cattle. Food production marked the first revolution in human history, and agriculture led to the growth of permanent settlement of agrarian communities. The first evidence of food producing community was noticed from Baluchistan, as early as the 6th millennium B.C., a fertile soil, abundant supply of water, and men and ideas from Iran resulted in the growth of agriculture at place like Kile Gul Mohammad, large village and agrarian community sprang into existence.[1]

The primitive people were not aware of the art of cultivation; they wandered from place to place in search of food and water. But the transition from a wandering and mobile life to a settled agricultural life was a long and eventful process. Finally land not only became the main source of livelihood but also a vital bond of union of all the members living in a particular place. It bound together all the inhabitants who guarded their land zealously from external aggression. This was how the agrarian communities came into existence.

Land classification: The peasants in ancient India were quite conscious of the nature of land and its relation to the production of a specific crop of economic importance. The vast knowledge acquired by experience has been handed over from generation to generation. It was very intelligently and ably moulded in the form of maxims, proverbs, etc., which were some sort of guidance to the peasants. Ancient Indian peasants were trained enough for the choice of a particular land for a particular crop and they were conversant with the principles of crop husbandry.

The land was classified mainly in two groups; i.e. (a) *Urvara* (fertile) and *Anurvara* (sterile). The fertile was further classified into different kinds according to their peculiar fitness for the cultivation of different kinds of crops, for instance, i.e. the land fit for the barley, for the sesamum, rice, mungo, etc. Sterile land was also further divided into salt ground and desert. The land watered by river were respectively called *naḍi-maṭrka* and *devo-maṭrka*.[2] D.C. Sircar is of the opinion that land may be classified as cultivable, cultivated and uncultivated, fellow, barren, jungly, hilly, marshy, low, high, etc. But from the king's point of view, it was classified into three kind viz. (a) State land, (b) land in the occupation of tenants who paid the king's dues according to agreed rates, and (c) land in more or less uninhabited areas over which state control varied under different circumstances.[3] Each of these type of land has its subdivisions. The state land in ancient India can be divided into the different kinds, such as (a) land attached to the king personally, (b) fiefs allotted to officers, subordinates and members of the royal family, (c) land cultivated by the state farms, (d) land cultivated by temporary tenants receiving half the share of the produce for their labour, and (e) uncultivated and waste land of various types.[4] Thus new settlements were usually founded in regions which were more or less uninhabited and uncultivated.

The exact chemical composition of different kinds of land was known to the ancient Indian peasants or agriculturists but they obtained a masterly knowledge regarding their characteristic suitability for the cultivation of different kinds of crops. The ancient India literary traditions speak of various kinds of lands, where works conducive to agrarian prosperity of the state could be undertaken. They are as follow: (1) fertile land, (2) watery and wet land, (3), plains, (4) marginal furrows, (5) low ground, (6) marshy, (7) land beaten by foam of river water, (8) land frequently overflown by water, (9) land in the vicinity of wells, (10) land watered by regular rain, (11) salty, fallow, barren and uncultivable tracts, (12) forest, (13) dry (14) rocky, (15) uneven, (16) desert, (17) fill of pebbles, (18) deep ditches, (19) elevated or high-table land, (20) grazing grounds, (21) garden-groves, mine and quarries, etc.[5]

The epigraphical traditions of early India refer donation of land, *kṣhetra* which means an arable field or tilled land.[6] Kauṭilya suggests that cultivation must be done according to the fitness of land, and peasant should bear in mind that all units of land were not of the same fertility.[7] The Arable land was preferred to all other kinds of land, for the very existence of people depended on it. The *Arthaśāstra* recommends that a limited land tract with water is better than mere plain; the former being more conducive to the crops and fruits throughout the year.[8] N.N. Kher states that "Kauṭilya gives importance to fertile lands. Thus the *kṣhetra* was a fertile land producing all kinds of agricultural products."[9] The terms such as *Akriṣhta, Ushara anurvara, bharma* and *khilā*, etc., were used for uncultivated barren, fallow, dry and salty kind of land in literary traditions of early India.[10] But Narada states that *Khilā* and *Ushara* lands were not completely waste land, unfit for cultivation, he explains that the plots of land not under cultivation for one year is called *ardha khilā* (half waste), and that which has not been tilled for the last three years was termed as *khilā*.[11] The *Arthaśāstra* refers jungle land as *bhūmi chchidravidthanam* which were reserved for the grazing of cattle, hermitages for the *Brāhmaṇas*, royal sport, and elephant land.[12] The rocky uneven and desert and land full of pebbles were not fit for cultivation.[13] The term *sthala* and *parvata* occur in the *Arthaśāstra*. When one branch of the Aryan ultimately settle down in the land of the five rivers, they adopted agricultural life and divided land into Arable land, Pasture and forest.[14] The land classification remained the same as it was during the pre-Buddhist period. In the centre was the inhabited portion containing the homestead of the peasants.[15] Around this inhabited portion was the arable field, the limits of which might be extended by fresh clearing of forest land.[16] The majority of the holding were probably small, though estates of 1,000 *kariṣas*, (one *kariṣa* = 8 acres) also occur in the Buddhist traditions.[17] Around the village lay its grazing pastures of herds of cattle. In the earlier period the pastures do not appears to have been organized in any particular way. But during *Jātaka* Age we come across an indirect reference to an enclosed pasture. A Brahman goat herd took a flock of goats and making a pen in the forest, kept them there.[18] The *Śattigvmba Jātaka* refers the heart of a forest where silk cotton trees were grown.[19] The *Arthaśāstra* refers meadow or grazing grounds in the outskirts of the village for the grazing of cattle.[20]

Land Rights in Ancient India

Question of land right in ancient India is a matter of controversy and unending debate. Different theories have been profounded both far and against the kings sole land right. There is hardly any unanimity among the scholars on this issue, because literary and epigraphical traditions of ancient India are not only confusing but also conflicting. These traditions have been interpreted by different scholars to suit their respective point of view.

The Ancient Indian kings were considered theoretically the sole owner of all land in his territory. But there was difference of opinions regarding this issue between two schools of thinkers. According to one school, represented by the Jaimini and Sabara,[21] the ruler was not the sole owner of land, and the question of king's right over whole land does not arise, but he was only entitled to levy taxes from the holders of land, and the state could acquire proprietary right on a plot of land under a tenant if only he purchased it from the latter.[22] Thus, in the opinion of this school of thinkers, the king collected taxes in exchange for the protection he offered to the subjects. The other school was represented by Manu, etc., was the view that the king's main responsibility was to provide protection to the state and regarded him as a god in human form and the lord of all land.[23] But the Vedic evidence prove beyond doubt that the office of the king was supreme commander, who rose to kingship.[24] But, here the question arises was the *Vedic* king the owner of the land of his realm? In the absence of categorical statement in Vedic traditions, who have to view this question in the light of the political development that took place in the fullness of time? The most important function of the king as we observed was to fight in order to protect his subject.[25] S.D. Singh argues that the advent of the Aryans in India synchronizes with the death and destruction of the cities of the Indus Valley and the office of the *Vedic* king, the supreme commander in battle, grew out of warfare.[26] Vedic deity, Indra is described as the divine prototype of the ideolised leader of the war, the saviour and the conqueror, who rises to kingship, and the institution of kingship originates in military necessity and deserves its validity from consent.[27]

It is argued that new land had to be required by the Aryan and same land was supposed to be distributed to meet the growing demands of the people. The *Ṛgvedic* hymns do not records any instance of land transactions or of inheritance of land or gift of land. With the expansion of the Aryan territory in the next period, extensive land came into the possession of the conquering Aryan, if the earlier inhabitants of the conquered regions had developed their land resources. The Aryan now secured the resultant benefits, former land rights ceased.[28] The *Vedic* kings are oftenly depicted as a rapacious person who could "devour" his subjects, has been variously interpreted. In the *Ṛgveda* the king has been described as devouring the people.[29] A similar notion can be traced in some other texts of early India.[30] It indicates that the king might have oppressed the peasants, that it obviously had its origin in a condition by which the king and his retinee were fed by the peasant's contribution, a plan with many parallels, and that probably the king could assign the royal right of maintenance to a *kṣhatriya* who was exempted from the royal bounty.[31] These statements show that the king devour the people has been interpreted to be an indication and almost a proof of the king's right of land.

But in the later Vedic period little change was noticed, where the king seems to be assumed some type of overall authority over land. It is evident that the application for donation of land as religious act or merit to the donees. The evidence may be multiplied in support of the fact that by the time of Upaniṣads,[32] the right over land had to be accepted. The growth of kingdom and the need for the coalescence in land of limitless horizons promoted the doctrine of universal conquest and universal ruler. In later *Vedic* India, king performed *Aśvamedha* sacrifice and marched on the neighbour and king was considered as the ruler of whole earth.[33] The *Śatpatha Brāhmaṇa* regarded king as the owner of the whole land and the cultivators were reduced to the tenancy.[34] This, of course, is not to say that all things were royally owned, and there was no freedom of private property. Royal land right over land did not thus mean the negation of the people's right in land. The further change in the land right is observed which differs from earlier conception. All ownerless land is described as king's land in *Jātaka*.[35] The king could replace those cultivators from his holding who had been declared defaulters. During Buddhist period king used his right over land quite effectively and cultivators used to get their land from the king for which they paid tax. He could increase the tax according to his own will,[36] the land donation to religious advisers and religious establishments proved the king's sole right over land,[37] and donees was entitled to enjoy the revenue of the villages granted by the king.

We come to know from the *Arthaśāstra* that the king experiences the ownership authority over all land,[38] it is stated that pastures, plains and forest were not subject to individual ownership. Right of alienation by the peasants by sale, mortgage gifts were subject to state interference. The right to receive a fine for the damage done to the farmer crops suggests that the king had control over all land.[39] The *Arthaśāstra* tells us that crown land (*Sītā*) was cultivated by the free working class without any claim to land. However, Megasthenes was probably the first foreigner who made categoric remarks about the royal land right. "The whole land was the property of the king and husbandmen till it on condition of receiving one fourth of the produce."[40] It is possible that Megasthenes had seen, during his stay at Pataliputra, only ruler land and hence made such a categorical statement. But *Arthaśāstra* clearly depicted two type of land within the Mauryan state; one type land belonged to the state and the other to private person. It is distinctly eluded to crown land and the portion of the produce payable to the state (*bhāga*) implying private property,[41] such lands were of two kinds; cultivated and uncultured. The cultivated tracts were suitable for various agricultural operations and when fertile were adopted for pasture ground, manufacture of merchandise, and other purposes attractive to Merchants.[42] Kauṭilya states that unprepared lands were not to be taken away from those preparing them for cultivation.[43] If such person did not cultivate those lands, land could be confiscated from those who did not cultivate them and given to other or they could be cultivated by village labours and traders lest those owners, who did not cultivate them properly, would pay less revenue to the state. If cultivators paid their taxes easily, they could be favourably supplied with grain, cattle and money, which they could return to the state at their convenience.[44] Ancient jurists also supported the royal land right. Narada suggests that in default of all heirs wealth should go to the state and used the word *bhōga* in connection with the ownership of land,[45] another ancient Indian jurist, Kátayana, describes king as the owner of the land and entitled him to one-sixth for that very reason.[46]

The epigraphic traditions of early India also depicted certain aspects of the problems pertaining to land. The

Satavāhāna land grants have the following immunities, such as immunity from interference and exemption from the salt tax and exemption from the entry from the police and magistrates of the district.[47] The Nasik cave of Vasithaputra Pulume records that the village has been donated to donee owned by a *Bhiksu* of fraternity—the *Bráhadayanyas* dwelling the king's cave to produce a perpetual rent for the care of the cave meritoriously excavated.[48] Another land donation was made by king Gautamputra Satkarni, consisting of one hundred *navaratanas* to a medicant ascetics with certain exemptions.[49] A Nasik cave Inscription of Sri Pulumayi Vasithiputra reveals that the great queen mother Gotami Balasire's grandson granted the village to a monk on mount Trirasmi.[50] This is the clear case of the transfer of royal land from the village is clearly called royal property. Another case of the royal land right or control can be traced from Nasik which, referring to the Kabhadi village,[51] as royal village, the Damodar Copper plate inscription (A.D. 443-44), tells us how a *Brāhmaṇa* approached a Board of state officers to make a gift, according to the *nividharma*, of *khilā* at the rate of three *dinarās* for each *kulya vapā*. The point to note is that this type of land was state property, which could be sold to private individual for a specified amount by the state authority through the Board of state officials or representative.[52] The Khoh copper plate of Jayanatha and other records the support the royal ownership of land.[53] We come to know from the Vakaṭaka records that even when donations were made, the absolute right was not bestowed the donee.[54] The post-Gupta inscription further testify to the existence of royal right over the land. The Madhuban copper-plate inscription of Harshavardhana testifies that king rejected the possession of the land and issued a new grant in favour of two people. This also confirms the royal right over land.[55]

However, the Royal land rights are clearly indicated in literary as well as in epigraphical traditions of early India but this view is not widely accepted by the nationalist school of historiography. Indian historians, both within and outside the nationalist historiography, questioned and negated some of the basic premises of colonial writings in early decade of the twentieth entury A.D. Issue such as a landowner and rights attracted the attention of N.C. Bandyopadhyaya, Pran Nath and U.N. Ghoshal. These scholars generally argued for the private land right, absence of oppressive taxation, the happy condition of the people and took a favourable view of the economic condition in early India on the basis of literary and epigraphic traditions. It has been pointed out by K.P.S. Jayaswal, that "there is indirect evidence to show that the king's title was given a wider meaning. In support of his argument he questions that how could it persist on tax-free lands and on villages of which revenue were assigned and which assignment he retained the right to Abrogate".[56] The cultivator's or peasants right to owe patrimony was limited, the limitation varying in degrees in different places and periods, and according to different legal opinion.[57] Thus, in theory at least the king right over lands may have been regarded as the ultimate right over all certain types of lands though in practice private property in land was recognized.

Private and Joint Land-Rights

During the *Vedic* period, the king was also acted as a guardian as he was expected to provide protection to his subject and for this service he was entitled to a payment called *bāli* (Vedic Tax). The king, on the other hand had undisputed right over all the land of his subjects. The question on his receiving *bāli* from his subject, could hardly have arisen. This position appears to have continued down to the *Atharvaveda* wherein we find prayers over all the land, the necessity for such a prayer was not either necessary or relevant.[58] It has been suggested that this measure was the result of the "lordship of villages through royal favour or through acceptance of the villagers".[59] According to another view, what the king in that period granted, was his regal or sovereign right of leaving contribution and probably nothing more.[60] But it shows that both these views are evidently without any sound foundation for it may well be argued, on one hand and on the other hand, that the villagers might as well have joined together for this kind of team work for their common welfare.

The position at this period can at best be only stated to be indeterminable and uncertain in regards to the royal rights over land, which cannot be considered to have developed entirely on the king. Vedic traditions also tell as about the idea of individualistic theory of landed property prevalent among the people.[61] Like all other institutions, the notion of private property in land must have been undergone some changes to emerge from its rudimentary stage of loose ownership to the more advanced right of absolute property.[62] During the *Śatapatha Brāhmaṇa* we do not find any direct reference or evidence to which can establish the king's sole control over all land.

We notice plethora of references to private land right in Buddhist traditions. The *Śatapaṭṭa Jātaka* gives the idea of private landowner and the *Maccha–uddana Jātaka* speaks of a Bodhisattva who was born in the family of a landed aristocrat. The *Mātarodaṇa Jātaka* depicted how, on the land of a wealthy merchant and his wife managed their family estate, the Buddhist traditions further conforms a economy which was based on private ownership of land.[63] The term *gahapati* was referred to in the sense of landowner. In one of the *Jātaka*, Bodhisatta was referred as a landowner who killed his nephew to become the sole owner of the estate and he uttered a verse to explain how silly it was to guard one's fortunes, whimpering mine, mine and the whole.[64] the *Mahāvastū* explain that, "if we were to divide the rice field and set boundaries to them? Let us allot this field to you and this to overselves." And so monks, they set boundaries to the rice field, saying, "this field is yours this is our".[65] Thus it indicates that these references to the portion of the landed property in Buddhist tradition dispel all doubt of non-existence of an individual right over the land. The donations of lands by the private persons were considered an act of religious merits. The elaborate rules regarding the sole mortgage of a land was fully recognized private property.

Therefore, the concept of private property in land was well established and well-acknowledged principle of civic life during Buddhist period. It is gleaned from these references and evidences that state neither claimed nor exercised any overall authority over private land right. But king's right over personal property like his royal garden was an admitted privilege and such property was termed as 'royal' over which his sole right was unquestionable but not overall the land.[66] Thus it can be surmised that the co-existence of state, private and ownership was established fact during Buddhist period. R.N. Saletore argues that the Buddhist concept of private land and its ownership as well as state or the king's right over his own property were not mere illustration of imaginary situations to Indian folklore, it can be corroborated at least to some extent by an examination of contemporary *Sūtra* traditions.[67] The author quoted in his support *Gautama Dharma Sūtra* who admits royal ownership of land when he states that, if the cattle damages crops in an unenclosed field near the road, its responsibility fell on the herdsman and the owner of the unenclosed field.[68] The allusion in this case apparently to a field owned by a private person but, it must be admitted that he does not explicitly state so. Nevertheless, he refers in another case to a specific case of passion. He laid down that the property of a person, who neither an adult is nor a minor, having been used by strangers, before his eyes for ten years, belongs to him who uses it,[69] but this limitation of adverse possession was not applicable in three cases. This was because he unequivocally declared that animals, land and women, are not to the owner through another's possession.[70] It is clear from above references that land was one of the items which an individuals could possessed.

Kauṭilya clearly indicates that king did not have exclusive right over all land, references are made to the private control of land that were difficult to be cultivated by the state.[71] He referred the purchase of land, which hardly have been possible if all the land had been state property. The tax paying peasants were entitled to sell or mortgage their peace of land to taxpayers only. *Brāhmaṇa* were entitled to sell or mortgage lands to those who were endowed with such land.[72] This was the legal position regarding alien land to ensure that taxes were regularly paid and that person, not entitled to certain kinds of lands, were not permitted to either purchase or even mortgage them. Alienation of land by private individuals and peasants were not rare when private parties could alienate land to their own accord, no reference to the consent of the king's, it may be presumed that they had the legal right to do so, which is an attribute to ownership.[73] Thus, not only was private land right of land in the Mauryan period acknowledged the principles in economic life but precise provision was made for settling dispute in regard to boundaries between two villages and also concerning fields among their respective owners. Kauṭilya recommends formation or creation of new agricultural settlements because of increasing population,[74] it obviously implies that demand for cultivable land was increasing in this period and simultaneously a keen necessity for some stable form of ownership must have been felt.[75]

The regulation made by the ancient Indian jurists as to the legal ownership of land, sale of land, dispute over landed property, alienation by gift or mortgage and so on speak of a society of a complex nature, where the right of private owners were safeguarded and there was thus no place for ownership which arouse out of mere occupation.[76] Kauṭilya argues that mere occupation of a boundary or any other property, etc., should not give person the right of possession.[77]

The dictum of Manu that land belong to him who first removed the weed, and dear to him who first killed it, and *Rāmāyaṇa* also depicted similar dictum.[78] This dictum through the analogy of land and dear in the maxim of Manu is not appropriate from the practical point of view, such loose type ownership or right of possession might have prevailed in ancient society at the time of first occupation and before the inception of the state. When, however, a stable government came into existence, this notion underwent a change. Other jurists of ancient India recommended certain lawful modes of acquiring property such as inheritance, purchase, partition, seizure and finding. Manu suggests seven mode of such ownership, viz., inheritance, purchase finding or friendly donation, conquest, lending at interest, performance of work and acceptance of gifts from virtuous man.[79] *Bṛihaspati* also recommends seven ways of acquiring immovable property.[80] Thus it is clear that our law givers were more or less unanimous as to be the legal modes by which ownership can be established. Even, elaborate rules were laid down by the ancient jurists to safeguard the right of lawful owner of the property.[81]

Certain land charters of early India also throw some light on the private land right. The Pathyar Rock Inscription of third century B.C. refers a belonging to private individual and similar evidence is recorded in the Kanhiara Rock inscription of third century A.D. where a garden of an individual named Krsnayasa is referred.[82]

These references to the private possession of a pond and a garden conform the notion of private property or individual land right in early India. The Mathura stone slab inscription refer a gift of a tank, a reservivor, a garden to private individual, and similar nature of donation of an entire village to the *Sañgha* (Monastery) by the *Mahārathi* Somadeva with its taxes, ordinary and extraordinary with its income, fixed and proportionate is recorded.[83] The idea to note here is that the donor was not either a ruler nor even an official but only a great warrior, who made this donation to a body of private person with all right including its taxes due to the state and its income occurring from. Thus one private individual granted even an entire village to a body of *Sañgha*.

Joint land rights: The notion of joint land rights are indicated in the *Śatapatha Brāhmaṇa*, referring that without the consent of a clan a *kṣhatriya* cannot make any donating of land, suggesting thereby the joint land right in later *Vedic* times. Even the *khilās* land during *Vedic* period does not necessarily indicative of private ownership; it was kept for the common use by peasant.[84] Comunal land or jointly controlled land was owned by the whole communal of the village or of the locality for the joint benefit. Such land can be classified under two heads: land within the village and outside the village, mention may be made of *Go-mārga, Gō-vāta, and Gō-patha Gō-cāra* etc. From these terms it is clear that the communal land within the village were particularly associated either with the cattle route or with the grazing fields. The *Gō-cāra* was undoubtedly, *Gō-cāraṇa-bhūmi*, i.e. the land the community moves and grazes.[85] Existence of *Gō-cāra-bhūmi* had been considered essential for an ideal village by the early writers. Kauṭilya suggests that each village must be surrounded by the *Gō-cāra-bhūmi*, and it has been laid that the cow-herds "shall graze the herds in the forest to which are allotted as pasture ground for various seasons,"[86] the cattle grazing lands around the village were held in common by the villagers from the *Vedic* times.[87] Manu mentions that king should make special provision for the common pasture.[88] Thus ancient Indian jurists lay down the law that the grazing field being common to all are being individual. Even *Jātakas* reveal that the belt of meadow land around the *grāmakhetta* (village land) and uncleared waste and woodland were enjoyed by the villagers in common.[89] The *Arthaśāstra* refers certain objects of common utility, such as the village pond, village gate, the mote hall, irrigation tanks, roads, bridge, parks, along joint and common defence village propriety and sometimes collective undertaking of cultivation of field, proves that communal land rights of landed property was also established notion in early India.[90] This co-operative spirit displayed in such economic activities has always been a feature of Indian village life.

It is argued that there were either communally owned lands lying outside the village, described in the epigraphical tradition as *Vana, araṇya* and *jangala-bhūmi*[91] (forest land). It is clear from these traditions that through these donation king wanted to bring more and more land under cultivation and by thus doing so new agrarian settlement were created. The *Tippera* inscription referred the establishment of 211 *Brāhmaṇas* settlements having joint ownership of land, and a similar nature of land donation is recorded in the Maliya copper plate of 571-72 A.D. which refers donation of 100 villages under joint ownership of land.[92] Thus the right of the transfer of immovable property was exercised by whole group of people, four donations were made by the people of (*Samastasthāna*) Gwalior a piece of land lying in a village and two fields to certain temples and both villages declared their collective possession. The piece of land donated are specified as belonging to village so and cultivated by so and so.[93] Thus these references to joint land right confirm the communal ownership of land existed in autonomous tribes and the republican state in early India.

REFERENCES

1. Excavation in the Quetta Valley and Archaeological Survey in the Zhob and Loralai district, West Pakistan, in the *Anthropological Paper of the American Museum of Natural History*, Vol. 45, pt. 2, pp. 169-401, and Vol. 47, pt., 2, pp. 277-448. Fresh Problem from Baluchistan, *Antiquity*, Vol. XXXIII, 1959, pp. 15-28.
2. R. Gangopadhyay, *Some Material for the Study of Agriculture*, *op.cit.*, p. 43.
3. D.C. Sircar, *The Land System and Feudalism in Ancient India*, Calcutta, 1966, p. 12.
4. *Ibid.*
5. *AŚ*, IX.1. 11.35; *Māhavastū*, 1.318; 1.352.
6. Luders *Inscription* No. 1000, 1024, 1042, 1073, 1125, 1126, 1130, 1158, 1166, 1667.
7. *AŚ*, 11.24; V.2; *Mahāvastū*, 1.355.
8. *AŚ*, VII. 11.
9. N.K. Kher, *Agrarian and Fiscal Economy*, Delhi, 1973, p. 22.
10. *AŚ*, 11.1, 11.24; 11.35, 111.10; VI.1. *Mahvāstū*, 11.295.
11. *Narada Smriti*, XI.26.
12. *AŚ*, II.35; II.2, III.10.
13. *Ibid.* VI.1.
14. *R.V.* III. 23-24, XIV. 10.
15. S.K. Das, *The Economic History of Ancient India*, Vol. I, Bagerhat, 1937, p. 190.
16. *Jātaka* No. 466.
17. *Ibid*, No. 389, 484.
18. *Ibid.* No. 413.
19. *Ibid*, Nos. 277, 430, 503.
20. *AŚ* III.10.
21. P.V. Kane, *History of Dharmaśāstra Poona*, 1962-63, Vol. II, pp. 865-66.
22. D.C. Sircar, *The Land System and Feudalism*, *op.cit.*, p.11.
23. *Manu*. S., VIII. 39, VII, 7-8; Mbh. XII. 68.40.
24. *R.V.* I. 103.5, I. 53.7, I.32.6, I. 33.12, I. 63.7, I.31.4,; I. 74.2; II. 200. 7-8.
25. *Ibid.*, III. 43.5; IX. 35.5.
26. S.D Singh, "Royal Ownership of Land in Vedic period", in D.C. Sircar, (ed.), *The Land System and Feudalism*, *op.cit.*, p. 26.

27. *R.V.* I. 103.5, V. II. 20.7-8; III. 34.1, IV. 30.20; VIII. 4-7, VIII. 35.17. Beni Parsad, *Theory of Government in Ancient India*, Delhi, 1927, p. 15.
28. Pushpa Niyogi, *Contribution to the Economic History of Northern India from the Tenth to the Twentieth Century A.D.*, Calcutta, 1962, p. 72.
29. R.V. I. 65.4, IV. 22.7.
30. *Śatapatha Brahmana*, IV.2.1 3.17; V. 3.8 12; 4, 2.3, X. 6, 2-1, XIII 2. 9,6.8. *Kausitaki Aitareya*, I. 8.2.17, IV. 12.
31. *Sat Br.*, XIII, 6.2, 18; 7.1.13.
32. *Chand up*. IV. 2.4-5; Sat. Br. XIII. 7.15.
33. G.C. Chauhan, *Origin and Growth of Feudalism in Early India,* (From the Mauryas to 650 A.D.), Delhi, 2004, p. 143.
34. Śat. Br., VII. I.1.8.
35. *Játaka*, I. 398, IV 485, VI. 348.
36. *Ibid.*, II, 240, IV, 169, 224, 329, 400, V. 98.
37. *Ibid*, I. 135, II, 428-29, IV. 105, 229, IV. 437.
38. *AŚ*, I.14.
39. *Ibid.*, III. 10, IV, 10.
40. J.W. Mccrindle, *Ancient India as Described by Megasthenes and Arrian*, London, 1877, p. 84. B.N. Puri, *India as Described by Early Greek Writers*, Varanasi, 1971, p. 101.
41. *AŚ*, II.6.
42. *Ibid.*, VII, p. 325.
43. *Ibid.*, II, p. 46.
44. *Ibid.*, *Manu S.*, X. 115, *Narada S.*, XIII.51, *Brahespati's*, XIX, 22-23.
45. *Narada S.*, XI, 84-85, XIII, 51.
46. *Katayana Smriti*, V. 16.
47. *EI*, VIII, No. 3. *Select Inscription* I, pp. 192-95.
48. Luder No. 1123-24.
49. Luder No. 1105, 1125-26, EI, VIII, pp. 67-74.
50. *EI*, VIII, No. 8, pp. 61-62.
51. *Ibid.*, p. 23.
52. *Ibid.*, XV, p. 131.
53. J.F. Fleet, *CIII*, III, No. 5, p. 29, No. 12, p. 47; No. 22, p. 100, No. 25, p.112, p. 119.
54. *Ibid.*, No. 55, p. 235, V.V. Mirashi, CII, Vol. V, No. 6, p. 22.
55. K.K. Thapyal, *Inscriptions of the Maukharis, Later Guptas, Pushpabhutis and Yasovarman of Kanauj*, Delhi, 1985. No. 8, pp. 182-85.
56. K.P.S. Jayaswal, *Hindu Polity*, Bangalore, 1943, pp. 174-83.

57. Pushpa Niyogi, *Contribution to the Economic, op.cit.*, p. 78.
58. R.N. Salatore, *Early Indian Economy*, Bombay, 1973, p. 459.
59. N.C. Bandyopadhyaya, *Economic Life and Progress in Ancient India*, Allahabad, 1980, p. 119.
60. MacDonell and Keith, *Vedic Index*, Vol.1, p. 246, R.N. Salatore, *Early Indian Economy, op.cit.*, pp. 459-61.
61. R.V. I, 100.18, III, 31.15; VII, 49.2, VIII, 91.56; X. 33.6; *Aitarya Brāhmaṇa*, III. 28.
62. *Jātaka*, II, 279, 288. III, No. 317.
63. *Ibid.*, I.92, 153, II 99, IV. 262.
64. *Ibid.*, No. 301.
65. *Mahāvastū*, I. 346.
66. *Jātaka*, IV. 281.
67. R.N. Salatore, *Early India Economy, op.cit.*, p. 464.
68. H.N. Apte (ed.), *Gautama Dharma Sutra*, with Commentary of Haradatta, Poona, 1910, (Tr) by G. Baler, 58E, II, XII. 21.
69. R.N. Salatore, *Early Indian Economy, op.cit.*, p. 464.
70. *Ibid.*
71. *AŚ*, 11.24.
72. *Ibid.*
73. Pushpa Niyogi, *Contribution to the Economic, op.cit.*, p. 76.
74. *AŚ*, II.1.
75. R.N. Salatore, *Early Indian Economy, op.cit.* p. 30.
76. *Ibid.*, p. 31.
77. *AŚ*, III.16.
78. *Manu. S*, XI. 44, *The Ramayana*, II, 32-30.
79. *Ibid.* X. 115.
80. *Brahaspati.S*, VII. 23.
81. *AŚ*, III. 5, *Manus.S*, IX. 104, *Vishṇu S.* XIII, 2-3 *Yajña S.* II. 117, 123; IV. 132.
82. EI, VII No. 16, No. 9.
83. EI, No. 2, VII, No. 14.
84. R.V. VII. 1.1.4, VIII 1.1.8.
85. S.R. Das, "Types of Land in North-Eastern India", in B.D. Chattopadhyaya, (ed.), *Essays in Ancient Indian Economic History*, Delhi, 1987, p. 61.
86. *AŚ*, II.2, III. 10.
87. *RV* X.19.
88. *Manu S.*, VIII. 237, *Yajaña S.* II. 667.

89. *Jātaka* I. 194, II, 358, III 130, IV, 359, V. 103. *Manu. S*, IX. 219, *Vishṇu S.*, XVIII. 44.
90. *AŚ*. II.1, III 10.
91. EI, XV. pp. 307, 311.
92. J.F. Fleet, CII, III, op.cit., pp. 176 and 289.
93. Pushpa Nigoyi, *Contribution to the Economic, op.cit.*, p. 78.

Paradigms of Land Tenure, Demarcation of Boundaries and Settlements of Its Dispute

5

The literary and the epigraphical sources of Ancient Indian history reveal us that lands have been under cultivation in India for more than 5,000 years. In the beginning, tribes exercised control over the areas they had taken possession off. This right of the conqueror was the initial form of land right. These tribes allotted to the individual families land for their utilization, usually by means of shifting cultivation.

The forest land covered unlimited land led to another form of land right, the right of the first tiller. Whoever tilled a plot of land in the forest area also enjoyed the right to use land. However, this private right of land was only valid as long as the land was actually tilled. As soon as the individual stop tilling the plot, the right over it reverted to the tribe. The strenuous work of clearing, the necessity of mutual help, small scale defence measures, and the expansion of the families led, in the course of time, formed the villages which assumed the regulation of land right and different forms developed.

The village having individual land right consisted of a group of families which had rights to the land on the basis of having tilled it. The claims of the families were limited to the cultivated land. The uncultivated land in the vicinity of the village was jointly utilized, but no claim was made to it. It belonged to the king, whom later times also granted permission to cultivate the land. In the case of villages which held land right jointly the village community claimed the right to all land within the village boundaries and allotted it to individual families for cultivation.

During fourth century B.C. literary tradition refers various paradigms of land tenures in the case of land donated to *Brāhmaṇa*, officials, taxpayers, for colonization purposes. The *Arthāśāstra* refers the term *Brāhmadeya* a kind of land tenure or land granted to those who performed sacrifies, spiritual guides, priests, and those who were well-versed in *Vadic* traditions. This kind of lands were fertile, productive, which yielded sufficient produce and were exempted from the payment of taxes and fine to the kings.[1] The second type of land tenure was under which land was donated to state officials for their services to the state such as superintendents, accounts, veterinary, surgeons, physicians horse-trainers and messengers, etc.[2] was called *atithya*. It was made very clear that these beneficiaries were free to alienate the land. The third paradigm of land tenure was when land was donated only for life and could not be made hereditary or otherwise alienated was called *ekapurāsikani*.[3] It was endowed only for the life-time of the donee and could not be transferred in any manner. These kinds of lands were cultivable lands and the peasants had to pay a specific tax (*Kārada*). The paradigm of land tenure which *Arthaśāstra* refers was waste land, *bhūmicchidrā-nyāya*, according to which, a person bringing it under cultivation was entitled to enjoy it without payment of taxes. The original meaning of the term *chhidra* in *bhūmicchidrā-nyāya*, however, may have been piercing (i.e. furrowing in course of cultivation). So the *nyāya* seems to have originally refers to the cultivators of waste land. But D.C. Sircar, is of the opinion that "Chidra was also understood in the sense of 'a hole' an opening or a gap", and therefore the same principle is mentioned in some cases as *bhūmicchidrā pidhaṇa-nyāya*, the maxim of covering up *bhūmicchidrā*, since a plot of waste land could be regarded as a gap in the cultivated area in one's possession, reclamation of such land might be technically known as covering up the gap.[4]

The *Arthaśāstra* of Kauṭilya refers another term *āyudhiya* which means the land donated on condition of a regular supply of troops in lieu of tax,[5] the arrangement of such military service by the people were made through revenue collectors appointed by the state.[6] But this paradigm of land-grant seems to be somewhat like feudal tenure of later period.

Buddhist literary source refers the term *bhoga-gāma* which is not depicted in other Buddhist literary tradition. The *bhoga-gāma* was for those villages which were granted for enjoyment, these villages donations were received and enjoyed by the king priest, *Mahāsethi*, merchant, and the member of the Royal family.[7] It appears that this kind of land donation was received by the donees in lieu of some services to the state. The priest held important position in the state during Buddhist period. As *Mahāṣetthi Anathapinḍika* was the head of the commercial community and performed official duties along with it and performed double duties,[8] the mercantile community was highly respected by in Buddhist state. It was therefore, the *bhog-gāma* was granted to *Anathapinḍika* by the king for his services. *Jātakas* refers the donation of a village as an act of royal favour, a reward for religious and secular services, etc.,[9] the donees in such cases were barbers, ministers, the crippled and *Brāhmaṇa,* etc. It is difficult to decide the question of the tenure of *bhoga-gāma*. The donation of a village under this *bhoga-gāma* tenure was taxable during the tenure of the services of the donees. The donee enjoyed some nominal dues in the form of food and drinks, and it is very clear that *bhoga-gāma* was not free from the royal taxes.

Ancient Indian epigraphical traditions reflected different paradigms of land tenures such as, *prakrtayah dharma*, *akṣaya-nivi*, *aprada-kṣayanivi*, *bhūmichdidrā* and *tribhoga*, suggesting public, private and joint types. The *Prakṛtayah dharma* tenure means common ownership of land which is referred in a grant of king Dharmaditya (551 A.D.). Therein no single private owner is mentioned. A *Sadhanika* (the agent) Vatabhoga wanted to buy a piece of land for donation to a *Brāhmana*. He approached the body of leading men, requested them to take price from him, divided land and gave it to him. The body of leading men and common man unanimously agreed to sale it for four *dinaras* per *kulyavapa*,[10] another paradigm of land tenure as reflected in epigraphical tradition is known as *Dharma-bṣaya Aṣankaya*, the donation of land was made to private person in joint ownership to behold the joint tenure basis. A land charter record refers to a donation of a village to a *Brāhmaṇa* called Cudamani, the son of Jaggata who was the eldest of four brothers. All these brothers were living together, and the grant was made in favour of the head of the family but it was intended to be enjoyed by all four brothers and their decendants,[11] this type of grant can be termed a *dharma kṣayaṣankaya* form of grant intended for the preservation of dharma.

The Mayidavolu copper plate inscription of third century A.D. and the Hirahadagalli copper plate inscription of fourth century A.D. and the Kondamudi copper plate prescription of third century A.D. record the complete denial of the right of proprietorship and the right to sale, mortgage and transfer to the donees.[12] The donation were made in favour of the association of the *Brāhmaṇas*, which signify that the system of collective tenure was also in vogue. Thus it can be inferred that through the *brāhmadeya* tenure land were granted to *Brāhmaṇas* for their perpetual enjoyment, but still their title to possess such land were formally renewed and conformed by every new king on the throne, and this probably depended on their good reciprocal relations with the ruling authority.

Akṣaya-nivi-dharma, and the *nivi dharma*[13] tenure of land seems to be almost identical, the land donated under this form of tenure *Satavāhāna* kinds to the Buddhist monks with its exemption of taxes and certain administrative right such as digging of salt, etc. They, however, cannot be considered as proprietors of such land. Land charter of Kumar Gupta (443-44 A.D.), refers a *Brāhmaṇ* who requested to the local district authority to make a donation of land according to the *Nivi-dharma*, so that it may be enjoyed forever as long as the moon and the sun and stars exist in the sky and its confiscation was condemned.[14] Herein the *nivi* has been interpreted as an endowment but what kind of endowment was not specified. But the nature of endowment was perpetual or permanent. This kind of land donated to donees under *akshayanivi* system, as perpetual enjoyment of state revenue by donees without actual transfer of proprietary right to the person.

Similar type of land donation was referred in the Hirahadagalli copper plates inscription to the donees as the moon and stars would shine in the sky.[15] Nasik Buddhist cave inscription of second century A.D. refers a land-grant of a village to the Monks, for the care and maintenance of the cave.[16] The grantee had rights of enjoyment of economic and administrative control over the donated village. But Satavāhāna period donees had no rights of transfer, sale and destroying the tenure, which were vested in the donors. Although during Gupta period donees had the right to transfer, sale and mortgage as the term *nividharma-kshaya* indicates.[17]

The Bihar stone pillar inscription clearly depicted the tenure of *akṣaya-nivi*, where a donation of a field was referred to a person.[18] Thus under the tenure of *akṣayanivi* system, the land right of donated land were transferred permanently to the donees, ultimately the state lost revenue as well as the control over donated land.

Another paradigms of land tenure in ancient India is referred in early sources of Indian history was *Apradakṣaya nivi-dharma*. This tenure was based on the principle of *dharma*. The Damodarpur Copper plate inscription of (488-89 A.D.) refers a donation of land as per the tenure of and *apradakṣaya-nivi-dharma*, where a prospective purchaser requested the district authority to make a donation of land according to the established rule by destroying the condition of *aprada-kṣaya-nivi-dharma*.[19] The Damodarpur copper plate inscription of Buddha Gupta records that the Sresthin requested the district authority for the purchase of four *Kalyavapās* of *aprada* land for donation.[20] R.N. Salatore state that if the *aprada* is to be understood as referring to land not given to anyone else before, or prior to the transaction under reference—viz., unsettled land, then the word qualifying the nature of land need not have been used in the present case and it could well have been granted to a specific had been granted to a specific person.[21] In this grant it is clearly stated that the land in question had already been given by the donors to another person previously, implying that this was second time that such a land was given away. This implies that land must have been once, in its uncultivated state, given over to someone who had cultivated it and it was again given to another party for second time, but not in an uncultivated state. The Buddha Gupta land-grant of (533-34 A.D.), refers that how an applicant requested for the grant of a piece of land as per the *aprada dharma* tenure, required it and donated it as perpetual donation,[22] this type of tenure indicates a transfer of its ownership from its owner to another to be enjoyed in perpetuity.

Brāhmadeya-Tribhoga-Dharma: The *tribhoga-dharma* type of land, grants were intended for the welfare of *Brāhmana* and the deity. The Alina copper plate of Siladitya VII, (447-67 A.D.) refers a donation of a village named Mahilabuli to a *Brāhmaṇa*, for the maintenance of the *bāli, carū, agnihōtra*, sacrifices and for other ceremonies. Similar nature of land grant is referred in the Khoh copper-plate inscription of Mahāraja Hastin (482-83 A.D.) a village was donated to a Brāhmaṇa with certain economic exemptions from taxes like the *udraṇga*, and *uparikara*, non-interference from the regular and irregular troops, and remission of all taxes.[23] The donees were entitled to get the tribute of customary taxes, etc., and in inhabitants of the donated village were bound to obey the order of the donees. This donation of land was permanent and irrevocable, this type of tenure seems to be identical with the *bráhmadeya* type of tenure which Kauṭilya has referred in *Arthaśāstra*.

The *Arthaśāstra*[24] of Kauṭilya refers the term *Bhūmichheridra vidhanam dharma* a type of tenure, or uncultivated land. This kind of practice appears to have originated from the system of permitting a person to cultivate for the first time a piece of uncultivated land or jungle land, exempted from rent. This type of tenure was often granted for increasing the spiritual merit of the donor. The Khoh copper plate inscription of (533-34 A.D.) records the donation of two villages by king according to the *Bhumichhidra*[25] rule. In this case the ownership of these villages got transferred to the donees permanently and confiscation was prohibited. Similar land donation is referred in the Maliya copper plate inscription of Maharaja Dharasena II (571-72 A.D.), where a village named Antraratra was donated.

Again, in the Alina copper-plate inscription of (266-67 A.D.), the similarities are mentioned.[26] Thus we can deduce from above evidence and references of different paradigms of land tenure that this system of land tenure was prevalent throughout the entire length and breadth of Ancient India from third century A.D. to the tenth century A.D.

Thus the *Bhūmichhidrā nyaya*, therefore, appears to have been a practice of permitting a person to cultivate, for the first time, an uncultivated, and fellow or jungle land, which was rent free. It can be surmised that the *bhūmichchidrā-nyāya* was a type of tenure by which virgin/fallow and cultivable land was brought under cultivation but its transfer of ownership was made permissible in certain cases.

Demarcation of Boundaries

In order to safeguard the interest of the landowners against frequent anomalies arousing out of land disputes, and the careful boundary demarcation of village or arable field was suggested or recommended in early India.[27] The *Arthaśāstra* refers detailed demarcation of village and land boundaries of cultivated, uncultivated, wet, fruit garden, pastures, and forest lands.[28] Ancient Indian jurist recommended the demarcation and fixation of village boundaries.[29] As boundaries disputes were common in early India, thus, ancient jurists recommended the proper demarcation of village boundary in order to reduce the possibility of disputes among the landowners.[30] Kauṭilya and Manu suggests that the village boundary should be demarcated by a river, mountain, raised mound, forest, cave, artificial buildings, tanks, wells, temples, fountains, trees having long life, such as '*Salmali palmyra*, silk cotton tree and different kinds of bamboos, etc.[31] It is also suggested that boundaries of village and a field should be demarcated both by natural and artificial marks, i.e. visible and invisible marks. The marks must be put in such a way as may not easily disappear.

The references to proper demarcation of a field or villages boundary are clearly referred in epigraphical traditions of ancient India.[32] The Jurnar Buddhist cave inscription of first century A.D. refers the demarcation of donated a field by a reference to the mount Manamukuda on its west. The similar demarcation of a donated village is referred in Nasik Buddhist cave inscription of 142 A.D., where donated village was located in the south west side of the mount Tiranha,[33] the village Sudisana was situated at the south of Govadhanhara.[34] Ushavardata donated a village demarcated on the banks of the rivers Barmasa and Prdhasa in Kathiawar.[35] The Mahad Buddhist cave inscription records a donation of a field to a donee which was located below the cave.[36] The Pallona inscription of fourth century A.D., refers the donation of a field to grantee which was located on the north side of the drinking well below the king stamps.[37]

Thus, it is very clear that the rivers, cave, tanks, well and mountains, etc., specified the demarcation of donated villages, piece of land and a field. *Manu Smriti* records certain invisible marks to demarcate the boundaries of a field by hidden marks, such as stones, bones, cow's hair, chaff, ashes pot, dry cow-dung, bricks, cinders, pebbles and sand. These things should be buried where boundaries meet,[38] it is understood that these articles did not last for a long time. The later law giver suggests these objects to be kept in jars or vessels.[39] Besides, plethora of references to partition of landed property, the proper demarcation of the field among the lawful heirs is suggested.[40] Thus the marks like stone, pillars, fences of sticks and branches, and water channels, etc., were set up around the plots of land which distinguished the land held by different owners.[41]

The village boundaries were marked or demarcated by a river, a temple, orchard and a neighbouring village. The boundaries, noticed in the Nowgong copper-plate inscription, were a well, pathway for the cattle, a dike, reservoirs, a pond and some trees.[42] The Gauhati copper plate inscription of Indrapala record that the use of ridges, maize-fields, granaries, ponds, clumps of bamboos, rivers, row of houses, embankments tree as demarcation marks.[43] The Mohoba plate records the donation of land; its boundaries were the *nālā*, belonging to the barber on the east, another *nālā* on the south and an embankment on the west and a *brāhmaṇa* holding, a tank-embarkment and a square of fifty-two cubits of land on the north.[44]

Thus, Ancient India had proper safeguards for the maintenance of such boundaries. Any uncertainty in this respect might cause a dispute between villages concerned.

The village/a field boundaries were held very sacred and any violation to them were severely dealt with. The *Arthaśāstra* refers a fine of 24 *pāṇas* for destruction of the boundaries.[45] But Manu is more rigorous in enacting that such destruction should be punished by mutilation.[46] *Vishṇu Smṛiti* depicts that if anyone destroyed the landmark they should be compelled to pay the highest amercement and asked to mark the boundaries again with the landmark.[47]

Settlement of Boundary Dispute

Kauṭilya refers the settlement of boundary disputes between two villages and also concerning fields among their respective owners. Kauṭilya further states that the settlement of land dispute by the neighbours and elders of five or ten villages were to be investigated into such disputes between any two villages while, in regard to fields, they were to be decided by the elders of the neighbourhood of the village concerned.[48] Indeed all the land within the territory belonged to the king could hardly have been any such dispute and the intervention by witness or elders for investigation would hardly have been necessary. The mediation was required to know the boundary mark and to give an evidence of his knowledge; he used to put on unusual dress incognito to and led the people to the place of dispute. He stated correct boundary marks; the encroaching party was heavily fined. But if he failed to give correct marks, he was similarly treated.[49] Ancient Indian juirist attached great significance to the verdict of the witnesses of different categories in deciding such boundary dispute.[50] The witnesses were to determine the boundaries with truth. Those convicted of false evidence were punished. In the absence of any witness knowing the facts on landmarks, the boundaries were fixed by the king himself.[51] Even the present day rural land demarcation still follow these rules with little modifications owes great debt to the ancient Indian jurists.

REFERENCES

1. *AŚ*, III.10.
2. *Ibid.*, II.1.
3. *Ibid.*
4. D.C. Sircar, *Landlordism and Tenancy in Ancient and Medieval, op.cit.*, p. 5.
5. *AŚ*, II. 35, V. 3.
6. *Ibid.*
7. *Jātaka*, I, 365, 412, 441, III, Nos. 104, IV 80, 473.
8. *Ibid.*, I.120, 209, 349, III. 119, 299, 475, IV. 63, V. 384, VIII. 116.
9. *Ibid.*, I. 138, 420, II. 429, III. 229, V. 541.
10. R.N. Salatore, *Early Indian Economy, op.cit.*, p. 496.
11. *Ibid.*, p. 497.
12. *EI*, I, p. 5, 9, 479, II. p. 485, Vi, pp. 84-88, S.I. Vol. I, pp. 433-37, Luder, No. 1200, 1205.
13. *Luder*, Nos. 1000, 102, 1073, 1100, 1105, 1112, 1328. S.1, Vol. I, No. 82, p. 186; EI. VII, Nos. 7-8, pp. 47-65; EI, X, No. I, pp. 16-19.
14. *EI*, XV, No. 7, p. 131.
15. *S.I.*, vol. I, *op.cit.*, p. 439.
16. *EI*,VIII. No. 67, *Luder*, 1124, S.I. Vol. I, *op.cit.* p. 201.
17. S.K. Maity, *Economic Life of Northern India in the Gupta Period*, Calcutta, 1957, p. 29.
18. *J.F. Fleet, CII; III*, No. 12, p. 50.
19. *Ibid.*
20. *Ibid.*
21. R.N. Salatore, *Early Indian Economy, op.cit.*, p. 499.
22. J.F. Fleet, *CII, III*, No. 39, p. 190.
23. *Ibid.*, No. 22, p. 103; No. 28, pp. 127, 132.
24. *AŚ*, III.2.
25. J.F. Fleet, *CII, III*, No. 31.
26. *Ibid.*, No. 38, p. 170.
27. R.V., I. 110.5, I, 100.18, V. 336.
28. *AŚ*, 11.35
29. *Ápastamba*, I.3.9, 9.16, I.3, 11.9 II.4, 9.4.
30. *Manu S.*, VIII, 246-48, *Yajaña S*, II. 151, *Mitakshara*, II.I, p. 4, *AŚ*, II.1.

31. *AŚ*, II.1, Manu, VIII, 246-48.
32. Luder, No. 1163.
33. *EI*, VIII, pp. 61-62, Luder, 1123.
34. *EI*, No. 68, Luder, 1124.
35. *Ibid.*, VII, No. 57, Luder No. 1099.
36. Luder, No. 1073.
37. *EI*, VIII, p. 143, Luder No. 1327.
38. Manu, VIII, 249-51.
39. *Brahspati S.*, XIX, 20-21.
40. *Gautama*, X. 39, XXVIII, 4, *Mahavastu*, I. 346.
    Manu, S., X, 111-112, X, 115.
41. *Jātaka,* I, 215, 336, II. 376, IV. 169, 281, 276, 281, V. 412, *Mbh.*, VIII.12.
42. Pushpa Niyogi, *Contribution to the Economic, op.cit.*, p. 47.
43. *JASB*, Calcutta, vol. LXVI, p. 285.
44. *EI*, XVI, p. 9, Pushpa Niyogi, *Contribution to the Economic, op.cit.*, p. 48.
45. *AŚ*, III.9.
46. *Manu S.*, VIII, 291.
47. *Vishṇu S.*, V. 172.
48. *AŚ*, III.9.
49. *Ibid.*
50. *Ibid.*, *Manu S.*, VIII, 245-55, 259-61.
51. *Āpastamba*, II,II, 29,7-8. *Gautama*, XIII. 16, *Manu S.*, VIII 99, 257, *Yajana S.*, II. 156. *AŚ* III.9, *Manu S.*, VIII, 245-48.

The Land Measurement as Reflected in Literary and Epigraphical Traditions of Ancient India

6

The history of land measurement can be pushed back to pre-Vedic civilization, the adoption of land measures have been reflected in the Harappan architectural style. The centralized measurement system served the agrarian interest of Indus peasant. Technical enebled gauging device to be effectively used in angular measurement, uniforms unit of length were used in planning of town.[1] Ian White Law holds that rolers made of ivory were used during Harappan period and excavation at Lothal have yielded one such roler calibrated to about 1/16 of an inch—less than two millimetres.[2] The fashion of measuring land was in use in Vedic period. We notice adequate reference in the *Ṛgveda* to measurement of land,[3] the *kūrudhamma Jātaka* records that how the driver of a chariot was "measuring a field". We are told how that a person gave one end of cord, which he had tried to a stick, to the owner of a field to hold and took the other end, himself. Thus it indicates that land measurement was certainly known and practiced and that such operations were undertaken by means of a measuring to rod called the *daṇdaka* to which was tied to a rope to assist in the measurement of land.[4] The *Kāma Jātaka* revealed that state officer was called *kammibas* who was entrusted with the duty of measurement of land.[5] The *Jātakas* refers the terms *karias* (one karias = 8 acres of land). The *Kariaṣ* was a normal measure of land.[6]

The Mauryan kings must have been quite familiar with land measurement. The *Arthaśāstra* refers that prior to the purchase of land and other buildings the accurate description of the exact boundaries of fields, gardens, and lakes had been declared or fixed before the elders of the neighbourhood,[7] this could only have been possible if a survey was made as it seems to have been done. Kauṭilya mentions a list of the measures, such as *kamṣa, angular, daṇda, rajju, aratni, dhanus, gorutu, bahu* and *yojaña*, etc. Each of those measuring has been defined and its particular length is given. The different measures referred by *Kauṭilya* came into common use especially in the measurement of land from early times.[8] Kauṭilya states that *Hasṭa* measure was equal to 24 *Angulas* in breadth or a cubit of the length from the elbow to the tip of the middle finger and probably may have been used for measurement of arable land.[9] Another unit of measure was the *Kamśa*.[10] The next measure more freely used for measuring land was *daṇda* (rod).

According to ancient juirist or authorities of law, as defined measurement standards, 4 *hastas* = 1 *daṇda*, therefore it would appear that 20 *hastas* = 50 *daṇdas* = 1 nivartana.[11] But the question between *daṇda* and *nivartana* cannot be regarded as a fixed one, as there are different views among early Indian authority on this point.

According to *Baudhayan Dharma Sutra*, 1 *nivartana* = 126 *daṇdas*, 50 *daṇda* to be = 1 *nivartana*. According to *Vayupūrāṇa*, 1 *nuvartana* = 25 *daṇdas*. It appears both the authority understood a *nivartana* to be invariably a square, the length and breadth being equal.[12] The *daṇda* (rod) used for the measuring the land granted to the *Brāhmaṇas* was 192 *Angula*,[13] on double the used length of the rod. The *dhanus* (bow was equal to 4 *Hastas* or 96 *Angulas*.[14]

Ancient Indian epigraphical traditions refers a measure called *Nivartana*,[15] similar measures is recorded in *Arthaśāstra* of Kauṭilya where one *nivartana* is interpreted to be equivalent to 360 feet. This measure was common in the north and as well as in the south. The Nasik Buddhist cave inscriptions records the grant of a field of 200 and 100 *Nivartanas* of Gurtamiputra to the mendicant ascetics.[16] Similar grant of a *Nivartana* was referred in the Hirahadagulli copper inscription of fourth century A.D.[17] The Gnnapadeya copper-plate inscription of the time of Srini jayskan davariman, records the grants of 4 Navratanas.[18] The Abhona plates of Samkaragana refers a donation of 100 *Nivartanas* of land by *Nivartanas* measures forty on both side.[19] This system of land measure was also current among the Eastern Calukyas. An inscription of 567-68 A.D., belonging to king Kirtivarmvan records a land donation of 25 *nivartanas*.[20] This measure was also in vogue among the Kadambas as can be seen from their grants. The land donation of 33 *nivartanas* was recorded, to Jains religious Shrines. Similar land-donation of 20 *nivartanas* to a spiritual teacher is recorded in the kudugene plates of Vijaya Siva Mandhatravarma.[21] *Nivartana* was the most popular land measures in ancient south India, especially among the Western Calukas and the Kadambas. Villages varying in area from 25 to 100 *nivartanas*, were given as donation during the time of the Western Calukyas.[22] During the Rastrakutas time this system of land measure became popular, the Twarkhed plates of Rastrakutas of 631 A.D., records of the *Nivartana* equal to 20 rods,[23] which has been considered equivalent to 200 cubits or 40 *hastas*, each *hasta*, as per *Arthaśāstra* was being equal to 51 *angulas* (each *angula* being equivalent to ¼th of an inch). The *koluvan* plate of *Yásovarman* refers to the system of *nivartana* measure.[24] The Banswara plate of Bhojedeva records a donation of 100 *nivartanas*[25] to the donees. Another unit of linear measures was the *mattals*, which was smaller than the *nivartana*, common land measure during the Western Calukyas. The Adur grant of 567-68, refers the donation of eight *mattals* of rice land to the donee.[26] The *Padavarta* measure of land which was used in Gujrat and Saurastra. The *Padavarta* measure of land has been understood to mean the turning of a foot the use of *padavarta* measure can be traced to the Gupta times. The Maliya copper-plate inscription of 571-72 A.D., records the donation of 100 *padavartas* land to grantees.[27] J.F. Fleet interpreted *padavarta* as the turning of foot, and explains that 100 *padavarta* meant 100 feet square each way, i.e. 10,000 square feet, which would measure only ten feet each way and would be rather a smaller area for a grant to say nothing of the still small areas mentioned.[28]

Hasta was the popular unit in ancient India for the measurement of land. It was not always the distance from the tip of the elbow to the middle finger. The *prajapatyahasta* or the synonymous *Aratni* was equal to 24 *angulas* in breadth,[29] or a cubit of the length from also to the tip of the middle finger and probably may have been used measuring arable land. But the *hasta* used for measuring pasture land was different from that used for timber forests. The former comprised two *vitastis* plus one Dhanurgraha or 28 *angulas* and the latter of 54 *angulas* or about 40½ inches,[30] thus, it can be surmised that in ancient India three standard type *hasta* of 24, 28 and 54 *angulas* respectively. It can be assumed that the *hasta* was taken the exact sense of the word, but it was a length of measure of different denominations used by the land surveyors. The people might have been using their *hasta* from tip of the elbow to the tip of middle finger for their own purposes. The *hasta* measurement can be traced during the Rudradaman period. It is mentioned in Junagrad Inscription that the breach made in the Sudarsana lake dam was 20 *hastas* long and 75 *hastas* broad. R.N. Salatore states that if second form of *hasta* measure is to be taken into account in estimating the area breached in the dam, than its length was 21 × 30 *angulas* or 420 inches or 35 feet and its breadth was 21 × 75 *angulas* or 1675 inches or 106½ feet in length.[31] It is clear that epigraphical traditions considered hasta form of measurement of land as one of the popular forms of measure in early medieval India. The *Siyadoni* stone inscription refers the term *hasta* measuring a field.[32]

Another form of land measurement in ancient India was *hala*, (Plough) measurement. But we cannot say only thing in precision that when and where this form of measurement came to be needed as a unit of measurement of land difficult to be determined. Manu, however, refers to various kinds of ploughs, such as the plough drawn by eight bullocks was interpreted as the lawful plough—the *dharma hala*, that was driven by six bullocks for the purposes of cultivators, the *madhyama hala*, that driven by four for house holders, the *grhaṣtahāla*, driven by the time was for the *brāhmaṇa*, the *brāhma-hala*.[33] Similar classification of plough types are mentioned by *Panini* who refers to the *hala* measure,[34] and the type of land measure he called as *halasya-korśa*, a field tilled by one plough and multiples of the *halya* land were expressed as *dvihalya* (two plough) and paramahialya,[35] eight *angulas* long and four *angulas* broad plough is referred by Brhaspati,[36] if an *angulas* to be considered 1/4th to this specification, a plough should have been 4 4/5 increased in length and 2½ increase in breadth. But such a small toy size plough could hardly have been the plough-length of a land measure in the sixth century A.D. This kind of *hala* might have been misinterpreted. The *hala* as a unit of land-measurement means that extent of land which could be cultivated by a pair of oxen, i.e. one plough.

But, however, different kind of *hala* measure was reflected in epigraphical traditions of ancient India. The term *Bhikhu-hala* is referred, which generally understood as monk, *bhikka-hala* when the peasants were provided bull as well as land for the cultivation by the *Sañgha*[37] (Buddhist monasteries). Another term *grāma-hala* is referred in the Paithan plates of the Rastrakutas king Govinda III 7th A.D., can be interpreted as arable land, or it can be interpreted as a village-plough,[38] the land was to be cultivated by such as plough. This kind of plough probably corresponded to the *madhyama hala* of Manu Smriti, which was drawn by six bullocks and meant for a village not for a family. The Udayendiram inscription of eighth century C.E. refers the term *bhoga-hala*, which can be taken as the counterpart of Manu *grhaṣta-hala* meant for householders. Another plough measure unit was known as *Vrhad hala* refered in Harsa Stone inscription of Chauhan king (970 A.D.). This type of plough was compared with the *dharmahala* of Manu, drawn by eight bullocks and considered the lawful. Thus, it can be surmised that plough measure varied from period to period, from king to king and from region to region.

The system of the plough-measure in connection with land-grant indicates that it was well-known that how much land could be usually cultivated with one plough in a day. What the area of a piece of land was in any particular case could be approximately guessed on the basis of the number of plough mentioned even in the absence of figures denoting the actual measurement of the land in question.[39] The Hathal plates refers to an area of land that was tilled with two ploughs in a day, and Charkhari stone inscription records of grant of land which could be cultivated by five ploughs in a day.[40]

It is difficult to ascertain the exact area that could be cultivated with one plough. The size of the plough and the physically of the oxen may not have been uniform. Land was different in qualities and different regions; the capacity of the plough depended on the variable feature of the land. As the grades of land were of different categories, the extent of land indicated by the plough measure could not have been the same every where,[41] thus, the cultivation depended in the size and weight of the plough as well as the quality of the land in different parts of the state. A healthy pair of oxen could plough even more than 5 to 6 acres of land, if the land presents congenial conditions and thereby involves less labour.[42] It can be deduced that the *hala* (plough) might have varied from 5 to 8 acres of land and the higher figures of 8 acres, though conjectural, does not seem to be very improbable.

Bhūmi: Another unit of land measurement utilized since the times of *Śatpatra Brāhmaṇa*.[43] Even *Arthaśāstra* refers this mode of land measurement as equal to fourteen *angulas* or ten and half inches.[44] But in Gupta epigraphical source it was recorded as a large measure unit. The *Cammals* copper-plate inscription of Maharaja Pravarasena II refers how the village of Caramanka was measured by 8,000, *bhūmi*.[45] The Dudia plate of Pravanasena II records the donation of 25 Bhūmi to donees and similar nature of land donation is recorded in the Hirnayaparobhoga to donee. Thus, it can be surmised from these reference of *bhūmi* in inscriptions that the *bhūmi* measure could hardly have been a large unit of measurement as it varied from 25 to 8,000 bhūmies.[46] R.N. Saletore does not considers *bhūmi* measurement unit in ancient India, "This measure of land had nothing to do with the *bhūmi chchhidra-nyáya* in which the word *bhūmi* is merely a reference to the earth and not a reference to unit."[47] But Pushpa Niyogi, considers bhumi measure of land as local measure unit which occurred in two Chamba copper-plate inscription of Somavarmedeva and Aṣatadeva.[48] The term *bhūmi* or *bhū* and *bhūmi-shaki* is referred in the Chamba land charters.[49] It is clearly shown in Chamba land charters that a *bhūmi* or *bhū* was divided into 4 *Mashakas* or *bhū Mashakas*,[50] where *bhū* is equivalent to about 17 acres. Thus a *bhū Mashaka* represents therefore, a certain portion, i.e. a quarter of a *bhūmi*. But the actual size of a *bhūmi* and its subdivision *bhūmi mashaka* is not known. Mahesh Sharma rightly angues that the Gupta and post-Gupta land measures were adopted, i.e. *piṭaka*, a fixed measure by volume of grain sown as mentioned in the Bhramour epigraph of Yugakara.[51] But *piṭaka* unit of land measurement seems to be commonly used in epigraphical tradition of Bengal; which is mentioned along with other local measures such as *drōṇas, adhavapa, unmanas* and *kakiniba*. If the measure were measure of yield of the land it is reasonable to hold that *piṭakas* was also used in the same sense.[52] The Gayaighar copper-plate inscription of 507 or 508 A.D. refers the *piṭaka* which was equal to 40 *drōṇas vapas* = 5 *kulyavapas*. This type of land measurement is reflected in the following land-charters such as the Belana copper-plate of Bhojavarmandeva which records 1 *Pataka* and 9¼ drones of land, the Ramapal copper-plate of Srichandra records 1 *piṭaka* of land. Similar nature of land donation is recorded in Barhackpur grant of Vijayasena, which refers 4 *piṭakas* of land to donees. The Shaktipur plate of Lakshmanasena refers the land donation of 6 piṭakas, each of which was given a name such as Raghvahatta Varahakina, Vallihita, Vijaharapura, Damaravada, and Nimapitaka, etc. These six individual names of six *piṭakas* might represented the different part of donated land in different villages, as Kielhorn has argued that the term *piṭakas* was a part of a village which had name of its own, but really belonged to a larger village.[53]

Kalyavāpa form of land measurement can be taken back to the Mauryan times, as *Arthaśāstra* refers this term as the countries where water channels were used in agriculture,[54] but directly in the sense of a unit of land measure. A *Kulya* was known as a cubic measure or basket full of seed. It is argued that so much land, was is usually sown with a *kulya* of seed.[55] Basak is of the view that one *kulya* was equal to 8 *drōṇas* and *vapa* may mean the place or area where the seeds are grown, viz., a field.[56] It has been suggested that seedlings from one *kulyavapa* of seed would require from 128 to 160 *Bighas* for their transplantation. An epigraph of fifth century A.D. tells us that the cultivate lands were sold at the rate of four *dinaras*, "for the area that can be sown with a *Kulya* of seed".[57] The term *kulyavapa* can be compared with other similar connotation in *pāṇiṇī*, who has argued that the size of a field was determined by the quantity of seed required for its sowing viz., tasya-vapah.[58] If one *prastha* measure of seeds was shown in a field it was called *prasthika* and likewise for one *drōṇa*, *drounika* and for one *khāri*, *khārika* like wise, if a field required a *praṣtha* measure of seeds, it was called patrika.[59] On the same anology, if a field required one *kulya* of seeds than it could well have been known as *kulyavapah*. Likewise, the *drōṇavapa* was also a unit of land measurement in fifth century A.D., as the Paharpur copper-plate land-donation of a field measuring four and two and half *drōṇavapa* in the village named *Prsthima-pottaka*,[60] Gostapunjaka and Nitva Gohali and a horse-stead measuring one and half *drōṇavapa* at Vata Gopali were donated to donees.[61] The Baijnath Prasasti refers the term *vaha* a local unit of land measurement which was equal to an area on which the quantity of seeds was to be sown equal to four *drōṇas*.

Thus, it can be deduced from the references and reflected in literary and epigraphical traditions of ancient India that the paradisms of land measurement differed from region to region as we did not notice any single land charter in which all the different forms of land measures are depicted together. Thus regional and local variations were observed. In most of the cases only one form of measure is depicted or referred, standard followed was not the same everywhere. An inherent difficulty is confronted in determining the exact size of particular area of land mentioned, in the absence of necessary details.

The different units of land measurement are referred in throughout the ancient Indian traditions, which include those of length, divided into several series, rising from those below the standard *angula*, defined as the middle joint of average size; middle finger of a man of average size; to those above including the span and the cubit, and ending with the rod (*daṇda*) or bow (*dhanuṣ*) of around 180 cm. and above this measurement of longer distance was measured in *goruta* or *kroṣa* and *yajaña*.

Thus the land measuring system in ancient India possibly was one of the most complex and archaic system. But, in India land dealings are still done in a number of archaic units. It appears that people are satisfied and comfortable with them.

REFERENCES

1. Helaine Selin (ed.), *Encyclopedia of the History of Science, Technology, and Medicine in Non-Western Culture*, "Shigco-Iwata", "Weights and Measures in Indus Valley", Springular, 2008, pp. 2254-55.
2. Ian White Low, *A Measure of All Things: The Story of Man and Measurement*, London, 2007, pp. 14-15.
3. *R.V.* I, 110.5.
4. *Jātakas*, III, 276.
5. *Ibid.*, No. 328.
6. *Ibid.*, 389, 484, 479.
7. *AŚ*, II. 20, III. 9.
8. *Ibid.*
9. *EI*, II, No. 230, X, Nos. 195, 416.
10. *AŚ*, II. 20.
11. *Mārkanday Pūrāṇa*, XZIX. p. 37, *Vāyū Pūrāṇa*, p. 116. CII, IV, pp. 43-46.
12. *Pushpa Niyogi, Contribution to the Economy, op. cit.*, pp. 97-98.
13. *AŚ*, II.20.
14. *Ibid.* Manu, S., VIII, 237, *Yajña*, II. 170.
15. *Luder*, Nos., 1125, 1126, 1200, 1327.
16. *EI* VIII, pp. 71-73.
17. *EI*, VI, p. 88.
18. *Ibid.*, VIII, p. 143.
19. *Ibid*, IX, p. 299.
20. *IA*, XI, p. 69.
21. *EI*, VI, No. 2, p. 15.
22. *IA*, VIII, No. 2, p. II, XLIV, pp. 216-17.

23. *EI*, XI, Non, 27, p. 290.
24. *Ibid.*, XIX, pp. 67-69, p. 105, EI, X10, p. 10, p. 69.
25. *Ibid*, XI, p. 181.
26. *IA*, XI, p. 69.
27. *J.F. Fleet*, *CII*, *III*, No. 38, pp. 169-70.
28. *Ibid.*, p. 170.
29. *AŚ*, II. 20.
30. *Ibid.*
31. R.N. Saldore, *Early Indian Economy, op.cit.*, p. 511. No. 7, p. 61.
32. *EI*, No. II, p. 110.
33. *Manu. S*, VIII, 119.
34. *Pāṇiṇi*, IV. 4.97.
35. *Ibid.* I. 1.72, 186.
36. *Bṛaspati*. S., X, 18.
37. *EI*, VII, No. 7.
38. *Ibid.*, I, No. 17.
39. *Ibid.*
40. *Ibid.*
41. *Ibid.*
42. N.M. Kher, *Agrarian and Fiscal Economy, op.cit.*, p. 59.
43. *Sāt. Brā*, XIII. 5, 4, 24; 6, 2, 2.18. Machdonell and Keith, *Vedic Index*, II, *op.cit.*, p. 108.
44. *AŚ*, II, II.20.
45. *J.F. Fleet, CII, III*, No. 88, p. 211.
46. *I.A.*, VIII, No. III, p. 44, EI, III, No. 35, p. 209. R.N. Saletore, *Early Indian Economy, op.cit.*, p. 570.
47. R.N. Saletore, *Early India Economy, op.cit.*, p. 510.
48. IA, XVIII, p. 7. Pushpa Niyogi, *Contribution to the Economy, op.cit.*, p. 98.
49. *Archaeological Survey of India*, Annual Reports, 1902-03, pp. 255-58. Mahesh Sharma, *Western Himalayan Temples Records State, Pilgrimage, Ritual and Legality in Chamba*, Leiden, 2009, p. 27.
50. *IA*, XVII, p. 7, ASR, 1902-3, p. 250.
51. Mahesh Sharma, *op.cit.*, p. 28.
52. Pupsha Niyogi; *Contribution to Economy, op.cit.*, p. 99.
53. *IA*, XVIII, p. 135.
54. *AŚ*, II. 24, p. 127.
55. *IA*, XXXIX, p. 215.
56. *EI*, XV, No. 2, p. 132.

57. *IA*, XXXIX, pp. 197-202, 205.
58. *Pāṇiṇi*, V. 1.45.
59. *Ibid.*, II. 3.87, V. 2.73.
60. R.N. Saletore, *Contribution to Economy, op.cit.*, pp. 511-12.
61. *EI*, XX, No. 5, p. 63.

The Economic Dimensions of Land Grants

7

Recent debate on land-grants in Early Medieval Northern India has centred on the propriety of its interpretation in terms of feudalism. It is argued that 'Land Grant' generated a landed aristocracy and brought about the transformation of political power, reduced the peasantry to bondage and subjection, degraded the artisans and ultimately paved the way for the conquest and subjecting of early medieval northern India by many foreign elements.

In order to determine the economic dimensions of 'land grant' in early medieval Northern India about seventh century A.D. onwards, we have to keep in mind the chief trends of historical development after the death of Harsha Vardhan, unleashed a storm of fissiparous forces which brought in its wake the Sino-Tibetan invasion led by Wang Hiuen't'se in 647-48 A.D. Out of this chaos the Maukharis emerged again their earlier glory but the Later Gupta wrested the paramount from them. In the eighth century the Varman king of Kanauj, Yasovarman probably representing the line of the Maukharis, again got the upper hand, conquered far and wide and cornered many of the contemporary chiefs. In the same period, the Muslims occupied Sind and Multan and from there launched raids in the South and the West bringing to the fore new forces of defence latent among the people."[1]

The Flotsam and Jestsam of old ruling dynasties created new patterns on political power and produced new ruling class that goes by the generic term 'Rajput'. This phase of chaos, disorder and turmoil made normal functioning of the economic machinery of the state difficult and called forth new ways and means of maintaining a remblance of peace and poise and ensuring a mobilization of military forces both for offence and defence. The phase of chaos and turmoil made normal agrarian life, economic, industry and trade, wholly disrupted and the advances in it made in the foregoing ages, completely lost, yet its full utilization for stabilizing the structure of state needed an atmosphere of placidity and repose which the rapidly moving kaleidoscope of events did not permit to grow. The newly ruling classes were not properly trained in administrative techniques. They devised quick and easy methods to attract and hosts of supporters and retainers. They got utilise the services of the right to collect revenues and dues from the people on their behalf and appropriate it to themselves in lieu of services that they rendered. This development robbed the state of its economic potential and all power, economic, taxes and other dues from the peasants, but the inhabitants were not attached to the land as they were in Western Europe. Thus feudal Lord eventually became a dominant force in the society and politics that guided and shaped the course of the history of ancient India thereafter. In order to understand and analyse the economic dimension of land-grants in its proper perspective, I would like to discuss first the early medieval land-charters of the time. We find very few references of land-grants in the later-vedic[2] and *Dharma Sutra*[3] periods. Land-grants were made as a *dana* (pious gifts) and donors wanted *punya* out of the *Bhudana* (Land-grant). But Manu in his work recommends that the land-grants were to be given to the *adhipati*[4] of the villages. Kauṭilya on the other hand suggests that land-grants should be sanctioned to the *Brāhmaṇa* and to other state officers.[5] *The Nirmand copper plate inscription of inahasamanta and Maharaja Samudrasena* (612-13 A.D.)[6] records that the village of Sulisagrama was granted by Samudrasena to a body of *Brāhmaṇas* who studied the *Atharva Veda* at the *agrahara* of Nirmanda near the bank of the river Satluj in the Kulu district of Himachal Pradesh, in the service of God *Tripurantaks* of Sive. This was considered necessary of the establishment of bali, *cara*, *settera* etc., and the facilitate the supply of materials required for the daily worship of the deity. This inscription also suggests that the grant was made to the *donees* along with plain and forestlands and to the inhabitants (*Sa-praja*) with the *urdranga* (land), which included the village boundaries together with grass, timber and springs.[7] This shows that the *donees* were given the right to collect taxes and other dues from the peasants. *Sanpaur Stone image inscription of Adityasena*[8] (seventh century A.D.) refers to the gift for religious purpose by Satapaksa in the *agrāhara* of Nalanda free from all hindrances. *The Banaskhera copper plate inscription of Harsa*[9] records the donation of the village named Markatasagar to two *Brāhmaṇas of Bhāradvāja gōtra.* They were exempted from paying all dues. *Madhuban Copper-plate Inscription of Harsa* (631 A.D.)[10] refers to the grant of the village called Somakundaka to Somavedi Bhatta...Vatasvarmin of *Samrni Gōtra and Ṛgvedi gotra.* It was away from the Vamarathya who had been enjoying it on the strength of a forged document. The village was donated to the donees with full right of inheritance by Harsa. The grant of Harsa states that a village was donated in favour of two *Brāhmaṇa* as an agrahara (rent free holding usually in the possession of Brāhmaṇa) in accordance with the custom governing its acceptance by *Brāhmaṇa* so that the customary privileges going with such holding remained understood. The villagers were asked to be obedient to the donees and to pay them the all dues (Pratyaya) including *tulya, meyabhaga, bhoga, Kara, hiraṇya*[11], etc.

We come to know from the Midnapore copper-plate inscription of the time of Sasanka (600-25 A.D.) which refers to the grant of 20 *drōṇas* (*drōṇavapas*) of ordinary land and one *drōṇavapa* of homestead land in favour of the *Madhyandira Brāhmaṇa.*[12] The Midnapore copper-plate inscription of the time of Sasanka,[13] refers the donation of the locality named *mahā-kumbharapadraka* in favour of the *Brāhmaṇa* of the *kaśyapa gōtra* with free from all hindrances. The Kailan Copper Plate Inscription of *Sridharanarata* (665-75 A.D.)[14] records the donation of 25 *pitakas* of land made by the king was transmitted to the *Vishayapatis* of the two *Vishaya* called *guptinatana* and *patalayika* and their *adhikama* (office) by the *kumaramātya* stationed at Devaparvata and by their adhikarna. The grant was made at the request of the *Mahasandhivigrahika jayanatha* and the gift land was dedicated to the *Bhāgavat Tathagataratna* (Buddha) or *Ratnatraya* for the worshiping of the Buddha, the reading and writing of Buddhist religious texts and the provision of food, clothing and other accessories for the *Ārya-saṅgha* as well as to a member of *Brāhmaṇa* for the performance of their *panch-mahāyajña.*[15] The Ashrafpur copper-plate inscription of Devakhadga (670-85 A.D.)[16] record the grant of several plots of land, measuring 9 *Pitakas* and 10 *drōṇas,* by king Devakhadya in favour of the Buddhist monastery. One of the plots of land stated to have been in the Jagir held by queen Prabhavati and another is that of the Samanta Vantiyoka.[17] *The Deo-Baranark Stone Inscription of Jivitagupto II* (c 700-10 A.D.) records the grant of a village in favour of the god *Varunavasi-Bhattaraka,*[18] the grant was made together with the *udraṇga uparikara*, proceeds of fines for ten offences, and other income.

The Khalimpur Plate of Dharmapaladeva (775-82 AD.),[19] records the grant of four villages to a temple of the god named Narayana, free from all hindrances. This copper-plate Inscription depicts that all the important dignitaries assembled at four villages, such as, the *Rājans Rājanakas, Rājapūtras, Rājamatyas,*[20] *Senapati visagnapati, Bhōgapatis, Sakastadhikritas*[21] *Daṇḍosaktis, Daṇḍaptyas, Chauradd-haranikas, Darhsadhasadhanikas, Deitas kholas,*[22] *Gangamikas, Abhituaramanus*; Inspector of elephant, horses, cows, buffalo-cows, goats and sheep, inspector of the forces *Tarikas,*[23] *Saulkikas, garlanikas* were dependent of the king's feet. Sometimes, some of them who belonged to the irregular and regular troops ask to present to the chief warrior[24] *Jayasthakayastha mahāttaras,* Dasagramikas[25] and other district officers were forbidden to enter into the donated villages.[26] Thus we notice that these four villages were donated with their *Lattika* and talapitaka[27] with the all type of exemption. The villagers and cultivators were directed to pay all kinds of revenue to the donee instead of paying to the state.[28] The *Nalanda copper-plate inscription*, (812-50 A.D.), records the donation of five villages, named Rajagriha (Rajpur) Nandivanaka, Manivataka, Natika and Hastigrama (in district Rajgir), and one in the Gay Visaya (district Gaya).[29] It shows that villages were granted with all kinds of exemptions, such as, exempted from the entry of the *Chāṭas* (villages-officers) and *Bhātas* with taxes dues to the king's family or court, nothing of these to be recovered, according to the *bhūmuchchhidranāya*, and last as long as the moon and the sun would shine on this earth.[30] *The Barah-copper-plate inscription of Bhojadeva* (c 836 A.D.)[31] refers to the donation of *agrāhara* named *Valakagrāhara* which lay in the *Udumbara Visaya of Kalanjara-maṇḍala, in the Kanyakubja-bhukti to the Brāhmaṇa* born of the family of Bhatta Kacharara Swamin belonged to the *Bhāradwāja-gōtra* and a student of the *Vajasaneya-Sakha* with all its income. The inscription tells us that owing to the incapacity of the controlling officer in the time of Ramabhadradeva, it was disturbed for the sometime and the *Bhojadeva*, the grandson of *Nagabhatadeva*, revived it on the old terms on 18th October 830 A.D.[32] and this document shows that the *agrāhara* was granted with all types of exemptions and residents of the village were directed to be obedient and pay all the dues to the donees.[33]

A. Cunnigham discovered two inscriptions in 1846 in the famous temple of *Śiva-Vaidhyanatha at Kiragrama* (Baijnath) in the Kangra district of former Punjab (now in Himachal Pradesh) from the Paleographical point of view, he assigned the date of these inscription about 804 A.D.[34] We find a reference to land-grant made by the secular persons to the temple of *Śiva-vidyanatha* at the village of Kiragrama.[35] The *Praśati* No. 1, records the grant of land which was made by a *Brāhmaṇa* named Ganesvara, son of Govinda and inhabitant of Kiragrama. He donated half a plough of land to the temple in Naragrama, where he possessed a field which required four drones of seed corn,[36] we notice in the same *Praśati* that a rich merchant Jivaka son of Depika and Mathika, donated his own land in Kirāgrama for the courtyard in front of the temple.[37] However, it has been mentioned in the *Praśati* No. II that Rajanaka Laksman Chandra's and his mother made a grant of one plough of land from a village on permanent basis.[38] It is clearly stated in the *Praśati* that grant of land must be protected as long as this earth exists.[39] We notice in the *Praśati* No. II, that two merchants named Manguka and Ahuka donated one plot of land cultivated by four plough along with oil mill and one shop in Kirāgrama to the temple for the maintenance of lamp,[40] it further suggested that land belonging to Naragrāma had been donated along with the inhabitants.[41] *The Monghyu Copper-Plate Inscription of Devapala*, ninth century A.D. refers the grant of a village Mesika situated in the *Krmila-Visaya* to a *Brāhmaṇa*.[42]

The Pandukesuar copper-plate inscription of Calitasura[43] (824 A.D.) records that *Parambhattaraka Maharajadhuja Paramesvara Lalitasuradev* informed all the officials assembled there, together with the officers in change of the township inhabited by the eighteen kinds of subjects, headed by the *Rājan, Rājanaka, Rajāpūtra, Rājamatya, Sāmanta, Mahāsāmanta, Thakkūra, Mahāmanasara, Mahākerthakritika, Mahāpratihāra, Mahādaṇḍanayaka, Mahārājapramātara, Sarabhanga, Kumaramatya, Uparika,—Tadayuktaka, Viniyaktaka*, superintendents of the elephant, horse and camel troops, *Duta, Presanika, Daṇḍhika, Daṇḍapasika*—cowherd, merchant, and foremen of guilds to all the inhabitants, to the entire people, to the regular and irregular soldiers, etc.; that some land which was laying within the jurisdiction of the administrative unit called Thappalasare forming a part of district was donated in favour of god with all type of exemptions. *The Partabgarh Inscription of the time of king Mahandrapala II of Mahodrya*, (c 946 A.D.)[44] records the various grants made by different authority to the monastery of Hari-Risisvara, who originally belonged to Dasapura. Under its management were the shrines of *Vata-Yaksini Devi, Indraditya or Inderajaditya-deva and Trailokya-mohanadeva*, which were situated at the village of Ghonta-varsika, where there was a temple dedicated to Nityapramditya-deva.[45] This inscription depicts that a village was donated by Mahārāja Mahandra Pala II in favour of *Vata-Yaksni devi*.[46] The second part of Inscription records a grant of village, in favour of

Indraditya-deva by Mahadeva, the provincial Government of Ujjain, at the request of Chahamana Indra-raja, a feudatory chief.[47] Third part of inscription of a field in favour of Indrarajaditya deva by Bhahtripatta, son of Khommana donated in 942 A.D.[48] and the fourth part of document refers to the land-grant to different deities by different persons, the gift of a field named Chhittullaka, in which 10 *Maṇis* of seeds could be sown, and which was irrigated by one leather bucket, in favour of Indraditya-deva, the donation of a field was made Indraraja to the god Tralokyamchana deva.

The donation of a field, in which 10 *Maṇis* of seed could be sown, and of Mochha field, requiring 10 Manis of seed was made to unknown diety.[49] The Paschimbhog Plate of Srichandra (c 925-75 A.D.),[50] records the various land-grants. D.C. Sircar, divides this document into three blocks, first block depicts the donation of 120 *pitakas* to the Gaurd *Brāhmaṇ for matha* or temple, it shows that the *matha* was a big religious establishment out of the said land, 10 *pitakas* were allotted to teacher for exposition of the Chandra.[51] (Chandrayakarana), 10 *pitakas* for the (maintenance) and *ghuṭika* (chalk, etc.) of 10 students, 5 *pitakas* for daily offering of food to 5 (guest) *apurva-atithe*, *1 pitaka* to *Brāhmaṇ* who built the temple, 1 (one) *pitaka* to the accountant or astrologer. 21 *pitakas* to scribe (*kayastha, 1 pitaka* to 4 florists (*malakara 22 oilmen*, 2 *pitakas* (*Kumbhakāra*), 5 players on the drum called *katala* 2 conch-shell blowers, (*Śankha-vadaka*), 2 players on the big-drum called *dhakka*, 8 players on the *dragada* (*Kettle-drum*), 22 servants (*Karmakana*) and Cobbers.[52] Two *pitakas* to the dancer (*nāts*), 2 *pitakas* to each the 2 carpenters (*sūtradhara*) to masons (*Sthapati*), 2 backsmiths, ¾ *pitaka* the land to 8 maids servants (*devadasi*), and 47 pitakas for repairs to be carried in the temple establishment.[53] The second block of inscription refers to the 280 *pitakas* of land in favour of the gods.[54] The details of the distribution of 280 *pitakas* is depicted in lines 42-47 of the document which speak of the following person—attached to the two groups of four *mathas*, 10 *pitakas* of land was donated to each of the 8 teachers of the four *kedas* (i.e. 80 *pi0takas* in all), 5 *pitakas* for each group of 5 students in each of the eight *mathas* (i.e. 40 *pitakas*, ½ *pitaka* to each of the following in each of the eight *mathas*—the flourist, the barber, the oilmen, and washermen, servants and cobbers (i.e. 16 + 32 = 48 *pitakas*, ¾ *pitakas* to each of 2 maidservants in each of the 8 *Mathas* (i.e. 12 pitakas in all), 10 *pitakas* of land for repairs to each one of the 8 *Mathas* (i.e. 80 *pitakas* in all),[55] two *pitakas* to *Matha* or *Brāhmaṇa* (chief priest) in each of 2 groups of *mathas*, 2½ *pitakas* to the scribe of each 2 groups of *mathas*, and one *pitaka* to the astrologer on account of each of the 2 groups of *mathas*, 3 *pitakas* to the physicians (*Vaidya*) attached to each of 2 groups of *mathas*, thus this account for 280 *pitaka*.[56] The *Paithan* Copper-plate of king Govind,[57] and the Sungal C.P. of King *Vielagdha* 1st quarter of eleventh century records the various exemptions to the donor.[58]

It has been argued that an inscription of the tenth century from Gorakhpur clearly says that the village which the minister granted to the goddess Durga had been received by him through the favour of king Jayaditya, most probably a feudatory of the *Gurjara-Pratiharas*. It would appear that sometimes the king pleased with an officer for some valuable service performed by him gave a village over and above the usual remuneration he was receiving.[59] An inscription which belonged to 973 A.D. from Harsa (Jaipur) indicates that under the Chauhan of Sakambhare the kinsmen of the king had in their private possession village and hamlets which they had received as assignment from the king and which they could dispose of at will.[60]

We notice that these donations have been made in accordance with the principle of *Bhūmichchhidranyāya* with libations of water as a permanent gift lasting as long as the moon, sun and earth would exist, with certain privileges, together with all the income enjoyed by the state in the shape of taxes in kind and cash. The cultivators and the peasants of the countryside are directed to be submissive to the donee and to pay hım the proper dues. The *bhoga-patis* (landlords, governors) of the future are also directed to approve that grant and protect it.[61]

From above literary traditions as well as epigraphical sources of early medieval Northern India, we are able to deduce that the grant of lands and villages with inhabitants, house-sites, cultivated, an uncultivated fields, genders, etc. to the *Brāhmaṇa*, monks, religious as well as educational institutions, such as, *Vihāras*, temples, *mathas* as the servants, and officers of the state or kings for various state services, had been donated as tax-free, donation by he kings, and private individual, subordinate rulers and sometimes state officials in lieu of cash salary. It is noticed that in the seventh century A.D. onwards the state officers were mostly paid in the form of land-grants, and this would appear to have been the common practice in our period as well.[62] D.C. Sircar inclined to accept the free land donation to donees.[63] On the other hand he admits that there are a few charters recording grants of land to people of the warrior and other classes for service rendered to the king. He also admits that early Indian rulers often granted Jagir for the maintenance of their officers and dependents. He too, qualifies his argument by adding that they were not under feudal obligations; he however, fails to explain the nature of obligation. His argument seems to be theoretical in nature. He states that Indian society was class and clan-ridden and left no scope for the development of feudal tendencies,[64] a suggestion which is more conjectural than factual. Om Parkash is of the view that besides their absolutely tax-free nature, the land-grants, have also been taken for granted for their entirely charitable character, bringing nothing in return to the state. He further argues that the study of the land-grants is incorrect and there are a number of instances of fixing a special tax in the land-grants themselves. The special tax has been variously termed as *trno daka, nikara, aruvana agrāhara-pradeyamsa*, *piṇḍa-dāṇa*, etc.[65] Om Parkash argues that the several grants do not only had the right to all taxes and other sources of income, announcing further, the ban on ingress and egress of the regular and irregular troops in the donated villages or land, nowhere mentioned that the donee will be paying nothing to the state or government.[66] His rejection of the concept of feudal land-grant is blunt but primarily based on whatever argument he could put forward in favour of his thesis. But he should keep in mind that it has not been recorded in any land charters that the donee will pay something to the state. We recorded large number of land-grants which depict various exemptions; and different sources of state income were transferred to the donees, like, grass-land and pasture land of the village, (*Sna-sima-trnayutigocara-paryanta*), the surface above the ground (*tāla*), the space above the ground (*uddesa*) the dug land and water of the village (*Jala-sthala*) and the pits and barren spots (*gant-osara*), salt pits, (*levaṇa*), market places and landing station (*haṭṭaghātta*). Records of some of rulers of the Himalayan areas mention besides boundaries and pasture lands, trees, orchards, springs and waterfall, etc.,[67] were the sources of revenue to the state which had been transferred to the donee and finally state suffered huge amount of revenue. Om Parkash states that early Indian land-grants were not a drain on the state economy, he further argues that religious grants were also converted into sources of state revenue by granting only partial exemptions implying thereby that the unremunerated taxes were to be realized from the donee.[68] But he refers only partially privileged grant but ignores full exempted estates or/and land grants.[69] It is clear that peasants could not leave cultivation and escape to other village, some villages were transferred to the donees along with artisans, herdsmen and cultivators, tied down to the soil. Perhaps the practice was rendered necessary by the scarcity of working population for running the rural economy.[70] Since, the fundamental function of the peasant is to cultivate the soil, there is no other way out except cultivating the land, and about the movement of the peasants from donated village to another village seem be that generally, people are emotionally and sentimentally attached to the soil, they would like to stick to their respective place under any circumstances? Om Prakash, however, argues that the state somehow left helpers under the pressure of immemorial tradition of the non-taxability of the *Brāhmaṇa* to abolish their honoured prerogatives,[71] but we did not get any idea regarding the helplessness of state which compels state to grant land to *Brāhmaṇa* and religious establishment with all type of exemption. He himself admits that there was feudal formation and hierarchy of officials were paid in terms of land assignments.[72]

It is evident from the early Indian traditions and archaeological sources that the king made donations to temple, monasteries, monks, *Brāhmaṇas* and their religious and other secular individuals as a reward and salary for their religious and other services. But land donation in India is still a matter of controversy for obvious reasons. Many questions were raised, e.g. why did early Indian King's supported land-grant; even the practice had invariably hit their economic interest, caused loss of revenue and loss of state control over the land granted to donees.

Generally two kinds of land were donated in lieu of cash salary for their services to the state, e.g. pasture on barren and land lying in the outlying regions of the state. The purpose of these land-grants may be many. The king might have sincerely desired to bring uncultivable land under cultivation, secondly by granting the land in the far-flung areas where the royal authority was little felt by the presence of central authority. Thus the king could exert its influence in such areas where the people were oblivious of central authority prior to the grant was effected. It is argued that the land-grants are noticed in such places where the circulation of coins were either minimal or absent. This argument although had relevance but we cannot say emphatically that it was because of absence of coins that land was granted. It might be owing to the desire of the king to bring more and more land under cultivation through donees.

While assessing the merits and demerits of land-grants in view of state position, we can say that the state could exert its influence in such areas where it was unknown, secondly by means of land-grants a new class of landed aristocracy emerged in the society and they were successfully rallied behind the state. However, the demerits of such land-grants can be seen in the light of loss of revenue that the state suffered and also the loss of state control over its land created the problem of sub-infeudalism.

We come to know from the study of various land charters that it is also ordered that not even the slightest oppression or vexation should be caused by any body to the donee or to his ploughmen, cowherds, maids, servants and dependants. It has been observed that overlords did not make any serious efforts to stop exaction of feudal chiefs. As the central authority in early medieval period had declined considerably and had to depend on the levies sent by the feudal chiefs, it could not afford to interfere with their high-handed exploitation.

The upshot of the above discussion is that the linking of the fashion of land-grants to the religious as well as secular persons in lieu of salaries for their services to the state, prevalent in early medieval Northern India, to the emergence of feudal economy seems historically sound. In stead of bothering to set the economy in order and gear those to the process. The kings found short-term of remunerating them through land-grant and assignments of revenues. The land charters record that the cultivators should attend on the donees and pay them the all type of taxes and revenues in cash '*hinaṇya*' and kind (*meya*). This custom shows that state in Early Medieval times faced economic losses in both the way whether donee is required to collect revenues from the peasants or donees were denoted land or village in lieu of salary for their services to the state, in both ways the state was looser. It is clear from the study of various land charters that the ownership of land-grant was transferred from the donors to the donees and the peasant, tilling it, was reduced to the position of a semi-serf.

It belies the earlier concept of enjoying land-grants, and certain kinds of land had been donated to different people religious as well as secular people as a remuneration for their services to the state or king. No doubt, the fashion of making land-grants in Indian history was as old as *Brāhmaṇa* and Buddhist literature, but it has been used in different perspectives in different periods. The early medieval traditions indicate significant changes in the relation of the donors and donees and consequently its impact on the early medieval Indian economy, since 8th century onwards, whereupon officials of the state were remunerated through land-grants.

REFERENCES

1. B. Parkash, "The Genesis and Character of Landed Aristocracy in Ancient India", in *JESHO*, Vol. XIV, 1971, pp. 201-02. Parkash argues that inland and overseas trade flourished during Early Medieval periods. He quoted *Kuvalayamalakaha* of *Uddyotanasuri* in favour of his above argument, but isolated references regarding the flourishing stage of trade is not enough to negate the theory of declining of trades perfounded by R.S. Sharma, D.N. Jha, Romila Thapar, etc.
2. *Aitareya*, Br. VIII, 21 *Sat Br*, XIII, 7.1.15, VIII, 1.18. 1,73.4. *Chand Up*, IV. 2, 4-5.

   D.C. Sircar, *Landlordism and Tenancy in Ancient*, p. 3. Those who are well versed in the *Sastras* admit that the owner of the land and water and that the people can exercise their right of ownership over all other things excepting these two—unprepared land shall not be taken away from those who do riot cultivate them and given to other; or they may be cultivated by the village labourers and traders; or the owners who do not properly cultivate them should pay for the loss of the state. *Ibid.*, pp. 2-4.

   Sircar argues that copper plate charters often speak of the grant of land as a rent-free holding in accordance with the *Bhūmicchidra-nyāya* or the principle of *bhūmicchidradaṇa*— when the governor or a small vassal chief wanted to create a rent-free holding in favour of a *Brāhmaṇa* or a deity, he applied to the king and apparently paid the price of the land in question at least on a theoretical basis.

   The granting of land in lieu of services was the central principle of feudalism in Western Europe. The king was regarded as the owner of all land, much of which he let out to his barons or tenants-in-chief who, in return for the property, agreed to perform certain service and to make some payments and supplies. M. Block Feudal Society (tr.) C.A. Mangon, London, 1961, pp. 165-67. This was usually to provide the king with a specified number of soldiers in times of war. The barons in their turn let outland to others on similar conditions and same process was continued downs the scale. It is argued that no other single phenomenon has been ascribed so much causal value in early Indian history as that of the land-grants. Feudalisation, ruralisation, regionalisation, stagnation and backwardness of early Indian society, economy and state are traced back to a single factor that of the land-grants.
3. *Āpastamba Sr.* 11, 10.26, *Gautama Dharmasūtra*, V. 19, XIX, 16, *Jātaka Stories*, I. 97-98, II, 42, Ill 104, 223, IV 473.
4. *Manu*, S. VII. 115-17.
5. *AS, II*. 1, II. 35. G.C. Chauhan, *Origin and Growth of Feudalism*, *op.cit.*, pp. 80-81.

6. K.K. Thaplyal, *Inscription of the Maukharies, op.cit.*, pp. 182-53. J.F. Fleet, CII, III. No. 80, plate X, p. 286. G.C. Chauhan, "Traces of Feudalism as Seen in the Nirmand Copper-plate inscription of c 612-13 A.D." in *Annals* of (BCRI), Vol. LXXVII, Pune, 1997, pp. 241-46.
7. J.F. Fleet, *CII. III*, *op.cit.* No. 80, pp. 86-89, p. 289, Lines, 8 to 10. G.C. Chauhan, *Loc. cit.*, p. 244.
8. K.K. Thaplyal, *op. cit.*, No. XIII, pp. 158-59.
9. *Ibid.* No. 17, pp. 176-82.
10. *Ibid.* No. 18, pp. 182-85.
11. D.C. Sircar (ed.) S.I. III. No. 3, pp. 24-25, Line, No. 9.
12. *Ibid.*
13. *Ibid.* No. 4, pp. 26-27.
14. *Ibid.*
15. *Ibid.* pp. 36-40.
16. G.C. Chauhan, *Economic History of Early Medieval, op.cit.*, pp. 71-72. Sima Yadav, *The Myth of Indian Feaudalism*, Delhi, 2005, pp. 41-42.
17. *Ibid.* pp. 41-42.
18. *Ibid.* p. 50.
19. *EI, IV*, No. 34, pp. 243-45.
20. *Ibid.*, p. 255. These terms literary means king's ministers, chiefs of the armies, chief of the *Visayas* (or districts), chief of the *bhoga*, where the *bhoga* is perhaps equivalent to *bhukti*, denoting a larger extent of the territory than a *Visaya*.
21. *Ibid.*, p. 253.
22. *Ibid.* The term khola literary denotes a messenger.
23. *Ibid.*
24. *Jyeśthakayosthas* means the chief writer.
25. The officers in charge of groups of ten villages.
26. *Ibid.*, p. 254, *Karana* denotes a writer, scribe, accountant.
27. *Ibid.* The term *hāṭṭika* might be described from *hātta*, a market.
28. *Ibid.*, p. 254.
29. *EI*, XVIII, No. 17, pp. 310-14.
30. *Ibid.*, p. 225.
31. EI, XIX, No. 2, p. 15. Mahesh Sharma "State Formation and Cultural Complex in Western Himalayas: Chamba Genealogy and epigraphs 700-1650 A.D." in *IESHR*, Delhi, 2004, pp. 400-01.
32. *Ibid.* p. 16.
33. *Ibid.*, p. 19.

34. EI, I, p. 97, II, pp. 482-83. G.C. Chauhan, "The Traces of Feudal Culture as Reflected in two Prasatis of Baijnath", *MDURJ*, Vol. 6, Rohtak, 1991, pp. 89-91.
35. *Ibid.* p. 107.
36. *Ibid.*
37. *Ibid.* Line 34.
38. *Ibid.*, p. 118.
39. *Ibid.* p. 115, Line 35, whatever pious gift has thus been made by anybody for the sake of Siva, may that last for his (benefit) as long as this earth exists.
40. *Ibid.*, p. 118, text, p. 115.
41. *Ibid.*
42. Bhagwant Sahai, *The Inscription of Bihar*, Delhi, 1983, 40-85, p. 75.
43. D.C. Sircar, *SI*, No. 15, pp. 668-69.
44. EI, XIV, No. 13, pp. 176-77.
45. *Ibid.*
46. *Ibid.*, p. 177.
47. *Ibid.* pp. 180-81. It was probably a local dynasty of the Chauhan which had entered into a subordinate alliance with king Bhoja Deva I, and helped him in his wars, thus giving the overlord great pleasure, Indra-raja built a temple for its upkeep.
48. *Ibid.*, p. 181.
49. *Ibid.*, p. 182.
50. *Ibid.* XXXVIII, No. 51, p. 289.
51. *Ibid.* pp. 294-95.
52. *Ibid.* p. 295.
53. *Ibid.* p. 296.
54. *Ibid.*
55. *Ibid.*
56. *Ibid.*, p. 297. D.C. Sircar is of the view that the third block of land was left over after the distribution of first and second blocks (measuring 120 + 280 = 400 *pitakas*) were donated in favour of 6000 *Brāhmaṇas*.
57. EI, Ill, p. 107. Sircar, *Land Lordism and Tenancy, op.cit.*, p. 72.
58. *Ibid.*, p. 74, *op.cit.*, pp. 167-69. EI, Ill, p. 107.
59. K.K. Gopal, "Assignment to officers and Royal Kinsmen in Early Medieval India," 700-1200 A.D., in B.P. Sahu (ed.), *Land System and Rural Society, op.cit.*, p. 120.
60. *Ibid.* pp. 127-28.
61. *Ibid.* pp. 297-98.

62. K.K. Gopal, *op.cit.* p. 118. V.K. Thakur, *Historiography of Indian Feudalism; op.cit.*, p. 25. T. Watter, *Onyuan Chawang's Travels in India*, London (Rep. 1973) , Vol. V, p. 176.
63. D.C. Sircar, *Landlordism and Tenancy, op.cit.*, p. 33.
64. D.C. Sircar, cited in V.K. Thakur, *Historiography of Indian Feudalism, op.cit.*, pp. 25-26. G.C. Chauhan, *EHENI, op. cit.*, pp. 76-78.
65. Om Prakash, *Early Indian Land Grants, op.cit.*, p. 2.
66. *Ibid.*, p. 3. Om Parkash argues that such grants possibly transferred, in effect, only the collection right along with the privileges and loc taxes to the donees who were still obliged to pay the dues and taxes or central government than collected by them.
67. D.C. Sircar, Landlordism and Tenancy, *op.cit.*, p. 49. And *El*, XXXI, pp. 281, 288, 296.
68. Om Parkash, Early Indian Land Grants, *op.cit.*, p. 282.
69. J.F. Fleet, *CII, Ill*, No. 80, p. 286. D.C. *SI*, , *op.cit.*, No. 3, pp. 24-25, No. 4, 26, 27, *EI*, IV No. 34, pp. 243-45, *E*, XVIII, No. 17, pp. 310-14. *EI*, XIX. No. 2, p. 15, *EI*, XIX, No. 13, pp. 176, *EI*, XXXVII, No. 51, p. 289, *EI*, XXI, pp. 281, 288, 296.Vogel Antiquities of Chamba State, Calcutta, 1911. Part-I, pp. 167-69, El, XXXII, pp. 122, 125, 217.
70. R.S. Sharma, *Indian Feudalism, op.cit.*, pp. 218-19.
71. Om Parkash, *Early Indian Land Grants, op. cit.*, p. 283.
72. *Ibid.*, p. 287.

    D.C. Sircar, confuses that the gift of a village without such income would be useless to the donees. He qualifies this point by stating that 'granting a village' and granting a village together with the villagers' thus mean the same thing. Thus granting a village by donor or granting a village together inhabitant does not make any differences to D.C. Sircar.

The Chauhan Land Economy

8

Among the thirty-six of Rajputs clans, there flourished a clan of Chauhan in early medieval times in northern India. The author of *Pṛthvirajvijay*, Jayanaka gives an interesting and witty interpretation of the word "Chauhan", which consists of these letters CA+HA+MA+NA, i.e of the first letter of *Capa, Hara, Maṇa* and *Naya*, representing: Strength, Religion, Reputation and Politics respectively. By this interpretation Jayanaka adroitly acquaints us with the characteristic attributes of the Chauhans.

There is no denying of the reputed strength of Chauhans which only could save them from so many onslaughts through the ages. These great warriors of Rajputana extended the boundaries of their kingdoms touched Punjab in West, Delhi in North and Gujrat in South. The Chauhans were one of the most glorious dynasties among the rulers of northern India in early medieval times.

Historians and scholars of Rajput history put forth different theories regarding their origin which still remain as matter of debate and great concern to among the scholars and historians of Rajput history. Indian and foreign scholars propounded various theories about the original home of the Chauhans, such as, *Agnikūlas* (as fire born), the *Kṣhatriyas* of Solar and Lunar races, *Aindera, Vaishnava, Malana, Brāhmaṇic* and descendants of some foreign tribes.[1] The theory of *Agnikūla*, given by Chand Bardai, goes like this, "once the sages—Visvamitra, Gautama, Agastya, and Vaistha, etc. performed a great sacrifice at Mount Abu. Ultimately, Chauhan originated out of that sacrificial fire, hence it contains a lot of incredible details which are baseless and apparently absurd. Scientifically, no living beings can bear from fire pit. The second most popular theory was put forth by V. Smith, James Tod and William Crooks and Baden Powell, etc., known as theory of foreign origin. In fact, Indian were being ruled by the Britishers and they tried their level best to consider the Indians inferior to them and interpreted the origin of Chauhans which suited them the best. It is for the aforesaid reasons, for me very difficult to subscribe the theories of *Agnikūla* and foreign origin of Indian and Western scholars. Whatever might be the theory of their origin, but certain early medieval literary and archeological traditions remind us of the contribution made by the Chauhans to Indian Society and culture.

It is argued that land-grants played very important and crucial role in the socio-economic and political formation of early medieval North India, which transformed money economy into a feudal economy through the issuance of land-grants and generated a landed aristocracy. Om Prakash rightly argues that no other single phenomenon has ascribed so much to causal value in early Indian history as that of the land-grants. Feudalisation, realisation, rationalisation, stagnation and backwardness of early Indian Society. Economy and state are traced back to a single factor, that of the land-grants.[2] There are very few instances of land-grants in later Vedic[3] and *Dharmasūtras*[4] period, land grants were made as a *dāṇa* (pious gifts) and donors wanted *pūṇya* out of that *Bhudāṇa*.[5] But Manu recommends the land-grants to the *adhipati* of villages. *Kauṭilya* suggests land-grants to *Brāhmaṇas* and some state officers.[6] It shows that the phenomenon of making of land grants in Indian history was as old as *Brāhmaṇa* and Buddhist literature. It has been used in different manner and capacity in different periods.

It is evident from the early Indian texts and archaeological sources that the king made donation to temple, monasteries, monks, *Brāhmaṇas* and their religious and other secular individuals as a reward or salary for their religious and other services, or recognition of their learning. In course of time the idea behind the donation of land got changed. It became an accepted phenomenon to donate land in charity during Chauhan's times. But land donation in India is still a matter of controversy for obvious reasons. Many questions were raised, e.g., why did early Indian king's support land-grants even when their own economic interest caused loss of revenue and loss of state control over the land? Land-grants were carefully drafted as legal documents of their times. Land-grants were taken highly reliable sources and their evidence was taken almost on its face-value, unless, however, there were unmistakable indication of fraud detectable in particular case.[7] The purpose of these land donations might have been manifold. The king might have sincerely desired to bring uncultivable land under cultivation also to enforce stamp of authority/ruler even in the far-flung areas so that people did not remain oblivious of central authority and the law of the land. It is for the aforesaid reason that it is difficult to subscribe the theory propounded by R.S. Sharma that "the land-grants are noticed in such places where the circulation of coins were either minimal or absent".[8] While assessing the merits and demerits of land-grants in view of state position, we can say that the state could exert its influence in such areas where it was unknown. Secondly by means of land-grants a new class of landed aristocracy emerged in the society, which always successfully rellied behind the state. Though, these land-grants did result in loss of revenue to the state but it implicitly promoted sub-infeudalism. This resulted in the vast unmanageable terrains being made manageable and the locales came to acknowledge the hither to unknown majestic power. It was common in early medieval North India that the villages/ plots of lands were granted to *Brāhmaṇa*, Jain Shriṇes, and temples and even to secular persons.

Again, the epigraphic sources of Chauhans times indicates different meanings and concept of land-donation and significant changes in the relation of the donors and the donees and consequently its impacts as the legal binding existed between the donors and the state officials. The Hansot plates of the Chauhan Bhartrivaddha[9] (c 786 A.D.), records a donation of a village Arjunaderigrama to a *Brāhmaṇa* named Bhaṭṭa-Butta, an inhabitant of Sanjrapadra by putting legal binding on the entry of state official in donated estate. Another land charter[10], (c 973 A.D.), inform us about the King Somharaja who after having bathed at Puskara tirtha donated some villages for the purpose of providing material for worship of god Harsa in the temple. Same land charter further tells us that Vatsaraja, younger brother of the king donated a village for the same. King's sons Govindaraja and Candraja gave two huts and king's officials also donated one village for the same.[11] The Copper-plates inscription of Chauhan Maharaja Ratnapal (c 1120 A.D.[12]) records a donation of a village to a *Brāhmaṇa* for the daily worship of God Siva. We have noticed a secular land-grant from the Nadol copper plate of Kirtipal (c 1160 A.D.[13]) that Alhanadeva and Kelhandeva were pleased to donate twelve villages to the Rajaputra Kirtipal, whereas the donee, in turns, is said to have donated a sum of 2 *drammas* per annum from each of these villages to Jain Mahavira shrine at the village Naddulai. To determine the nature of this land-grant is very difficult. It can be assumed from a sheer enjoyment grant, to governorship of the villages donated to him, as rewards for his services. In fact nothing can be surmised. It is a question of deep concern that the prince donated only a portion of income from the villages, did not alienate any plot of land, whether the prince was put under economic obligation by the donor to pay 2 *drammas* per annum from each village to Jain shrine?

Another copper plate which can be dated to (1163 A.D.)[14], from the paleographical point of view, refers a religious donation of a village in favour of god Tripurusadeva. The land-charter tells us that king Alhana, in fear of the ten sins, went on a pilgrimage while worshiping lord Siva with flowers, etc. He bathed his image with *Pancamṛta*, while holding water in his hand made a donation of Ṅandana village. Similar land-grant is recoded in Bamnera copper plate of the same year where Ajay Singh donated i.e. Dholika that is any piece of land. However, the Sanderav Stone Inscription of Kelhanadeva (c 1164 A.D.[15]) inform us about a land donation of one *hala* of land by queen Analadevi to the God Mahavir and one *hala* land was donated by a group of *rathakaras*[16] to celebrate the *Kalyanika*.

The Bijholi Rock Inscription of Chauhan Somesvara (c 1169 A.D.)[17] tells us about the donation of two villages named as Morajhari and Revana to the temple of Parsvanath by Prithvibhata and Somesvara respectively to get religious merits.

This land charter further informs us about certain land-donation to the shrine by certains persons, the inhabitants of different villages such as Guhila-Putra Raval Dadhara and Māhatmā Ghanasimha donated a *Kṣhetra- doholi*, lying midway between the village of Kamua and Revana. Gauda Somva and Vasudeva, inhabitants of the village Khaduṃvara gave one *Kshetra-dohalika*. Parigrahi Alhana, residing in the village of Vadauva donated one *Kṣhetra-dohalika*, Guhila-Putra Raval Vyaharu and Mahatma Mahana associated with the village of Lagher-Vijholi, donated a *Kṣhetra-dohalika* to the shrine of Parsvanatha.[18] The Lalrai stone inscription of Kelhanadeva (c. 1176 A.D.[19]), describes Rajputra Lakhanpal and the Rajputra Abhayapala as the proprietors of certain landed estate, but do not get any information regarding how these princes got this estate. It seems that Chauhans land-charter also testify to the apportionment of landed property among the kinsmen of ruling chief, but one land-charter of Chauhan tells us about the queen Sri-Tihunake enjoyed a village as *giras* (for food and clothing). Although queen did not belong to kin of the family in which she was married, but she was given a personal estate commensurate to her statues. Similar sort of land donation was enjoyed by *Dhandhika* who he donated to Śiva temple, its seems that this police officer had been granted several other villages besides this, but he was not entitled to make religious grant without taking prior permission of his master, his was a limited assignment. It seems that king did not assign the absolute right to the donees over the donated villages.[20] But a literary source of Chauhan times describes Kadambavasa, the mahāmantri of Prithiviraj III, who had the title of *Sarvadhikari* and *maṇḍaleshvara*, which indicates that he was donated a whole *maṇḍala* by way of salary or support this dignity.[21] Even donors donated a bazaar building or warehouse for storing goods to be exported and donee was asked to pay some money out of the rent occurring there from was to be offered the *pamchami-bāli*[22], every year in the temple of god Parsvanath. Another Chauhan inscription records (c. 1347 A.D.)[23] the donation of *Dhikuyan* (machine well) together with orchard to the same. Sanchor Stone Inscription of Pratapasimha (c. 1387 A.D.),[24] also remind us about the donation of a field, and 2 *paials* on every maund of each commodity form the custom house, for daily offering of the god Veyesvera. It is gleaned from the inscriptions of Chauhans that the rulers had several feudatory chiefs under them. These feudatories had their own states or Jagirs as the case may be, which were duly controlled by them. However, they were not free in external affairs; they actively participated in the battles of Chauhan rulers.[25]

In spite of the presence of feudal sort of relationship between paramount rulers and *Sāmantas* during Chauhans times on the one hand and revival of money economy, urbanization, flourishing trade and commerce are gleaned from the literary and epigraphically traditions of Chauhans times. A considerable number of towns and towns full of movement are reflected in Chauhans inscriptions. This is further corroborated by *Tarikh-i-Frishta*[26], which tells us about the urban life, the development of towns, forts, courts, sacred sites, points of strategic and commercial significance. Another literary source of Chauhans informs us that Chauhan dominions were full of temples, multistoried houses, and steep wells. Tanks and *prapas*, markets and towns full of commodities from various parts of the country.[27]

In fact, the shrinkage of trade or decline in commodity exchange in term of money economy did not mean the complete decline of trade and commerce. It refers to a situation in which they are not the consequential partner of the overall economic patterns. The Chauhan Inscriptions inform us about the flourishing trade in wheat, *mudga*, resin, oil, betal leaves, Kiradu, spices, *rathas*, salt and horses, etc. Horses were imported from *Uttrapatha*.[28] The literary and epigraphic sources of Chauhans further inform us about the traders who went about making money and storing cereals, cotton, salt, wool and buying lac, trading in jaggery, pressing oil, manufacturing Charcoal, clothing, cutting down forests, telling lie and cheating their customers by using false weight and measures.[29] Above detailed description of trading in various goods, suggest that trade and commerce during Chauhans times did not disappear.

However, within the Chauhan regions there seems to be no shortage of coins in market. The Chauhan inscriptions inform us about the numerous coins, such as *dramas Vimsopakas*, *rupayka, raukma* and *draela*, etc., uptill the tenth century A.D. The Chauhans remained the vassals of the Pratiharas of Kannauj. But for the first time we learn about Ajayadevas coins in the Dhod inscription of Somesvars times. Copper and silver coins were also issued by the Chauhans whose regions give indication of growing rural and urban trade. Billon coins seem to have been issued in good numbers by the Chauhans.[30] Thus, it is abundantly clear from the study of Chauhans land-charters that coins were freely used and further shows that development of trade and urbanization, which are fundamental features of money economy. It has been argued that early Indian Land-Grants generated landed aristocracy which ultimately transformed money economy into closed economy. But we can glean from the study of Chauhans land-grants a complete different meaning and purposes in the realm of early medieval Indian society, culture and religion.

To conclude, it can be categorically stated that the Chauhan land-grants differed in a big way from the traditional grants which were based on feudal economy, whereas the latter included permanent abrogation of the rights of the donors in favour of the donees, it was not so in the case of the former. No doubt, the Chauhans committed themselves and the state to the legal status of such grants, but certainly gave themselves the right to revoke any such land-grants in case of misuses and its abuse. Perhaps it origin had roots in ever flowing beliefs of the Chauhan that charity was a religious act meant to accelerate respectfully and public welfare. Their commitment to public welfare helped in growth of urban centres and the development of trade which was ensured by the easy transition through the currency floated by the Chauhans. Therefore, there are reasons enough to believe that the Chauhans were much medieval as well as advanced in perception and innovated a strong moneyed economy that laid the foundation of a new economies, never thought of before by the typical feudalism.

A Tabular Statement of Classified Details of Chauhans Land-Grants

	Inscriptions	*Donors*	*Donees*	*Purpose*	*Village or plot of land*
1.	The Hansot Plates of Bhartrivaddha c.786 A.D.	Prince	Brahanam	Charity	A village
2.	Harsha Stone Inscription of the Chauhan 973 A.D.	Simharaja Ruler, his younger brother and his two sons	Temple of Harsa	For the maintenance of lamp in Temple	2 villages and two huts
3.	Copper plate inscription of Chauhans Ratnapala 1120 A.D.	Ratnapal ruler	A Brāhmaṇa	For worshiping of Siva	A village
4.	Nandol copper-plate inscriptions of Kirtipal 1160	The rulers Alhanadeva-Kelhandeva	Rajaputra princes	Not clear	12 villages 2 drammas out of the revenue
5.	Nanana grant of Alhanadeva 1163 A.D.	King Alhana	To the temple of Tripurisadeva, 4 drammas from the custom houses	For the maintenance of shrine	A village of Nandana three haelaka land from village Cavodhi
6.	Bamarcha copper-plate of the Kilhandeva 1163 A.D.	The ruler	Tripurisadeva	For the maintained of the shrine	*Dholika* of land i.e. any size piece of land
7.	Sandehav stone inscriptions of Kelhanadev 1164	The king	God Mahavira	To celebrate the *kalyanika* of Jain festival	Two *haels* of land

(*Contd*...)

Inscriptions	Donors	Donees	Purpose	Village or plot of land
8. Bijholi rock Inscription of Chauhans Somasvara 1169 A.D.	The king, princes by the certain persons	To the temple of Parsavnath	Charity	A village Revan, 2 villages, certain *Kshetra-dohalika* of any size
9. Kalrai stone inscription of Kelhanadeva, 1176 A.D.	The ruler	Princes Lakhanpala and Abhayapala	For personal enjoyment	One village by each prince 1+12 (2)
10. Phalody inscriptions of Prithviraja 1276 A.D.	Seems to be a ruler but the name of the donee is not given	To the temple	In the memory of Prithviraja for charity and public utility	A field land and plots where boundaries of the field are also specified, along with the money donation.
11. Kot-solankiya Inscription of Vanavira 1347 A.D.	The Ruler is donor	To the shrine of Parsavnath deva	For the spiritual merit of the donor parents	An orchard (*vadi*) along with Dhikuyau
12. Sanchor stone Inscription of Pratapasimha 1387 A.D.	The king Paratapasimha of Chahaun dynasty	To the shrine of Vayesvara	For the daily offering to the god	A field, along with 2 *pailas* on every maund of each commodity from the customs house.

REFERENCES

1. *EI*, IX, p. 74, X, p. 103, XXXI, p. 302, *Indian Historical Quarterly*, Calcutta, Vol. XXIX, 1940, p. 746, G.H. Ojha, *Rājpūtana Kāltihas*, Vol. 1, Ajmer 1927, p. 64. D. Sharma, *Early Chauhan Dynasties*, Delhi, 1959, p. 50. *Prithviraja Vijaya of Jayanaka* (ed.) G.H. Ojha and Guleri, Ajmer, 1941, and *Nagari Prachini Patrika*, Vol. XII, part III, p. 264. *Prithvirajraso of Chand Bardai Nagri Pracharini Sabha* Part I, Banaras, pp. 40-41. *Hammiraraso of Nayachandra Suri*, NPS, Banaras, pp. 8-14. Lallubhai Bhimbhai Desai, *Chauhan Kula Kalpadruma*, pt. II, Baroda, 1927, p. 201. *Sisana Inscription of the Chauhan of Bedla*, in Anita Sudan, *A Study of Chauhan Inscriptions of Rajasthan*, Jodhpur, 1989, D. Sharma (ed.) *Kyamkhn Rāso of JAN Rajasthan Puratatava Granthmala*, No. 13, Jaipur N.D. *Proceeding of the Asiatic Society of Bengal*, Calcutta, May, 1973, p. 94. *Indian Antiquary*, Calcutta, vol. XVI, p. 19, Vol. XXXIX, p. 191 (hereafter IA). James Tod, *Annals and Antiquities of Rājasthān,* reprint, Vol. II, Delhi, 1971, (hereafter *Antiquities of Rajasthan*), pp. 356-57, 80. R.B. Singh, *History of the Chauhans*, Varanasi, 1964, pp. 11-12. J.N. Asopa, *Origin of Rajputs*, Delhi, 1976, pp. 94-95.

2. Om Parkash, *Early Indian Land-grants, op.cit.*, p. 1, D.C. Sircar, *Land Lordism and Tenancy, op.cit.*, p. 3. M. Block, Feudal Society (tr.) C.A. Mangon, London, 1961, pp. 165-67, V.K. Thakur, *Historiography of Indian Feudalism, op.cit.*, p. 25.

3. *Āitreya Br.* VIII, 20, *Sat. Br.* 16, 1972-78. *Chand.Up.* IV. 2, 4-5.

4. *Āpastamba Sr.* 11.10.26, *Gautam* V. 19, XIX. 16.

5. *Manu, S.* VII. 115-117, XXIV, *op.cit.*, p. 125.

6. *AS II.I.II.35,* II. I, II.35.

7. Om Parkash, *Early Indian Land-Grant, op.cit.*, p. 2. R.S. Sharma, *Indian Feudalism, op.cit.* pp. 61-62, 71-72, 136, 148, 171, 186 *EI*, Vol. XXXIII, p. 50.

8. R.S. Sharma, *Indian Feudalism, op.cit.,* pp. 54-55, G.C. Chauhan, *Economic History, op.cit.*, pp. 68-69, G.C. Chauhan, *Origin and Growth of Feudalism, op.cit.,* p. 41, R.S. Sharma, *Urban Decay in India*, Delhi, 1987, pp. 124-25.

9. *EI*, Vol, XII, No. 23, pp. 197 to 201. The occasion of the grant was a solar eclipse. D. Sharma's, *Early Chauhan, op. cit.,* pp. 14-15. *JBBRS,* XVI , p. 105. R.L. Mishra, *Epigraphical Studies of Rajasthans Inscriptions,* Delhi, 1990, pp. 3-4 time. *Progress Report of the Archaeological Survey of India*, Western Circle , March 1908, p. 47. *EI*, Vol, V, p. 216, VIII, p.130, IA, Vol. XIll, p. 77.

10. *EI*, Vol. II, pp. 116-29, Amta Sudan, *Chauhans Ins, op.cit.*, pp. 236-237, R.L. Mishra , *Epigraphical Studies, op.cit.*, pp. 53-62. *IHQ*, Vol. XV, p. 623. IA, 1913 , p. 64. J.N. Asopa, *Origin of Rajputs, op. cit.*, pp. 96-97.

11. *EI*, Vol. II, pp. 128-129. Anita Sudan, *Chauhan Ins., op.cit.,* p. 25 RB. Panday, *Historical and Literality Inscriptions*, Varanasi, pp. 216-21. R.S.

Sharma, *Indian Feudalism, op. cit.*, pp. 143-44, 199. Om Parkash, *Early Indian Land-grants, op. cit.*, p. 186.

12. *EI*, Vol. XI, p. 308, Durga Lal Mathur, *Rajasthan ki Chauhan Abhilakh*, Jodhpur, N.D., p. 1827. G.L. Shrimali, *Rajasthan Ki Abhilakh*, Jodhpur, 2000, pp. 9 1-96.
13. *EI*, Vol. IX, pp. 66-70. Om Parkesh, *Early Indian Land-grants, op.cit.*, pp. 186-87. Anita Sudan, *Chauhan Ins., op. cit.*, pp. 38-39. IA, X, p. 746. Durga Lal Nahar (ed.), *Jam Lakha Samgraha*, Vol. II, III, Pt. I, Calcutta, 1918, p. 210. Durga Das Mathur, *RCA, op.cit.*, pp. 58-63. G.L. Srimali, *RKA, op.cit.*, pp. 135-37.
14. Anita Sudan, *Chauhan Ins, op. cit.*, pp. 237-38. Vol. 23. G.L. Srimali, *RKA, op. cit.*, pp. 146-49. *EI*, Vol. XIII, pp. 206-08. G.L. Srimali, *RKA, op.cit.*, pp. 150-53. *Benera Copper Plate of Kelanadeva*, 1163 A.D.
15. *EI*, Vol, XI, pp. 46-48, P.C. Nahar, *JLS*, Vol. I, p. 229. G.L. Srimali, *RKA, op.cit.*, pp. 154-55.
16. *EI*, Vol. XI, p. 47. This inscription records the names of various *rathakaras* who donated a piece of land of jam shrine, were named as Dhanapala, Surapala, Jopala, Sigada, Amiyapala, Jisahada Delhana, all were the inhabitant of Shamderaka.
17. *EI*, No. 9, Vol. XXVI, pp. 84-98. *Bijholi Rock Inscription of Chauhan Somesvara*, 1169 A.D. *JRASB*, Vol. LV, Part I, Calcutta, 1886, pp. 14-15, 28-32, 40-46. H.C. Ray, *Dynastic History of Northern India*, Calcutta, 1936, Vol. II, p. 1082. *Antiquities of Rajasthan, op. cit.*, Vol. 11, pp. 1752-59, 1796-1805. *Cunnigham, Archaeological Survey Report*, Delhi, Vol. VI, p. 292. G.H. Ojha, *RKI*, 11, *op.cit.*, 1198.
18. *EI*, Vol. XXVI, pp. 105-112. Anita Sudan, Chauhan Ins, *op. cit.*, pp. 240-243. *Antiquities of Rājasthān*, Vol. III. *op.cit.*, pp. 1800-805. H.C. Ray, *Dynastic History, op.cit.*, Vol. II, pp. 1079, *IA*, Vol. XX, p. 202.
19. *EI*, No. XVI, Vol. XI, p. 49. Om Parkash. *Early Indian Land-grants, op.cit.*, p. 187.
20. *EI*, Vol. II, No. 8, IX, No. 9, Bll, 17-29. R.S. Sharan, *Indian Feudalism, op.cit.*, pp. 143-44. EI, Vol. II, No. 8, verse-49, Vol. XI, No. V, 1.2. A. Rudra, 'Against Feudalism', *Economic and Political Weekly*, Vol. XVI, No. 52, 1981, pp. 2133-46. M.R. Tarafdar, "Trade and Society in Early Medieval Bengal", *IHR*. Vol. IV, 2, pp. 274-84.
21. *Kharatargachchha-pattavali of Jinepada*, Singhi Jaina *Granthmala*, Bombay, 1950, pp. 25-33. R.V. Somani, *Prithviraj Chauhan and His Times*, Jaipur, 1981, pp. 87-88. D.C. Sircar (ed.), Calcutta, 1966, pp. 11-23. *Journal of Indian History*, Vol. XLIV, 1966, pp. 351-57. H. Mukhia, "Was there any feudalism in Indian History", in the *Journal of Peasant Studies*, Vol. 8, No. 3, pp. 273-310.

22: *EI*, No. XXIII, Vol. XI, pp. 60-62. K.K. Gopal, "Assignment to officers and Royal Kinsmen in Early Medieval India" in B.P. Sahu (ed.), *Land*

System and Rural Society, op.cit., pp. 118-34. G.C. Chauhan, *Economic History, op.cit.*, pp. 67-79. D.C. Sircar, *Landlordism and Tenancy, op.cit.*, pp. 4-7.

23. *EI*, No. XXIV, Vol. XI, pp. 62-63. K.K. Gopal, "Assignment officers", *Loc. cit.*, p. 121. B.P. Mazumdar, Merchants and Landed Aristocracy in the Feudal Economy of Northern India: Eighth to Twelfth Century in B.P. Saha (ed.), *Land System and Rural Society, op.cit.*, pp. 142-49. G.C. Chauhan, *Economic History, op.cit.*, p. 73.

24. *EI*, Vol. XI, XXIII, pp. 225-29. B.P. Mazumdar, *Merchant and Landed Aristocracy, Loc.cit.*, pp. 144-45. *IHR*, X, p. 321. K.K. Gopal, "Assignment of Officers", *Loc.cit.*, pp. 132-34. G.C. Chauhan, *Economic History, op.cit.*, pp. 24-25.

25. *Kharata, Pattavali, op. cit.*, p. 27. R.V. Somani, *Prithviraj Chauhan, op.cit.*, p. 86, *EI*, Vol. XXXV, pp. 239-42. The Pushkar Inscription of 937 A.D. K.G. Sharma, *Early Jain Inscription of Rajasthan*, Delhi, 1993, p. 2. B.P. Mazumdar, *Socio-Economic History, op.cit.*, p. 29.

26. J. Briggs (tr.) *Tarikh-i-Firishta*, Calcutta, 1911, p. 177. D. Sharma, *Early Chauhan, op.cit.*, p. 296. R.S. Sharma, *Indian Feudalism, op.cit.*, p. 198. Sharma argues that 131 Chauhan towns are not enough in numbers, but this number is quite considerable and one of the fundamental features of urbanization.

27. *Prithvirajavijaya*, V. Verses, 119-90. *Upamitibhavapra panchakatha of Siddharishi* (ed.), P. Peterson, Calcutta, 1899, pp. 7-9, 34-35, 105, 137, 312, 385.

28. *EI*, Vol. 11, p. 19, *Harsa Stone Inscription*, V.K. Thakur, *Historiography of Indian Feudalism, op.cit.*, p. 79. Inscription of Vigraharaja II, Kelhana of Nadol. *Inscription of Udayasimha, Inscription of Jalor and Mammata Inscription of Hastikundi. Upamiti-katha, op.cit.*, pp. 38, 427, 500, 554. R.S. Sharma, *Indian Feudalism, op.cit.*, p. 198.

29. *EI*, Vol. XI, p. 28, pp. 43-58. Anita Sudan, *Chauhan Ins, op.cit.*, p. 212. D. Sharma, *Early Chauhan, op.cit.*, p. 299 *Kiradn Inscription of Alehana, Nadol Inscription of Rajapala. Sevadi Inscription of Katukaraja.* K.G. Sharma, *Early Jain Inscriptions, op. cit.*, pp. 58-60.

30. Johns Deyell, *Living Without Silver, op.cit.*, pp. 144-80. IA, 1912, pp. 210-11, D. Sharma (ed.), *Rājasthān Through the Ages*, Bikaner, Vol. I, 1966, p. 498. D. Sharma, *Early Chauhans, op.cit.*, p. 339, K.G. Sharma. *Early Jain Inscription, op.cit.*, p. 61. R.C. Agarwala "*Madhyakalina Jams Sahitya Mein Mudra Sambandhi Samagri*", Jam Siddhanta Bhaskar, Vol. XXI, No. 1, pp. 6-16. (Anita Sudan, *Chauhan Ins, op.cit.*, pp. 215-16). *EI*, Vol. VI, p. 28. *EI*. XI, p. 41, R.S. Sharma, *Indian Feudalism, op.cit.*, p. 277.

Feudal Economy of Early Medieval Northern India

9

An accurate definition of the term 'Feudal Economy' is not practically possible. The word 'Feudal Economy' was originally coined in early seventeenth century A.D. and used in a political perspective. The kind of economic activity we see today in the industrialized cities and towns of India did not exist to any significant degree during early medieval period in India. The early North medieval economy was a natural economy, where peasants produced mainly for their own consumption and rarely market goods, but due to exchange of their services local needs were locally catered. In subsistence economy of early medieval India traders rarely resorted to trade, except for luxury goods because everything people produced by self-labour. The feudal economy consisted of subsistence agriculture in a society bound together not by a market but by tradition, custom and authority.

The society during early medieval age was fragmented into groups such as landlord, *Brāhmaṇa* landed intermediaries and *Sāmanta*. All sections of primary producers used to live in the villages. Hence there was a lack in the circulation of the coins, which restricted the growth of money economy. Since, the declining process of money economy gave rise to exchange of services and barter system.

Land-grants played very vital and crucial role in socio-economic formation of early medieval northern Indian economy. The state controlled economy was transformed into a feudal economy through the issuance of land-grants, ultimately, generated a landed aristocracy who enjoyed the revenues of one or more villages. The feudal fashion of donating land brought political fragmentation, reduced the peasantry to bondage and subjection, degraded the artisans and ultimately paved the way for the restrictions on the mobility of peasants and other humble folk.[1] The feudal elements might have gained importance in early Medieval North India, with the growing tendency to remunerate the officers in the form of assignments of land. We come to know from the *Si-Yu-Ki*,[2] and the *Harsacarita*[3] of Bana that during the seventeenth century A.D. the state officials were mostly paid in the form of land-grants for their service to the state. The Nalanda *Vihāra* owned one hundred villages and its number went up to two hundred village during the time of I. Tsing,[4] its number increased to five hundred village in ninth century A.D.[5] Large number of *Brāhmaṇas* were endowed with villages on permanent basis,[6] which shows that land-grants in early Medieval North India had become a feudal fashion.

Daulatpurva plate of Bhojadeva (706 A.D.) records large number of land-grants to *Brāhmaṇas*, individual, priest and temples by both rulers and their feudatories,[7] another copper plate of 930 A.D.; speaks of the grants of 600 *agrāharas* and 800 villages to the religious establishments[8] have emerged as important intermediaries between the state and the subjects. A record of 832 A.D. speaks of the donation of the village named Vallurika to a *Brāhmaṇa*.[9] Similar donation of a village is recorded in Tokhede-Copper plate grant of Govindaraja of the time of feudatory of the Rastrakuta Govinda III, dated 812 A.D.[10] The land-grants of 812 A.D. and 832 A.D. speaks of revenue free donation to feudal lord, but land-charters did not throws light on how the *Mahāsāmanta* acquire the land donation. This donation seems to be secular grant from the king with all kinds of exemptions.

The Chalsa inscription of Baladitya (725 A.D.)[11] from Rajasthan records, the donation of a village to a temple, without taking the approval of his overlord,[12] and certain secular intermediaries were rewarded with donation of villages for their services to the state.[13] Although epigraphic records show that their number was not as many as that of religious grantees. But if religious services were rewarded with land-grants, what could have been the other possible modes of rewarding secular services, especially when coins were not in common use.

The records of the *Rashtrakuta* king Krisna II dated A.D. 910-11 from Gujrat a group of 84 villages appears in the midst of other administrative division of longer and smaller number of villages which would suggest an attempt to incorporate the unit of clan monarchies in existing territorial system.[14] We notice a reference to a paṭṭa of 84 villages in the set-Mahet grant of the Gahadavala king Govindracandra,[15] and the same term *Caturásika-paṭṭala* is mentioned in the Badera Pattals plates of *Mahanadaladeva*[16] a feudatory of the Gahadavalas. Pattals come to be used in some part of northern India as the term for a territorial division, but basically it meant the territory which the king gave to chiefs as their *Jagirs*.[17] A Gujrara-*Pratihara* records referred to the reference to the system of 84 villages. In this record the chief is said to have acquired 84 villages by the might of his own arm, probably suggesting thereby that it was not because he belonged to the same tribe that he received it but in the sense that his overlord had to accept his claim in view of his military strength.[18] A Paramaras records of the eleventh century A.D. refers to a *Sāmanta* of the Ganga family enjoying a district which was a feudal grant of 84 villages.[19] It has been argued that whatever the differences between the two sets of grantees there is no doubt that they together constituted important intermediaries in land between the king on the one hand and the actual tiller of the soil on the other. For all practical purposes they became the occupiers and enjoyers of the villages, gave the rise to a class of landed barons who grew at the cost of peasantry.[20]

The early Medieval North Indian grants were generally permanent as has been clearly percieved in some cases. It also indicates that these villages were donated to the donees in lieu of their salaries. These grants gave to the officers the status of the feudal chiefs. We deduce that the regular officials were often paid in the form of village grants.[21] A ruler[22] had donated land to a *Brāhmaṇa* officer out of his own possession with the permission of the overlord, seems to be the land donated to him as a service tenure. The similar kind of land-grant is referred in the Pala records which seems to be allotted to the *Kaivarṭṭas* as remuneration for their services.[23] However, in the epigraphic records from different parts of Northern India we often find that the state officers had title of *rāuta, thakkura* and *rāṇaka* attached to their names. These titles stood for feudal assignments in lieu of their salaries.[24] We notice the term *rajanaka* which seems to be a title of a feudal chief in Chamba state[25] as well as in Kashmir. We can deduce that the officials were paid in terms of feudal assignments which ultimately generated a strong class of landed intermediaries or *Sāmantas*, officials and *Brāhmaṇa* which proved a drain on state economy.

The basic feature of western feudal economy was serfdom, where peasants were attached to the soil but did not own it. R.S. Sharma rightly argues that the religious donees, particularly the managers of big monasteries such as Nalanda, got their land cultivated by others, and their rents were collected through their agents.[26] In early Northern India donees enjoyed not only their power of subinfeudation but also eviction.[27] In their dominions the donees had been given the right to cultivate his benefice or get it cultivated, to enjoy it or to get it enjoyed, to do it or get it done.[28] This shows that position of peasants in donated villages looks like serfs in Western Europe. The *Skanda Pūrāṇa* a work of eighth and ninth century A.D., provides us very interesting information regarding the attachment of peasants to the land. According to this story king *Rama* had donated a number of villages to 18,000 *Brāhmaṇa* with 36,000, *Vaisyas* as well as *Śūdras* after performance of certain religious rites.[29]

The inhabitants of the villages, the *Vaishyas* and *Śūdras* were directed to serve the donees,[30] who later divided the villages amongst themselves. Rama asked the people to obey the command of the donees and serve them devotedly.[31] The *Śūdras* and *Vaishyas* were asked to render services and pay dues to the donees and not to leave or transfer allegiance from them.[32] We come to know from an inscription that the donee was empowered to collect from the villagers all kind of taxes. Thus, it is very clear that vassal treated his fellow tribemen as tools meant for his personal enjoyment, capable of having being burdened the peasant with all type of fair and unfair dues, which reduced them to the position of serfs. Thus the restrictions on the migration of peasants, which could only strengthen the hands of the landed intermediaries and ruling chiefs keeping peasants and working folk under subjection.[33] During eighth and tenth century A.D., owing to feudal tendencies, localism backed by somewhat closed economy because so much accentuated that there developed a set of special local observances and obligations which differed from village to village.[34]

The paucity of coins in early Medieval North India is a very popular debate among scholars. The notion of scarcity of coins in early medieval India was questioned and negated by Johns Deyell, who located huge quantity of silver coins in religious establishments, but coins are portable item and could be offered or donated by religious devotes during their visit to religious shrines. He argues that the *Dramma* coinage was in wide circulation during *Gujrara-Pratihara* rule,[35] he admits that its area of circulation was limited and the currency did not survive for long period. It makes his arguments is self-contradictory.

But the *dramma* was not used in any appreciable quantity prior to the ninth century A.D. Although Rashtrakuta ruled for two hundred years, and their kingdom touched the sea-coast, same was the case with the Pala to whom not even single coin can be ascribed indisputably inspite of their rule for about four centuries. Nothing can be said in precision regarding the minting of copper coins in Kashmir,[36] due to the relative isolation of the country, its coinage had little impact beyond the sphere of feudatories.[37] Thus it shows that chances of the scarcity of coin is early medieval Northern India cannot be ruled out.

The metallic currency was almost absent in most part of northern India between eighth century to 1000 A.D. The decline of trade and the grants of land to high officials in lieu of cash payment did away with the need for coins. Moreover, there is evidence for barter and the use of cowries as medium of exchange in daily transactions.

Forced labour was an important feature that contributed to the rise of feudal economy in early medieval Indian history, The term *Viṣti* was used in the sense of labour, which the villagers were obliged to provide to the state and landlord or vassals.[38] The labour was used for the construction and maintenance of irrigation system, for road works, fortification and other works required for the king or vassals. This labour required by the state in early Indian society cannot be referred to as forced labour in the strict sense of the term but it was by no mean a voluntary decision of an individual to work for the king or vassal.[39]

We notice *Visti* in some of the literary works of early medieval period. The *Rājatarangiṇi* speaks of forced carriage offloads to be exacted from the villagers. In the *Kāthasaritsāgara*, villagers are mentioned as being directed by the king's officials to pluck dates from a fallen date.

Some inscription of eighth and ninth centuries A.D. inform us that the village headman known as *grāmika, grāmakuta, grāmadhipati*, etc., were frequently, (feudal lords) running their own estates with the help of forced labour,[40] some inhabitants of the villages (*Varika*) were asked to work three days a month in the monastic estate. They had to do all kinds of agricultural works to repair and to erect monastic building.[41]

Thus, it appears that the peasant had been reduced to a state of serfdom by the extension of the practice of forced labour, and during the Pala period the peasants were subjected to the *Sarvapida*.[42] We further observed that vassals in eastern Kathiawad had the right to imposed forced labour from the villagers, this practice was continued in subsequent times of both *Pratiharas* and *Rastrakuta territories*.[43] The donee had been given the right to cultivate the lands to get it cultivated to enjoy it and get it enjoyed. Whatever might be the factors or circumstances for the prevalence of *viṣti* (forced labour). It was very much prevalent in a considerable scale in early medieval Northern India.

One of the ingredients of the feudal economy in early medieval India was the decline of trade, both internal and external. Silk, and spices were important items in the Indo-Byzantine trade. The Byzantines, however, learnt the art of growing silk-worms in the middle of the sixth century A.D. Consequently the silk trade was badly affected,[44] the migration of silk weavers from Gujarat and their taking to other vocations acquired meaning in this content. It has been argued that trade in the silk declined because Byzantine merchants stopped importing silk from India.

During the post-Gupta time the position seems to have substantially changed on account of decline in India's export and further stoppage of the supply of gold from Central Asia and the Roman Empire. R.S. Sharma is of the view that Asia was completely destroyed by the *Huṇa* invasion; and no gold coins are found in India for about three hundred years. When they reappear around 1000 A.D., the colonies of the pre-Turkish Muslims, who are called *Tādjiks* (Iranian), appeared in various parts of the country except in Kashmir, but no Indian colonies are reported in Persia or Central Asia from this period.[45] The Chinese account of ninth and tenth centuries refers to the presence of Indian merchants in China and Chinese merchants in India in the seventh century A.D. but trade seems to be confined to luxury articles and the use of common articles in internal transactions referred to by this Chinese account could not have helped foreign trade.

It has been suggested by Mohd. Habib that the Hindus were not supposed to travel overland into countries where the *munja* grass does not grow and the black gazelles do not graze practically handed over all foreign commerce to outsides, along with the domestic commerce incidental to it.[46] L. Gopal argues that India's share with the China was gradually declining probably because of the competition of Arab and Indonesian merchants. India is not mentioned among the countries which according to *Suug Annals* were trading at Canton in 971 A.D.[47] The Liang-Shu does not include China in the list of countries with which central Tien-Chu had much sea trade. Obviously sea trade with China had ceased to be an important item in India's sea trade activities,[48] the frequent feudal wars of the period were also responsible for much destruction of the economic prosperity of the country.

The records of this period indicate that the invaders often attempted to cripple the trade and economy of their enemy and to destroy the lives and property of their subjects.[49] It has been observed that coastal areas of India carried on some trade with countries of South-East Asia and China, but this interaction does not seems of any intense kind. Decline of trade was not just limited to foreign trade. Long distance internal trade too suffered owing to the weakening of links between coastal town and the interior town and further between of towns and villages. The decay of town and shrinkage in Urban Commodity production and the decline of trade were related problem. We come to know from the *Kathāsaritasāgara*,[50] a work of later period, that traders moved through forest to avoid the multiple payment of duties. Sea voyages and long distance travels were taboo. Such attitudes did not promote the cause of trade. Early Northern Indian economy experienced the rise and development of a number of rural settlements which had not been linked to exchange networks and long-distance trade. Although the exchange networks did not entirely collapse, the transfer of settlements to various kinds of donees had created a congenial atmosphere for the emergence of self-sustaining closed units of production and consumption. Local needs came to be met locally. The growing sense of localism and self-sufficiently of the villages is reflected is expression such as *grāmadharma, ghamacāra*, and *sthānacāra* all referring to village or local practices in contemporary puranic literature.

It is clear that early Indian villages were based on a self-sufficient economy where production approximated to local requirement, which little attempt at producing a surplus to be specifically for trade or exchange, surplus production would hardly have benefited the peasant, since it would have led to a demand from the landlord for a longer share. The existing system led to accepting the standard of minimum production, since the incentive to improve production was absent.[51] Limited production and lack of trade led to decrease in the use of coins, and trade was further hampered by the emergence of a wide range of local weight and measure, making long distance trade more difficult.[52] The Puranic literature recommend the observation of *grāmacāra*,[53] *grāmadharva* and *sthānacāra*[54] with the terms *disadharma* and *jātidharma*. The feudal aristocracy was actively connected with the accentuation of localism and regionalism.[55] R.S. Sharma rightly argued that the fundamental characteristic of feudal economy when local needs locally satisfied, which did not leave scope for specialized production market.[56] During this period Pala villages were inhabited by all types of people, i.e. villages were populated by artisans, merchants and cultivators. An inscription of the 882 A.D. reveals that peasants were not only tax payees in the remote area, it includes artisans and traders who use to pay *kāra*, *hiraṇya*.[57] Thus for the upkeep of the self-sufficient economy of the village it was necessary that all sections of primary producers should live in the village.[58] This inscription further records a donation of a piece of land for a flower garden, two fields, for a monthly supply of lamp-oil to be made by the guild of oil millers, and a monthly supply of flower-garlands to be made by the guild of the gardeners.[59] It seems that artisans were forcibly attached to the religious shrine of donated village. It has been depicted that, grain, cloth, oil, flowers medicine and requisite labour for the repair of building were supplied by the villages; it shows that the villages helped in sustaining the self-sufficient economy of the big monasteries by making various kinds of services available to them.[60]

The decline of towns in north India is attested by the account of Hiuen Tsang who visited India during the time of *Harshavardhana*. He further writes that the kingdom of *Rāmagrāma* was waste and dissolate for many years, and that its towns were decayed having a few the few inhabitants.[61] He further states that the town of Ganga was in bad shape, "this town is naturally strong. It has but few inhabitants; there are about 1,000 families of Brāhmaṇas only,"[62] he argues that the region called *Suughna* located 400 Li (miles) north of Thanesan, lay on the western side of river Yamuna was ruined.[63] It has been depicted that Arab geographers of ninth and tenth centuries, refer to town in some part of India but point out their fewness in the country as a whole. Merchant Sulaiman (851 A.D.)

states that the greater part of India was without towns, and it has been further confirmed by Ibn-Al-Fakin Hamdani who complied his book *Kitabul Buldān*, state that China has large town but India does not have towns.[64]

Initially the land was the property of the state or king but feudal lords, *Sāmanta-Brāhmaṇa*, and religious establishments began to acquire land through donation made by the kings. Kings tracts of land came into the hands of the *Brāhmaṇa*, *Sāmanta*, Monks and religious establishments, which now became a strong supporter of the kings. The Kings donated the land among *Brāhmaṇas* and *Sāmantas* on perptual basis. Now the villagers were dependent on their new masters (donees), who imposed manifold duties on them. The villagers of early northern India and the donees underwent a long and slow process of adjustment leading to varying social, economic and political foundations but did not extend uniformly to the whole of ancient India.

However, the basic feature of a feudal economy was its agrarian character and petty production, based on the peasant family where every villagers denoted a certain quota of his labour or his produce to his master. The surplus produced by the peasant was appropriated by a class of landlords who did not fulfill any economic function. Thus the peasantry seems to be economically and juridically dependent on the landlord or on their master. The agrarian property was privately controlled by a class of landed aristocrats who extracted a surplus from the peasants.

Decline in trade, paucity of coins and absence of coin moulds indicates economic decline and fall in demand for finished products. The decline of towns and cities life forced the *Brāhmaṇa* and Artisans to migrate from city to villages in search of new-sources of livelihood, where they were attached to their patrons and paid in kind for their services. But decline of ancient town life in early medieval northern India cannot be considered an indicator of decline in overall economic growth. Urban decline and stagnation resulted in agrarian expansion, which was further promoted by land-grants. Thus closed economic system, where the regrouping and reorganization of social relationship affected by urban decline led not only to the rise of a class of landed intermediaries but also to the spatial and occupational immobility of the artisans by making them integral part of closed economic system, they were firmly attached to the soil and their patrons, paid for their services in kind at the time of harvesting. Thus the custom of exchange of services became common practice in the feudal fashion in early medieval north India. Thus the fundamental characteristics of early medieval India economy was marked as individual ownership of land, subjection of peasantry, conversion of income and village self-sufficient economy, exchange of services, supremacy of landed aristocracy and fragmentation of royal authority, leading inevitably to economic disorder.

REFERENCES

1. B.N.S. Yadava, "Immobility and Subjection of Indian Peasantry in Early Medieved Complex", in B.P. Sahu (ed.), *Land System and Rural Society, op.cit.*, p. 329.
2. T. Watters, On *Yuan Chwang Travls in India*, I rep. Delhi, 1961, p. 169.
3. *Harṣacarita*, ed. J. Vidyasagra, Calcutta, 1892, p. 93. L. Gopal, *Economic Life of Northern India, op.cit.*, p. 14.
4. J. Takukusu (tr.) *A Record of the Buddhist Religion*, Oxford, 1896, pp. 41-45.
5. *EI*, XVII, 17, 11, 33-40.
6. K.K. Gopal, "Assignment to Officers and Royal Kinsmen in Early Medieval India 700-1200 C.A.D. in B.P. Sahu (ed.), *Land System and Rural Society.*
7. *EI*, XIX, 2, 11. 1-16, V. 24, 11-6-9.
8. R.S. Sharma, *Indian Feudalism., op.cit.*, p. 92.
9. *EI*, 1. VIII, pp. 52-58. Om Parkash, *Early Indian Land Grants, op.cit.*, p. 4.
10. *EI*, III, pp. 53-55.
11. *Ibid.* XII, p. 11.
12. *EI*, XXXII, pp. 31-44.
13. R.S. Sharma, *Indian Feudalism, op.cit.*, p. 92.
14. K.K. Gopal in B.P. Sahu, *Land System and Rural Society, op. cit.*, p.130.
15. *EI*, XI, pp. 20-26.
16. K.K. Gopal in B.P. Sahu, *Land System and Rural Society, op.cit.*, pp. 130-31.
17. *Ibid.* Secular grants might be as many or more than religious but might be inscribed on palm-leaf on cloth and therefore have perished with the passage of time.

18. K.K. Gopal in B.P. Sahu, *Land System and Rural Society*, *op.cit.*, pp. 130-31.
19. *EI*, XIX, No. 11, 8-9, twelveth century refers to Ratnapura. It would appears that Ratnapura was a feudal estate of 84 villages which originally some king had appointed to a chief of his tribe.
20. R.S. Sharma, *Indian Feudalism, op.cit.*, pp. 92-93.
21. K.K. Gopal in B.P. Sahu, *Land System and Rural Society, op.cit.*, p.121.
22. *EI*, XIX, No. 8.
23. *Ibid.* No. 5.
24. K.K. Gopal B.P. in Sahu, *Land System and Rural Society, op.cit.*, 123.
25. *Rājatrangiṇi of Khalana* (trans.) M.A. Stein West Minister, 1900, VI, 117. J. Ph. Vogel, *Antiquities of Chamba State*, pt. 1, p. 144.
26. R.S. Sharma, *Indian Feudalism, op.cit.*, p. 96.
27. *Ibid.*, pp. 96-97.
28. *EI*, IX, 1 plate (a) 1, 19, plate (6, 1.63, 111, p. 264).
29. *Skanda Pūrāṇa (Brahmakhanda)* 3.3.35.44.
30. *Ibid.* 3.2.36.47.
31. *Ibid.* 3.2.35.56.
32. *Ibid.* 3.2.40.59-60.
33. B.N.S. Yadava, "Immobility and Subjection of Indian Peasantry in Early Medieval Complex" in B.P. Sahu (ed.), p. 331.
34. *Ibid.*, p. 334.
35. Johns Deyell, *Living without Silver, op.cit.*, p. 65.
36. Y.B. Singh, "Copper Coins and their Minnting in Early Medieval Kashmir, A. Problem", *JNSI* Varanasi, XLIX, 1982, pp. 180-184.
37. Johns Deyell, *Living without Silver, op.cit.*, 65-66. L. Gopal, *The Economic Life, op.cit.*, p. 215.
38. D.C. Sircar, *Indian Epigraphical Glossary*, Delhi, 1966, p. 379.
39. Marlexe Niammasch, "From the Ancient labour to the Feudal Corvee, A Marxist Approach to the study of Visti", in B.P. Sahu, *Land System and Rural Society, op.cit.*, p. 261.
40. Marlene Niammasch, *op. cit.*, p. 270.
41. *Ibid.*, p. 272.
42. *EI*, XXIX, I.b.I., 42. R.S. Sharma, *Indian Feudalism, op.cit.*, p. 99.
43. *EI, XVIII*, 26, 11, 66-67. XXII, 13, 1.59.
44. R.S. Sharma, *Indian Feudalism, op.cit.*, p. 54.
45. R.S. Sharma, *Urban Decay in India, op.cit.*, pp. 135-36.
46. H.M. Elliot and J. Dowson, *History of India as told by its own historian* London, 1866-77, Vol. I (Introduction) p. 46.
47. L. Gopal *The Economic Life, op.cit.*, p. 133.

48. *Ibid.*
49. *Ibid.*, p. 254.
50. *Kathāsaritasāgara*, *Somadeva* (ed.) C.H. Tawney, London, 1924-28, pp. 191, 218, 227.
51. Romila Thapar, *History of India*, Vol. 1, Delhi, 1990, rep., p. 244.
52. *Ibid.*
53. *Brāhannaradya* 22.11. *Sakand Pūrāṇa*.
54. *Devibhāgavata Pūrāṇa* (tr.) Vijanananda, Allahabad, N.D., p. 325.
55. B.N.S. Yadaya, in B.P. Sahu, *op.cit.*, p. 335.
56. R.S. Sharma, *Indian Feudalism, op.cit.*, p. 103.
57. *EI*, III, No. 36, 11, p. 154, 160.
58. R.S. Sharma, *Indian Feudalism, op.cit.*, p. 104.
59. *EI*, III, No. 36, pp. 154, 160.
60. *Ibid.* Monasteries and temples formed wider economic unit. It has been mentioned in Nalanda grant of Dwapala that five villages were donated for providing articles for warship, clothing bedding, food and medicine of the monks, *EI*, XXIII, 47.11, 39-40.
61. T. Watters, *op. cit.*, 11, p. 26.
62. *Ibid.* 11, p. 113.
63. *Ibid.* I, pp. 137, 318.
64. Quoted in R.S. Sharma, *Urban Decay in India*, *op.cit.*, p. 119.

Epilogue

10

In Epilogue, it can be safely surmised from this detailed and critical study of the literary and epigraphical records of ancient India, no doubt vouched on agrarian expansion, but it left the peasantry an easy prey to the feudal lands and landlords. Though it resulted in polarization of *Varṇa*, yet it left them as 'Cannon fodder' in modern parlance. The study, therefore, present a deteriorating grim scenario, about the economic condition of the people of ancient India. The study of Agrarian Economy of Ancient India which we have made in the pages that precede has been offered in the hope that thereby we may be enabled to envisage, in answer to contemporary economic quest, the material agrarian background of the economic life and changes as reflected in the literary and epigraphical sources. The anthropogenic pressures in response to climate change have brought significant change in the human life. Domestication of plants and animals refers to the process of reciprocation, by which animals and plants species come to depend on human for their survival, while providing humans with numerous benefits in turn. By domesticating plants, human being gained control over the primary food source for animals. But by domesticating animals, man gained control over living organisms that eat plants and greatly concentrated the energy they derived in the form of animal's protein. Thus human being taped the primary source of food energy by controlling plants. This led to security in food requirements of human being and hense sustained their lives and civilization on the earth.

Thus it can be surmised that Harappan-Vedic society appears to be less agrarian and more non-agrarian pastoralism was a primitive economic activity which involved the care of herds of domesticated cattles in Harappan-Vedic periods. In its primitive forms it was either practiced as the main mode of subsistence or combined with Agriculture pastoralism and agriculture during Harappan-Vedic times were interconnected and interdependent. Men and cattle herds lived a symbiotic community; the human component of this community took the forms of a settled village life composed either entirely of pastoralists or of some specialized pastoralists living among farmers communities.

Kauṭilya was not directly associated with the economic policy of the Mauryan state. As a matter of fact, the economic thought depicted in *AŚ* might not be the innovation of Kauṭilya, these might be derived from earlier traditions. The *Arthaśāstra* of Kauṭilya prescribed the model of mixed economy, in which private and public sectors played their important role. Some of the features of the Kauṭilyan economy are adopted by many states of modern world. The state had monopoly in the production of several goods and participated with private entrepreneurs in the exploration of mines. Fixed rate of interest and profit were prescribed. Traders were compelled to use standard weight and measures, the implication of a comprehensive programme of social security measures. Utmost care was taken to promote economy and the welfare of the people which was the main agenda of Kauṭilya, his economic thought keep relevance in the present-day economic scenario. It is very clearly depicted in *Arthaśāstra* that *artha* a much wider significance than merely 'wealth'. The material well-being of an individual was a part of it.

The question of land rights in ancient India is still undecided and remained most debatable and controversial among the historians of ancient Indian economic history. Different theories are propounded by different law givers in their respective writing regarding the land rights. Thus after critical analysis of ancient literary and epigraphical sources or texts we can surmise that no single system of land rights prevailed in ancient India, but royal, private and joint land-rights are clearly reflected in the literary and epigrahical traditions of ancient India simultaneously.

Another ingredient of agrarian economy in ancient India was land measurements. The paradisms of land measurement differed from region to region as we did not notice any single land charter in which all the different forms of land measures are depicted together. Thus region and local variations were observed. In most of the cases only one form of measure is depicted or referred, standard followed was not the same everywhere. Thus an inherent difficulty is confronted in determining the exact size of particular area of land mentioned, in the absence of necessary details.

The land-charters reflected not even the slightest oppression or vexation should be caused by any body to the donee or to his ploughmen, cowherds, maids, servants and dependants. It has been observed that overlords did not make any serious efforts to stop exaction of feudal chiefs. As the Central authority in early medieval period had declined considerably and had to depend on the levies sent by the feudal chiefs, it could not afford to interfere with their high-handed exploitation.

The upshot of the above discussion is that the linking of the fashion of land-grants to the religious as well as secular persons in lieu of salaries for their services to the state was the fashion of early Medieval North India.

It is very clear from the analysis of land-charters that the Chauhan land-grants differed in a big way from the traditional grants which were based on feudal economy, whereas the latter included permanent abrogation of the rights of the donors in favour of the donees, it was not so in the case of the former. No doubt, the Chauhans committed themselves and the state to the legal status of such grants, but certainly gave themselves the right to revoke any such land-grants in case of misuses and its abuse.

The basic feature of a feudal economy was its agrarian character and petty production, based on the peasant family where villagers denoted a certain quota of his labour or his produce to his master. The surplus produced by the peasant was appropriated by a class of landlords who did not fulfill any economic function. Thus thc peasantry seems to be economically and juridically dependent on the landlord or on their master. The agrarian property was privately controlled by a class of landed aristocrats who extracted a surplus from the peasants.

Decline in trade, paucity of coins and absence of coin mounds indicates economic decline and fall in demand for finished products. The decline of towns and city life forced the *Brāhmaṇa* and Artisans to migrate from cities to villages in search of new-sources of livelihood, where they were attached to their patrons and paid in kind for their services. But decline of ancient town life in early medieval northern India cannot be considered an indicator of declined in overall economic growth. Urban decline and stagnation resulted in agrarian expansion, which was further promoted by land-grants. Thus closed economic system, where the regrouping and reorganization of social relationship affected by urban decline led not only to the rise of a class of landed intermediaries but also to the spatial and occupational immobility of the artisans by making them integral part of closed economic system, they were firmly attached to the soil and their patrons, paid for their services in kind at the time of harvesting.

The agrarian economy in ancient India, witnessed the long and gradual process of feudalization. However, feudal agrarian relation differed from area to area because agricultural and landless labourers, manual servants, artisan, etc., were dependent on agriculture and were remunerated mostly in the common lands of the village though their status was not better than that of semi-serfs.

The social agrarian aspect of feudal system in early medieval India was intimately connected with the transformation of the *Śūdras*. It seems that the older settled regions *Śūdras* were provided with land and in remote parts the tribal peasantry was annexed to the *Brāhmaṇical* system through grants. It cannot be assumed that the burden of heavily increased taxes was to put on the villagers. Many charters clearly indicate transfer of artisans and traders to the beneficiaries. The charters clearly shows that the peasants, villagers and other inhabitants of the donated villages carry out the orders of the beneficiaries. Thus, if the piece of land or village is transferred the peasants are automatically transferred. From the eigth century A.D. onwards sub-infeudation has become a common phenomena in India history, which gave the rise to graded types landlords, different from the actual tiller of land, deteriorated the economic condition of the peasants. Some charters record that the donees were authorized to enjoy the land, to get it enjoyed get it cultivated. Thus with the increase in the number of intermediaries, and peasants seem to be forced to pay additional taxes. It also traces the causal complexities which forced the peasant to accept their fate passively and without a murmur. It, thus, becomes abundantly clear that Ancient Indian villages were based on a self-sufficient economy which produce approximated to local requirements with little attempt of producing a surplus for trade and exchange. Surplus production would hardly benefit the peasant, since it would have led to a demand from the feudal lords for a larger share. The re-grouping and re-organization of social relationships led to the rise of not only a class of landed intermediaries, but also to the spatial and occupational immobility of the artisans by making them intergal part of the *Jajmāni* system.

Appendix

EARLY INDO-CHINESE COMMERCIAL ROUTES: LINKAGES AND INTERACTION

From the very dawn of civilization commercial routes followed by the 'Buddhist Monks' played a leading role to harmonise the unevenly distributed economic resources over the earth. Through certain trans-countries commercial routes particular goods tended to flow from places, where they were plentiful, to those in which scarcity existed to balance the surplus production. The main protohistoric commercial routes between early China and India became the great commercial trans-continental link routes. Therefore, this appendix is an attempt to establish the commercial linkages and interaction between the two ancient cultures of Asia with emphasis on various trans-countries routes, through which the Indians and Chinese exchanged their trade goods. This can be established from the study of various secular and non-secular traditions of the two civilizations.

However, certain questions like who discovered the commercial routes between India and China; who traded through these routes for the first time; still linger in the minds of scholars. Any way, these are the difficult questions to be answered, and even the probable answers shall not be able to satiate the first of the inquisitive researchers. Therefore, the question regarding the ancient routes taken by the Indian to China and by the Chinese to India is still unsettled. Equally more baffling and mysterious is the fixing up of the first commercial contact between Chinese and the Indian. Though some of the scholars did try to trace and establish the commercial contact between two ancient civilizations as back as to the fourth century B.C.,[1] but there is no definite historical record as yet to establish this.

It is certainly an accepted belief that the commercial and the spiritual contacts between these two ancient societies took place through the silk routes. The most significant proof and evidence of these relations, and linkages lie in the establishment of Buddhism in China. The early Indo-Chinese linkages and interactions were established by the selfless Buddhist monks of both ancient societies who used to carry and spread the message of love and peace, which Buddha delivered to balm the ailing and suffering mankind. The cultural interactions between the these great societies was primarily initiated by the Chinese. Hence, source materials of its history are to be found in Chinese only, but unfortunately, such references of those noble Indian scholars, who went to China with purely missionary spirit and whose names are interwoven with the history of Buddhism in China, are not available. Thus, the great achievements of these iconoclasts are not recorded in Indian history or much detailed. These unsung torch-bearers of Indian civilization in China remain unknown.

For many centuries the Chinese society was predominantly agrarian in nature, with no urbanization. But this, closed economy of China was transformed into trade economy by these trans-continental routes and it led to development of urban centres. The Chinese silk was in great demands from all over the world, and China fulfilled this demand of the world market, sometimes through Indian traders—who served as middlemen,[2] yet no convincing and definite conclusions can be drawn.

The *Arthaśāstra* of *Kauṭilya* refers to Chinese silk, which clearly throws light on the regular commercial linkages between early Indo-Chinese times. *Kauṭilya* specifically depicts two types of commodities of Chinese origin, silks and fabrics of Chinese manufacture.[3] It is supported by the report given by the Chinese envoy Chang Kien—being the first to traverse the route across Chinese Turkestan and sojourned in Bactria (127 B.C.). He found to his great surprise that bamboos and textiles from southwestern China were sold in the local market but were not exported by China itself. He learnt that these were brought to eastern India through upper Burma, and then carried the whole way across north India.[4]

The early Indian secular and non-secular traditions inform us about two kinds of commercial routes between China and India—land and sea—through which trade was carried on. But this trade was regularly hampered on account of constant wars. The trade, therefore, remained confined within the frontiers of the country and later on extended to the boundaries of the other countries. This is reported by the Medhatithi who speaks of land and trade links and interactions among the now called Asian countries.[5]

The overland routes played very significant role between early Indo-Chinese commercial and cultural linkages and facilitated interaction between the two countries. The Indo-Chinese pilgrim routes, the Indo-Assam-Burma-China route and Indo-Tibetan-China routes were the major routes of commercial and cultural exchange. The merit and demerits of overland routes like those of the sea appear to have been realized as early as fourth century B.C. by both Kauṭilya and his preceptor though both differed on certain issues. The question of overland routes was also subject of difference when his preceptor held that overland routes, *vis-à-vis* the sea routes, were more expensive and less productive in realizing profits, Kauṭilya too disagreed with this view as he firmly held that overland routes were not liable to obstruction were permanent and were never in imminent danger and capable of defence.[6]

Early India had several mountain Passes in the North-East and North-West frontiers through which overland commercial linkages and interactions were experienced between early China and India, Burma and other Indo-Chinese countries on the North. From the North-Eastern frontiers of India, i.e. from the Assam hills, several overland commercial routes connected early India with China. Pellicot is of the opinion that a regular trade route by land between Eastern India and China lay through upper Burma and Yunnan at least as early as the fourth century B.C.[7] It is important to recall the report of Chang-Kien, the Chinese ambassador to the Yue-Chi country, wherein he testifies this. He also agreed that this route passed through India and reached upto Afghanistan and thence to Balkh. B.R. Deepak, states that Assam-Burma and Yunnan route originated in Chengdu, Sichuan province of China and entered Dali, Baoshan and Teng Chong of Yunnan province. From Yunnan it passed through the northern part of Burma and entered Assam in the North-East of India. The Southern silk route finally merged with the Central Asian route.[8] It is believed that this was the earnest route for Indo-Chinese interaction and commercial linkages. Long before second century B.C., Chinese cotton was carried through this route to Bactria via Uttrapatha, Campa was the emporium of Chinese goods. From Campa Chinese goods were dispatched to all commercial markets of early India. Through this overland route, Chinese silk came to Bharakaccha which later was exported to the markets of Alexandria.[9] P.C. Bagchi, argues that the Assam-Burma route to China which started from Pataliputra passed through Campa, Kajangala and Pundravardhana and extended to Kamarup. From Assam three commercial routes went to Burma, one, through the valleys of the Brahmaputra upto Patkoi range and then through its Passes upto upper Burma, and second through Manipur upto the Chindwin Valley, and the third through Arakan upto the Trawadi valley. These three routes converged on the frontier of Burma near Bhamo and then moved further over mountains and across river valleys to Yunnan-fu, i.e. Kunming, in the Southern province of China.[10]

From Bactria, the western gateway of India several routes led to China through Central Asia. Thus, the commercial interaction between early China and early India took place through Central Asia. China explored the trade routes which crossed that territory in order to export to India and the west. It was through this great commercial interacting carvan of business that India and China came to know each other so well. China contributed to early India and West. The exports include porcelain, paper, ginger and various fruits, as well as the treasured silk which was so important an industry, as to give its name to the silk road, or Central Asian Road,[11] across which silks were carried to Indian market or west through Indian market.

The founding of this carvan trade through the commercial route led to the exploration of the long and dangerous route across the desert stretch which is known as Gobi. It was by means of this commercial linkage and interaction that symbiotic and friendly relationships were established between people who otherwise might have never met. This commercial route between early China and India however did not only carry traders, merchants and patient, camel-drivers but also a different class of sacred men, i.e. Buddhist monks whose hearts were not set on gaining any economic and political advantage from China, nor were they interested in the subjugation of any small kingdoms by a great and strong empire, even though that great empire were their own native land. They were pilgrims, Buddhist monks, who craved for knowledge and were convinced that the source of knowledge lay in the distant land of India where the young prince Gautama had lived. These inquisitive minds trod the length of this commercial route from India to the cities of China and from China across the Pamirs to India. They became the medium for the spread of Buddhism through silk route from India to China. Thus, the Buddhist ideology revolutionized the cultural commercial life of the people of Indian and Chinese,[12] the Chinese traveler, Fa-Hien, had also taken this route from Ch'ang-ngan, passed through Lung and Western part of ShenSe and eastern part of Kan-Suh, crossed the mountain of Yang low to reach the emporium of Chang-yih. From there, he visited the kingdom of Shen-Shon, to the south and not far from Lake Noo into which the Tarim flows.

After a month and five days, he arrived at Yu-teen (Khotn), a large district on the south-west of Gobi desert. Khotan, according to Hiuen-Tsang, was a colony of Indians settled there by Kunala, the crown prince of Asoka. Its capital was Yotkan, from where the routes passed through Danalan, Ulik, Niya, Endre and others centres of Buddhism and commercial contacts with India.[13] Another important routes passed through the southern basin of the Tarim river of Tun-huang, which was the western port confine of China proper. Stering argues that this routes passing through the Lopnor had been used as a main line of interaction with China from time of Han dynasty. Hieun-Tsang and centuries after him even Marcopolo had followed this track through the desert,[14] besides these, even the northern routes was also important from the point of Indian commerce, cultural interaction and contact with China. The route between Kashgar and Kuch was an important trade colony,[15] that passed along Faizabad, Mahalbashi, Ueh Turfan and Aks. From Kuch, this route merged with the main route coming via Khotan to Tum-huong.[16]

Another overland commercial route was the Indo-Tibetan Chinese land route. This route was more difficult to access than central Asian route. This route came into being only during the seventh century A.D. We learn about this from the experience of a Chinese pilgrim, Hieun-Tsang in 627 A.D. On leaving China, he traveled across the desert, finally reached Tibet. There with the aid of King Strongbtsan Syampo's Chinese wife, he was safely escorted to Jullunder in the Punjab. This reveals that he was not well aware of that route for he seems to have traveled upto Nepal. It appears to have been in conformity with these conversant practice, which emphasized the return backwards in an easterly directions traversing the central steppes upto Kashgar and Khotan and through the Shipki pass near Shimla to enter India. This route was abandoned during seventh and eighth centuries because of political tension between China and Tibet; but appears to have been current only in tenth century when a Chinese traveler, Ki-Ye returned to China through this route.[17]

The existence of sea routes for commercial contacts and linkages has been the hallmark of early Indian traditions. Therefore, it is difficult to accept the Kauṭilyan belief that the water route was liable to destruction was not permanent, and a source of imminent dangers as it was incapable of defence.[18] R.N. Saletore rightly argues that, "it is surprising that Kauṭilya symbolic of royal power, should have held such a view and could only have come to such conclusion in the absence of a strong sea-power and probably from an ignorance of the real position of sea-ways".[19] The main threat at sea were the pirates whose ship, bound for the country of an enemy as well as those which violated the customs and rules in force in ports towns, were recommended to be destroyed, who thus could have both obstructive, destructive and dangerous. But sea routes could hardly have been dubbed indefensible unless the sea power of the government was extremely feeble to cope with their defence.[20] If these objections had been really genuine and had actually existed during Mauryan supremacy then the foreign trade, about which Kauṭilya has given so many details could hardly have been feasible.

There were specific periods of the year during such sea voyages could be undertaken between India and China. Villages on the seashores and lakes or rivers had to pay a fixed amount of tax[21] (Klrptam). This could not be interpreted to mean that there were no harbours from which a ship could not sail out to the seas. Kauṭilya tells us that ships at harbours or on their way, may be requested to pay toll.[22] It is very clear in *Arthaśāstra* that foreign traders, who often visited the country and those who were known to local traders were allowed to land on ports.[23]

Early India had an extensive sea board, since its borders were bounded on three sides of the sea. It had a network of navigable rivers free from the freezing effect of the cold climate. It is also noticed that the Western as well as the Eastern coasts had a number of good commercial harbours and emporium which were the trade units and partners of early Indian foreign trade. The early medieval literary traditions of the Sino-Indian interface could be traced to the Han dynasty (206 B.C.-220 A.D.). The first information is provided by Si Maqion (145 B.C.-90 B.C.) the Great Chinese historian in his master piece *Shiji*. The traditions depict that Zhang Qian who was Han envoy in the western regions returned to the court of Chinese emperor in 122 B.C.,[24] through the sea route. The *Jātaka* refers to some merchants who undertook the voyage to Suvarnabhumi (Land of Gold) for wealth and profit, [25] wherefore, certain commercial routes between India and China were noticed. One commercial sea route started from Bharakaccha to the coast of Suvarnabhumi.[26] Ptolemy informs us about another sea route, which was generally adopted by the merchants and traders of Kalinga. The ships set-sail from Polura, near the mouth of the Ganjam, would cross the Bay of Bengal for the Eastern Peninsula in the Far-East.[27] Balram Srivastava argues that for the traders of Mathura, Kausambi, Varanasi and Campa the most convenient port was Tamralipti. From Tamralipti the ships sailed on the open sea for *Suvarṇabhūmi* and other countries like Yanadvipa, Campa and Kamboja. It established a regular sea route between early India and China which became popular and the port of Tamralipti came to be the most suitable destination for a trader from China wishing to trade with northern India."[28] Mission from Funan, which started from India, in the first century A.D. actually landed on the part of Tamralipti.

The Malayan Peninsula also played a very important part in the maritime activities of the Indian in the Far-East since long before the Christian era. It was the central place between India and China, Its famous port was Takkola, which may be identified with Takua Pa.[29] A Chinese ambassador during the Wu dynasty while going to India come to the port of Takkola and then took the route to India through gulf of Martaban.[30] Java also played an equally important role in the trade between early India and Far-East.[31] It was colonized in the first century A.D. by Aji Saka of Gujrat. Later on, Indian traders developed their direct commercial relations with China in the second century A.D., during the regime of Deva Varman a Hindu king of Java.[32] According to the Chinese tradition, the king of Campa sent an ambassador in about 240-45 A.D. It took nearly one year to reach the mouth of Ganga from Campa,[33] the commercial route from Campa to Southern China was a direct one.[34] The trader from Tabal in Kamboja could reach Canton, the most important emporium of Southern China, within a few days.[35]

The Chinese travelers, who visited India and returned to their home through sea routes, often recounted their journey.

One such, probably the best Chinese description is given by Fa-Hien, who tells us how he left Tamralipti (Tamlak) for Ch'ang Kwang sailing down to Ceylon with a favourable wind, he embarked on board a ship which had more than two hundreds merchants and it had a trailor-boat which was small in size and tied to the larger vessel to serve as a life-boat in cases of emergency. The traders in extreme and difficult sea condition were constrained to throw overboard many of their heavier cargoes, which involved considerable losses to the unfortunate merchants.[36] The utter helplessness and the agonies of these miserable merchants, who had obviously secured neither on adequate ship nor a proper pilot, have been graphically described by Fa-Hien thus: "The merchants were full of terror, not knowing where they were going. After more than ninety days, they arrived at country called Javadvipa." Again, embarking there from in another merchant who was also carrying more than two hundred men, they transported provisions for fifty days and they continued the voyage on the days of the fourth month. Then they took a course to the north-east intending to proceed to Kwang-Chero.[37] Fa-Hien took 172 days or five months and twenty-two days from Ceylon to reach Kwang-tung in China. In 453 A.D. a Chinese Buddhist called Dharmakrama, had also undertaken the sea route from Southern India on his way back to China. The sixth century saw a continued development of many such interactions and linkages between early India and China. In 526 A.D. Bodhidharma, the great patriarch of Indian Buddhism, who was the son of a King of Southern India, "reached Canton by sea". He was received with the honour due to his age and character, and invited to Nanking, where the Emperor of South China held his court.[38] Beal while referring to the life of Hiuen-Tsang alludes to Baskarvarmana as having asked the great teacher that he would be escorted by his officials if he preferred returning back to China by the Southern sea route,[39] it indicates that the king of Assam Baskarvarmana had his control over the commercial sea-route leading to China.[40] Evidences of a regular sea-service from Kwang-Tung and the capital of Sri Vijaya, can also be found in history. I-Tsing tells us that it took him more than ten days to reach Kwang-Tang from here he left toward north-westernly direction, reached Tamralipti in "about half a month time". He further states that from Sri Bhoja they sailed to Ka-Cha and, after a voyage of more than ten days they came to the country of naked people and from there proceeded to Tamralipati.[41] I-Tsing seems to have taken about four months to reach from Tomralipti to Kwang-Tang by sea. A Japanese text of the mid eighth century A.D. states that heavily laden merchant ships from India and Malaya regularly visited the part of Canton.[42] An Indian monk named Bodhisena, a Brāhmaṇa of south India, set out for China by sea, and met on the way a priest of North India named Buttetsu a stranded victim of ship wreck. They arrived together in China in 733 A.D., and then went to Japan in a ship in 736 A.D.[43]

During the Tang period (618 A.D. to 907 A.D.), the commercial interaction and linkages with early India reached he highest peak in China. Thousands of Indian travelers thronged the principle cities in China. The period also witnessed a great development of the sea-borne trade interaction between India and China. An account written about 749 A.D. refers to the numerous traders and merchants belonging to the Poloman (i.e. Brāhmaṇa of India) sailing in the river of Canton. Coins of Tang dynasty have been discovered in South India.[44] The Chinese annals contain references to a kingdom called San-fo-tsi (Sailandra empire) sent embassies to China in 904, 960-62, 971-72, 974-75, 980 and 983 A.D. for strengthing of trade relations with China. In 971 A.D. a regular shipping-house is said to have been opened at Canton and two more subsequently at later periods, came up. These were frequented by the merchants from San-fo-tsi and other places in the East-Indies.[45]

The journeys of Buddhists scholars and monks between India and China provide a convenient background for the understanding of commercial linkage and interaction between two ancient societies. In the second century B.C. the Chinese traveler Chang K'ien found that Chinese silk was imported into Bactria via India, suggesting that even at this stage the Indian had not yet fully mastered the art of spinning and weaving fine silks, which they certainly did later. Besides silkworms another insect of commercial importance was the lac-insect, which provide both the resin used for shellac, and also the dye known as *Iaac*. The above fact was also established by the great Chinese historian in his masterpiece *Shiji* Xinanyizhuan. The record narrates that Zhang Qian who was Han enemy in the eastern regions returned to the royal court in 122 B.C. he reported to the Emperor, that while in Bactria, he saw clothes made in Shu and the walking sticks of bamboo. When asked where these things came from the man answered, "these are from Shenda (Sindhu) served thousands Li from here in the south-east, we bought them at the Shu merchant's market there".[46] From this statement, it can be surmised that, during the times of the emperor Wu in 122 B.C. and the Bactrian traders used to go to India and trade in Chinese cloths and bamboos which were sold in India by the Chinese businessmen of Shu.[47] This establishes the fact that Chinese goods must have been sold in Indian market, and Chinese businessmen had their own shops along with their Indian counterparts. This also shows that Indian traders had pronounced close commercial linkage and interaction with their Chinese counterparts, who seem to have been given the facility of setting up their own shops in Indian Territory. The records of grand historians of China throw some further light on the commercial aspiration of Bactria which was eager to open trade relation directly with China apparently through the northern routes but, as the Huna were blocking that route; such a course was not feasible. The Chinese emperor, Wu, tried to reach to the Bactrians through the South-western land route to India but the South-Western barbarians of K'un-ming did not let it happen. It shows that north and south routes were controlled by the barbarians and to that extent the trade of China, particularly in silk, must have been affected. But for them a trade might, therefore, have been conducted, which would have proved prospers for the inhabitants of China. China was actually cut off from both the northern and southern land routes, Chinese goods from the Shu province came to India where Chinese traders or businessmen sold them and these were purchased by the merchants from Bactria.[48]

The Kauṭilyan policy regarding the import and exports of goods involved two main principles. The first being public welfare and second being the public prosperity. The import of such goods which were not easily available for production purposes like seeds and goods of daily needs, etc., were exempted from payments of toll-charges which, if levied, would have only inflected the price of a large number and variety of goods, intended for public consumption. Kauṭilya states that if any commodity which was not considered beneficial to the welfare or the public, and any commodity easily available, than its import was not permitted into the country. In fact, the objective of public welfare is summed up by Kauṭilya in his estimate of a king's happiness. Thus, "in the happiness of his subjects lies his happiness; in their welfare, his welfare; whatever pleases him he shall not consider as good, but whatever pleases his subject he shall consider as good."[49] The Superintendent of Commerce (Panyadhykṣa) had specific duties in fixing the prices of merchandise imported from a distant country.[50] The Office in-charge of boundaries (Antapata) after carefully examining foreign goods as to their quality and stamped them with his seal before sending them on to the Superintendent of Toll (*Śulk adhyakṣa*).[51]

During the Mauryan times special concessions were granted to foreign traders, who come into the country for selling their goods.[52] Whenever weather-beaten ship arrived at a port-town, the superintendent of Ships had to show fatherly kindness to it. As regard quality of foreign goods of the village Accountant (Gopa) and the district officer (*Sthanika*), puts spies, in the guise of merchants determined to such goods arrived there, had to ascertain the amount of toll, road cess, conveyance cess, Ferry-fare and one-sixth portion, the charges incurred by them for their own subsistence and for the accommodation of their goods in werehouses.[53] Thus it is clear four *Arthásāstra* that concerned officials had to observe that foreign traders were granted certain concession but not spared in cases of offences. The state policy of bestowing concessions to traders engaged in foreign trade seems to have continued down to the early medieval terms. An Inscription of a king named Visnusena (592 A.D.) refers that traders staying abroad for a year were not to pay the entrance fee in the shape of toll while returning to their native place, but were to pay an exit tax when they went out again. This kind of an exemption can be considered an attempt to encourage foreign trade.

This section deals with the various goods imported into India and exported to China by land as well as sea during early periods and how their commercial implications may be classified under various heads. Xinru Liu informs us that the Chinese standard histories from the Han through the Northern dynasties (206 B.C. to 534 A.D.) are the obvious places to look for information about trade.[54] The official histories, as well as unofficial sources, record numerous instances of tribute to the Chinese emperor as acknowledgement of submission and as token of good will, or to a trader's payment to the emperor for permission to trade in China,[55] the donated items never went outside the palace in Chinese markets. Various items such as, Coral, pearls, glass and certain kinds of fragrances appear to be the important items exported from early India or through India to China; Silk was the major item exported from China to India.

Chinese silk was the only Chinese item which had reached the Western regions of Central Asia before the T'ang in large quantities, and because much silk was transported to Roman market through India in order to bye pass the strife-ridden Roman and the Persians empires.[56] The Buddhist traditions reveal us that silk was used as s status item in decoration in Indian royalty[57]—as industries, semi-culture and weaving, were well established in India during the Gupta periods. The wealth of the well-known Mandason silk weaving guild testifies to the prosperity of the silk trade.[58] In the early seventh century when Hiuen-Tsang visited India, he listed silk as one of the most popular materials for clothings in the country. But he used the word *Kauṣeya* for the commonly worn silk fabric because it was obtained from a species of wild silk worm.[59] Hiuen-Tsang clearly distinguished between the two kinds of silk. Obviously the difference between *Kauṣeya* and Chinese silk was quite clear.

China exported both fine silk textiles and silk yarn to India, which controlled part of the silk trade between China and Byzantine. Before the Byzantians acquired the knowledge of semiculture, their silk industry was heavily dependent on Chinese yarn, which they obtained from the Persians. The Persians in turn bought silk yarn from the Central Asian and Indian traders. The Persians had to buy the Chinese silk from India, and the Persians had no direct trade links with China as the Indians dealt in Chinese silk yarn. The Chinese silk Cinamasuka was used by the Indian elite; it was woven from Chinese yarn in India. But during the Gupta periods, the Chinese had already lost their monopoly over the silk market. The decline of the Roman market for the silk might have slowed down silk export and production in India. It was due to the rise of the Byzantian Empire that almost made up for the loss of Roman trade. Along with it many other luxury goods from Asia, came to occupy importance in the Byzantian Court and Church.[60] The Byzantian's emperor tried to get Ethopian merchants to buy silk from India, but the Ethopians could not reach the source since, Persia monopolized the Chinese silk trade via India and its seas.[61]

It is important to recall the shift in trade tendencies and which resulted loss to the Indian merchants as the Byzantians traders came to have a direct commerce deal with their Chinese counterparts. These shift further loss back to the Indian-Chinese traders as the Byzantians came to develop their own technology in semiculture—as was the basis of trade monopoly late in the century.[62] Inspite of these setbacks the silk industry continued to prosper in India. Bana Bhatt (646 A.D.), refers to coconuts balanced on loops made of slips of China silk hanging from yoke.[63] This shows that silk from China apparently continued to come to India, was in great demand especially on festive occasions. This, however, should not be interpreted to mean that there was no local industry of silk in the country as can be proved from the words of Hiuen-Tsang himself.[64]

Silk consumption in India was closely related to the lives of elite social groups—especially the urban and monastic elite, and also certain religion needs and social customs, ritual and standards. This is evident from the Mandasor inscription on the silk-weaving guild which prohibits a woman from meeting her lover in privacy until she has put on two silken garments.[65] Kalidasa described its customary significance during weddings in his works—*Kumarsaṁbhava* and *Raghuvaṁsa* where both the bride and bridegroom wear silk outfits.[66] Silk banners were indispensable during Buddhist ceremonies. Fa-Hien observed silk banners hung over monks' seats at a grand Buddhist ceremony held in Chieh-Ch's. In Kashmir, silk banners were donated to the Buddha's garden near Śravasti and were also hung in the parade of the Buddha image in Patliputra.[67] As official participation/delegations were rare, most of these banners were donated by traders passing by or, by people who bought these banners.

Another, item Storax, was imported into India from China, which was used for perfumery and medicine. It was utilized as an ingredient for manufacturing ointments and unguents.[68] Aromatic, items of like clove were also imported into India by Chinese traders.[69] Aloe another ingredient for perfume was also imported into India from China.[70]

Arthaśāstra of *Kauṭilya* further refers to two types of goods of Chinese origin, skins and fabrics with regard to skins he points that *Samura, Cinaṣi* and *Samuli* were procured from Bahlava. The Samuli were procured from Bahiava. The Samura type was thirty-six angulas (inches) long, and black, Cinasi was reddish black or blackish white, while samuli was of a wheat colour.[71]

This two-way traffic of commercial exchange and linkage between early India and China saw the export of "Sugar" from India to China. Although China grew sugarcane since long but did not have technology of making sugar. It is important to state that the term sugar was not to be found in China's first dictionary *Shuowen Jiezi* compiled by Xushen as early as that 100 A.D. The sugar manufacturing is beyond doubt the technology traveled to China from India, as word sugar, later on, came too referred in the supplements of the above mentioned dictionary. More convincing evidence to this effect was found in Xin Tangshu (*New Tang Annals*) which informs us that the Chinese Emperor T'ai Tsung (647 A.D.) sent a mission to India to acquire the recipe of sugar making. This technology was later adopted and improved by the sugar-cane groups of Yun-Cou, and resulted in the improvement of its colour and taste.[72]

The crystal was yet another precious metal from early India which was exported to a China, during the sixth century A.D. Chang's Yue work *Mirrors of Four Lords of the Lian Dynasty*, informs us that huge quantity of fine crystal "which belonged from western India, arrived in China" by some merchants.[73] It is argued that mirror offered for sale was of a particular standard, i.e. twelve inches by four inches across its surface and forty catties in weight. It was pure white had transparent surface and in the interior and displayed many coloured objects on it's observe when held and examined against light. Its substance was not discernible. When Chinese inquired about its price the sellers often quoted one million strings of copper coins. The Chinese emperor ordered his officials to raise the sum as the treasury did not hold enough to pay this amount. This reflects that such mirrors were highly expensive.[74]

The Sanskrit terms *Vaidurya*, which means lapis lazuli, beryl or cat's eyes gem, is the origin of *Ilu-li* before Buddhism spread to China, the Chinese name of lapis lazuli, a precious stone from the north-west, was *miu-lin*. From the Han to the Northern dynastics *miu-lin* and *liu-li* came to be interchangeable terms for a few kinds of blue or green precious stone. In the Buddhist texts, *Ilu-li* also denoted blue or green precious stone, primarily Lapis Lazuli.[75] It is noticed that the Han period onwards Indian empire produced *Ilu-li*, and the official history of former Han described *Ilu-li* as a product of the Kashmir and early India is considered as one of the exporters of crystal to China,[76] finally it can be surmised that Indian artisans must have been familiar with the technology of processing glass. B.B. Lal viewed that glassed titles in Texila reveal that Indian were skilful at moulding large pieces of glass.[77] The crystal or glass seems to be associated with Buddhist stupa. The glass titles were used to pave the sacred path around the stupa, the glass bottle, boards and small artifacts were buried along the reliquaries under Buddhist stupa.[78] In similar fashion of burning crystal items and beads in China suggests that, because they had similar religious value to Buddhists, glass and beads, were exported from India to China together with other beads.

Various other items of Indian export are referred in early Indian traditions, such as Coral and Pearls. These items could gradually spread from the royal court to the houses of other members of the elite, the Chinese aristocrats, Shih Ch'ung and Wang K'ai vied each other to display their wealth. Wang K'ai boasted to Shih that he had received a beautiful piece of Branch Coral two feet tall from emperor Wu of Chin.[79] This indicates that after Chin period Chinese rulers of small states continued to acquire Indian Coral. There were three possible commercial routs to ship the Coral to China from India. The most frequented route was the southern route to India the periplus informs us that the primarily destination of Coral in Roman Cargoship was India and then India to China. Pliny mentions that Coral was an highly treasured in India as Pearls were in Rome.[80] Hirth states that from the first century to sixth centuries, the Syrian merchants continued to export Indian Corals along with other goods for sale to Parthia and China.[81] Coral beads along with beads of other precious materials have been found in north Indian cities,[82] still coral continued to fetch high prices in the Gupta and post Gupta's times, which appears that it was a item of luxury in early China and India. Coral was also one of the treasures in the house of the rich courtesan Vasantsena.[83] Dikshitar states that Coral necklaces, conches were largely in demands in China and the Chinese emperors were fascinated by the product of western India.[84] Since, the India was the main market for Roman Coral, it follows that Coral beads which have arrived in China passed mainly through India, or through Red Sea to South China. S.K. Mainty argues that Coral was transferred to North India from South during Kalidasa times but M.S.

Shukla negated his argument and informs us about the fishing in and ornamental Coral was missing on the shores of South India.[85] From where did it originate? Is an unsettled query, but certainly north India was the major exporter of Coral to China before T'ang dynasty.

Pearls (*Maṇi*) the most important export item from India in early times was the source of commercial linkage and interaction between these two ancient civilizations of the world. The political disturbance in Rome probably checked in the third century A.D. the export of pearls from India to Rome, but in India the demands of pearls continued unabated and might have diverted the export to China. Fa-Hien informs us that the treasures of the Buddhist communities in Ceylon and India, were full of many priceless pearls (*maṇis*).[86] The Periplus reveals that the pearls from Persia were lower quality than Indian Pearls, exported to Far-East.[87] Marshal found a casket full of various kinds of beads, including pearls, inside a stupa at Taxila, verifies the association of pearls with Buddhist building remains. In North China pearls were also associated with Buddhist remains. A few hundred pearls were found in a casket under the foundation of a Northern Wei monastery, and also around the foundation of a famous Yung-ning *stupa* in the Northern Wer Loyang.[88] Thus, the finding of Indian Pearls under the foundation of Buddhist shrines suggests the trade in pearls between early China and India.

Thus, from the above exhaustive discussion, it can be conveniently inferred that trans-countries commercial routes played a leading and decisive role to harmonise the unevenly distributed economic resources between the Indian and the Chinese—the two ancient civilization of world from the fourth century B.C. The referred different commercial and cultural routes facilitated the flow of luxurious goods from places—where they were plentiful, to those where scarcity prevailed. This set right the balance of surplus production. With the growth of agriculture, the village economy of the people gradually changed its character because of the plethoric growth of towns, especially on the land and riverine routes and the centres of pilgrimage, commercial linkages and interaction between China and India. The Chinese standard histories, with such interdevelopmental reforms, detail the goods like Coral, pearls, glass, sugar and certain kinds of fragrances that were exported from or through India to China, with silk being the major item of import from China.[89]

This active trade between the two ancient societies funneled the transmission of Buddhism to China in the first century A.D. The increased intellectual communication of the Buddhist monks helped in spreading of knowledge, cultural communion and understanding of the two civilizations. Mutuality came to be the hallmark of the age because besides traders, the pilgrims and monks, traveled in carvans on the arduous routes. The Buddhist monks became agents of commerce and carried goods viz. silks, corals, pearls, Buddhist texts, irons, relics to defray their travel coasts, and thereby patronage and received hospitality because of self-sufficiency. Silk, corals, pearls and crystal acquired sanctity as these were pursued for religious purposes, especially in relic worship. The relic of the Buddha gained in commercial value when there was a market demand for it. Since the Buddhist relics came to be valued as treasures, the otherwise luxury goods trade thus came to play special role in the development of Buddhism. This developed a desire to donate and enlarged the market for goods listed as the seven treasures, even though these had to be transported from India. Thus, without the trade in non-indigenous goods such as corals and pearls from north India, and without the foreign market which raised the value of products controlled by Indian, such as lapis lazuli and crystal, the maturation of the concept of seven treasures would have been impossible. The Buddhist theological developments, therefore, provided a new market by creating the ritual needs for certains goods. The concept of sharing merits encouraged lay devotes to worship and denote, therefore, increased the demands for the exchange of gods between India and China via trans-countries routes.

The trade between China and India even though, was only for the satisfaction of a small elite segment of both the ancient societies, yet its impact on the economy of these societies was a reaching and permanent. Simultaneously, it also alludes to the social and economic disparities in both ancient societies of the world, which were/are suggestive of the class war, as did finally take place in the modern age. It can be, therefore, conclusively said the twentieth century went into the twenty-first century—with a shift which extenuates the ancient concept of mutuality and self-reliance through—once the old, and now the modernized commercial routes, linkages and cultural interaction. History yet again repeats itself but with an ostensible difference.

REFERENCES

1. Subramanian Swamy, *India's China Perspective*, Delhi, 2001, pp.1-2. R.N. Saletore, *Early Indian Economic, op.cit.*, pp. 94-101. Latika Lahiri (tr.), *Chinese Monks in India*, Delhi, Introduction. Xinu Liu, *Silk and Religion*, Delhi, 1996, *Introduction*. E.H. Schafer, *Great Ages of Man, Ancient China*, Netherlands Rep. 1995, pp. 38-39. A.L. Basham, *The Wonder that was India*, Delhi, ed., 1994, pp. 198-99. S.K. Dass, *Economic History of Ancient India*, Vol. I, Calcutta, 1937, p. 162.
2. P.C. Prasad, *Foreign Trade and Commerce in Ancient India*, Delhi, 1977, pp. 66-67. B.R. Deepak, *India-China Relations in the First Half of the 20th Century*, Delhi, 2001, pp. 1-3. Mansura Haidar, *Indo-Central Asian Relation from Early Times to Medieval Period*, Delhi, 2004, pp. 253-59. Mildred Cable, "The Central Asian Buddhist Road to China", in *Journal of Royal Central Asian Society*, Vol. XXX, London, 1943, pp. 275-83. Om Parkash, "India's Foreign Trade between 300 B.C. and 1000 A.D.: Assumptions and Issues", *Proceeding of Indian History Conference*, Kurukshetra, 1982, pp. 109-14.
3. *AS* 11.11, II. 30. Latika Lahiri, *op. cit.*, pp. XIX-XX. Xinru Liu, *Silk and Religion, op. cit.*, pp. 8-11, E.H. Schafer, *op. cit.*, p. 38.
4. K.A.N. Sastri, "The Beginnings of Intercourse between India and China", *The Indian Historical Quarterly, IHQ*, Vol. XIV, No. I, Calcutta, 1938, pp. 381-82. Om Parkash, "India's Foreign Trade between, *op.cit.*, pp. 109-13. R.N. Saletore, *Early Indian Economy, op.cit.*, p. 94.
5. *Manu S. VIII*. 153, 406.
6. *AS* VII. 12, *Jataka Stories*, 11. 243. III, 385 IV, 495, V. 520, 536.
7. R.N. Saletore, *Early Indian Economy, op.cit.*, p. 389, B.R. Deepak, *op. cit.*, p. 2, S.M. Devi, *Economic Condition of Ancient India*, Delhi, 1987, pp. 156-57. P.C. Bagchi, *India and China*, 2nd (ed.), Calcutta, 1981, pp. 5, 16. Latika Lahiri, *op. cit.*, p. XIX. P.C. Prasad, *op. cit.*, p. 146. Balram Srivastava, *Trade and Commerce in Ancient India*, Varanasi, 1968, pp. 112-13.
8. *Proceeding of American Orientat Society*, New York, Vol. XXXVII, 1917, p. 89. B.R. Deepak, *op.cit.*, pp. 2-3. Zhang Chuanxi (ed.), Zhongguo Gudaishi Gngyao (*An Outline of Chinese Ancient History*) Vol. II, Beijing University Press, Beijing, 1989, pp. 76-78. *Collection of South Asian*

Historical Materials from Chinese Sources, Vol. I, Shanghi Guji Publishing House, Shanghi, 1994, pp. 4-5. Geng Yinzeng, Hanwen Nanya Shiliaoxue (*Historical Data of South Asia from Chinese Sources*), Beijing, 1990, pp. 6-8. D.C. Sircar, *Early Indian Trade and Industry*, Calcutta, 1972, p. 2. A.A. Bokshcharin, "Sino-Indian Relations from Ancient Times to Sixteenth Century" in *China and her Neighbours*, Moscow, 1981, p. 124. W.H. Schoft (tr.), *Periplus of the Erythraean Sea*, London, 1912 (hereafter Periplus), 46.

9. P.C. Bagchi, *op.cit.*, pp. 16-17, Periplus, 46, 49, W.W. Tarn, *The Greeks in Bacteria and India*, Cambridge, 1951, p. 364.
10. P.C. Bagchi, *op.cit.*, p. 17. Balram Srivastava, *op.cit.*, pp. 12-13. R.N. Saletore, *Early Indian Economy*, *op.cit.*, pp. 389-40. P.C. Parsad, *op.cit.*, p. 146. S. Beal, *Hiuen Tsiang, Si-Yu-Ki, Buddhist Records of the Western World*, London, 1888, I, pp. 17, 19, 24, 30-38, 69, 172, 173, 176, II, pp. 198-99. Chhan Chunaj, Chhan, *Si-Yu-Ki* (Ti) Hindi (Maha Thang Rajavams Kat Mein Pishcham Kee Teerth Yatra ka Vrantant), Beijing, 1991, pp. 267-71.
11. L. Gopal, *The Economic Life*, *op.cit.*, pp. 107-08. Mildred Cable, 'The Central Asian Buddhist Road to China', *Loc. cit.*, pp. 275-77. P.C. Prasad, *op. cit.*, p. 146. Sir Hanry Yule, *Cathay and the Way Thither*, Vol. I, London, 1918, pp. 61-70. Xinru Liu, *Silk and Religion, op.cit.*, pp. 19-20. Balram Srivastava, *op.cit.*, p. 115. P.C. Bagchi, India and China, *op.cit.*, pp. 13-17. B.R. Deepak, *op.cit.*, p. 2, Xinru Liu, *Ancient India and Ancient China*, Delhi, 2nd (ed.) 1999, pp. 25-57.
12. L. Boulnas, *The Silk Road*, London, pp. 223-33. Mildred Cable, *Loc. cit.*, pp. 275-76. Xinru Liu, Silk and Religion, *op.cit.*, pp. 22-23.
13. Balram Srivastava, *op.cit.*, p. 117. A Stein, *On Ancient Central Asian*, Tracks, London, 1933, p. 157.
14. *Ibid.*, p. 116. Moti Chandera, *Trade and Trade Routes in Ancient India*, Delhi, 1977, p. 12.
15. P.C. Bagchi, *India and China, op.cit.*, pp. 14-15, E.H. Cutts, "Chinese Indian Contacts", *IHQ*, Vol. XIV, part I, Calcutta, 1938, pp. 487-502.
16. A. Stein, *op.cit.*, pp. 281-82. K.A.N. Sastri, "The Beginnings of Intercourse between India and China" *IHQ*, *Loc. Cit.*, pp. 381-87.
17. R.N. Saletore, *Early Indian Economy*, *op.cit.*, p. 390, P.C. Bagchi, *India and China, op.cit.*, p. 21. B.R. Deepak, *op.cit.*, p. 2, Latika Lahiri; *Chinese Monks in India, op.cit.*, pp. 213-21. P.C. Bagchi, "Sino-Indian Relations the period of United Expires 618-1100 A.D." in *Sino-Indian Studies,* Vol. Part-I, Calcutta, 1944, pp. 66-84.
18. *AŚ* VII, 12. R. Champaklakshmi, *Trade, Ideology and Urbanization in South India*, 300 B.C. to 1300 A.D., Delhi) 1996, pp. 101-07.
19. Ranbir Chakravarti (ed.), *Trade in Early India*, Delhi, 2001, *Introduction*, pp. 1-110.
20. *AŚ* 11.28. Kauṭilya further dilates, in pursuance of these principles, on the actual routes to be taken in the sea for commercial purposes.
21. *AŚ* II.28.

22. *Ibid.*
23. *Ibid.* E.H. Cutts, "Chinese-Indian Contacts" in SIS, Vol. XIV, No. 1, Calcutta, 1938, pp. 381-87.
24. B.R. Deepak, *op.cit.*, pp. 2-3. Institute of South Asian Studies, Beijing University (ed.), *Collection of South Asian Historical Material from Chinese Formers*, Vol. I, p. 4. Mildred Cable, *Loc.cit.*, p. 277. P.C. Prasad, *op.cit.*, p. 148. Balram Srivastava, *op.cit.*, p. 109.
25. *Jāt*, Vol. III, p. 188, IV, pp. 15, 17, 158, VII, pp. 30-40.
26. *Jāt*, Vol. III, p. 188. R.C. Majumdar, *Ancient Indian Colonies in the Far-East*, Vol. 1, Pts. I-I, Decca, 1937-38, p. 4.
27. G.E. Gerini, *Researches on Ptolemy's Geography of Eastern Asia*, London, 1909, p. 743.
28. Balram Srivastava, *op.cit.*, p. 109. G.L. Adhya, *Early Indian Economic*, Bombay, 1966, p. 169.
29. R.C. Mazumdar, *Hindu Colonies in the Far East*, Calcutta, 1944, p. 16. E.H. Warrington, *Commerce between Roman Empire and India*, Cambridge, 1928, p. 127. R.K. *Mookerji*, *Indian Shipping*, Delhi, 1962, pp. 114-15.
30. Ptolemy's *op.cit.*, p. 93. T.W. Rhys Davids (tr.), *Milindapanho*, Sacred Books of the East, SBE, London, 1880, Vol. II, 269. P.C. Prasad, *op. cit.*, p. 37.
31. R.C. Mazumdar, *Hindu Colonies in the Far-East*, *op.cit.*, p. 19.
32. *Ibid.*
33. Balram Srivastava, *op.cit.*, p. 112. Moti Chandra, *Trade and Trade Routes*, *op. cit.*, p. 19.
34. E.H. Warrington, *Commerce between Roman Experience and India*, *op.cit.*, p. 129.
35. *Ibid.* pp. 125-26, R.C. Majumdar, *Hindu Colonies in the Far-East*, *op.cit.*, pp. 8-9. H.C. Clifford, *Further India*, New York, 1904, pp. 6-7. He points out, "The Sea route to China via the straits of Molacca was no longer unknown to the mariners of the East." P.C. Bagchi; India and China, *op.cit.*, p. 27, P.C. Prasad, *op.cit.*, pp. 151-52.
36. Fa-Hien, *A Records of Buddhistic Kingdoms*, being an account of the *Chinese Monk*. Fa-Hien's *Travels in India and Ceylon*, (Tr.) James, Legge, Oxford, 1886, pp. 111-12.
37. *Ibid.*, pp. 113-14. R.K. Mookerji, *Indian Shipping, op. cit.*, p. 116.
38. Eukins, "Chinese Buddhism", in *Journal of Royal Asatic Society*, London, 1896, p. 100.
39. S. Beal. *Si-Yu-Ki*: Vol. II, p. 188. *Si-Yu-Ki* (tr.) in Hindi, *op.cit.*, pp. 1-7.
40. *Ibid.*, Introduction, pp. XXV-XXVI.
41. I-Ising (tr.) J. Takakusu, *A Record of the Buddhist Religion, as Practised in India and the Malay Archipelago*, Oxford, 1896, pp. XXX-XXXIII.
42. S.M. Devi, *op.cit.*, p. 151. *Epigraphia India*, Government of India Publications, various volumes (hereafter EI), XVII, p. 310.

43. Pellicot, *Loc cit.*, pp. 24-26.
44. P.C. Bagchi, "Chinese Coins from Tanjore", in *SIS*, Vol. I, Part I, Calcutta, 1944, p. 60, P.C. Bagchi, "Report on a New Hord of Chinese Coins", *SIS*, Vol. IV, Calcutta, 1953, pp. 194-96.
45. R.C. Majumdar (ed.), *The Age of Imperial Kanauj*, Vol. IV, Bombay, 1955, p. 413. S.M. Devi, *op. cit.*, p. 152, V.R.R. Dikshitar, "South India and China" in *SIS*, Vol. 11, Part-I, Calcutta, 1946, pp. 157-82.
46. A.L. Basham, *Wonder that was India, op.cit.*, p. 199. H.P. Ray, "Trade and Contacts" in Romila Thapar (ed.) *Recent Perspectives of Early Indian History*. 2nd Revised (ed.), Bombay, 1998, pp. 158-59. I.W. Mabbett, "The Indianization of South-East Asia", *Journal of Southeast Asian Studies*, Vol. VII, No. 1-14, 1977, pp. 143-61. Moti Chandra, "Revenue, Trade and Society in the Kushana Empire", *IHR*, Vol. 7, No. 1-2, Delhi, 1980-81, pp. 29-53. S.G. Darian, "The Economic History of the Ganges to the End of Gupta time," *JESHO*, Vol. XIII, pp. 62-87.
47. Burten Watson (tr.), *Records of the Grand Historian of China* (Ssu-MA chlen-shin chi), London, 1961, Vol. I, p. 269.
48. *Ibid.*, pp. 270-74. Xinru Liu, *Silk and Religion, op.cit.*, pp. 6-18, V. Mishra, "Sea and Land Routes in India as Revealed in the Buddhist Literature", *Journal of Indian History*, Vol. 32, 1954, pp. 117-29. H.P. Ray, "Early Maritime Contacts between South and Southeast Asia," *Journal of Southeast Asian Studies*, Vol. 20, 1989, pp. 42-54.
49. *AS* 1.19.
50. *AS* 11.11.
51. *Ibid.*, 11.12
52. *Ibid.*, 11.25.
53. *Ibid.*, XV.51.
54. *EI* XXX, p. 171.
55. Xinru Liu, *Ancient India and Ancient China, op.cit.*, p. 53.
56. *Ibid.*, p. 63. H.P. Ray, "Trade and Contacts", *op.cit.*, pp. 166-68. E.H. Schafer, *Great Ages of Man Ancient China*, *op.cit.*, 166-72. Balram Srivastava, *op.cit.*, pp. 109-17. The Silk Road, *op.cit.*, pp. 223-34.
57. *The Buddhacarita of Asvaghosha*, *SBE*, Delhi, Rep. 1985, Vol. 49. The Buddhacarita (ed.) E.H. Johnston, New Delhi, 1995, IV 49. The Mahavastu, (tr.) J.J. Jones, 3 vols. London, 1949-56-I, 149, 11.175, III, 141. IV, 49, VIII, 21. Mahvastu, 1, 149, 11.175, III. 141. R.K. Mukherji, *Indian Shipping*, *op.cit.*, 118-19. Mansura Haidar, *Indo-Central Asian Relation from Early times to Medieval Period*, *op.cit.*, pp. 257-58.
58. J.F. Fleet. CII, pp. 84-85, Vol. III. S.K. Maity, *Economic Life of Northern India, op.cit.*, p. 113.
59. S.K. Maity, *op.cit.*, p. 178.
60. Xinru Liu, *Ancient India and China, op. cit.*, pp. 65-66.

61. *Ibid.*
62. R.S. Sharma, *India Feudalism, op.cit.*, p. 55.
63. *Harsacarita*, E.B. Cowells, F. Thomas (tr.), London, 1997, p. 242.
64. Hiuen Tsang had observed in 639 A.D. that the garments of Indian were made of *Kauseya* which he added was the product of the wild silk worm.
65. J.F. Fleet, CII, Ill, *op.cit.*, p. 332. Nancy Lee Swan (tr.), *Food and Money in Ancient China*, The Earliest Economic History of China 25 A.D. Princeton, 1950, pp. 65, 198, 231.
66. M.R. Kale (tr.), *Kumarsambhava*, Delhi, 1967, VII, 7, 26, 73. R. Anotine (tr.), Calcutta, 1972, *Raghuvamsa*, VII, 18, 19.
67. Xinru liu, *Ancient India and Ancient China, op. cit.*, p. 68.
68. R.N. Saletore, *Early Indian Economy, op.cit.*, p. 114.
69. *Ibid.*, p.115.
70. *Ibid.*, p. 120.
71. *AS* II.11.
72. W.H. Schoff (tr.), Periplus, 14. B.R. Deepak (tr.), *Ji Xianhin, "Zhongyin Wenhua Jiaoliu yuanyuan liuchang"* (Endless flow of Cross Cultural Current between *India and China in Indian Horizon, Indian Council of Cultural Relations*, Delhi, 1995, pp. 5-6.
73. J. Bostock and H.T. Riley, *Pliny, the Elder. The National Histoly*, Vol. 6, London, 1855-77, VI, p. 380, Periplus. 5. H. Rackham (Tr.), *Natural History*, 10 Vol., London, 1940
74. Ximnru Liu, *Ancient Indian and China, op. cit.*, p. 59. P.C. Parsad, *op.cit.*, p. 213.
75. *Pliny*. XXX VII. 8, 10.
76. *Pliny*. 66, Periplus, 49. M.G. Diskshit, *History of Indian Glass*, University of Bombay, 1969, p. 25.
77. B.B. Lal, "Examination of some Ancient Indian Glass Specimens", *Ancient India*, No. 1, 1952, p. 22.
78. John, Marshall, *Taxila*, Vol. I, Cambridge, 1951, p. 238. M.G. Dikshit, *History of Indian Glass, op.cit.*, p. 36. R.S. Sharma, *Urban Decay in India, op.cit.*, p. 149.
79. Xinru Liu, *Ancient India and Ancient China, op. cit.*, p. 54. Ranbir Chakravarti (ed.), *Trade in Early India, op.cit.*, p. 39.
80. *Pliny*, XXXII.II Periplus 28, 39, 49, 56. Nayanjot Lahiri. *The Archeology of Indian Trade Routes upto 200BC*, Delhi, 1999, pp. 79-85.
81. F. Hirth, *The Ancient History of China*, New York, 1911, pp. 73-74. Om Parkash, *Economy and Food in Ancient India*, Part I, Delhi,1987, pp. 97-112.
82. A.K. Narain and others, *Excavations at Raghat*, pts. I-IV, Varanasi, 1976-78, Pts. II, p. 12.

83. P.B. Kane (tr.), *Malvikagnimitra of Kalidasa*, Bombay, 1950. C.R. Devadhar (ed.), *The Works of Kalidasa*, Delhi, 1986. verses, 164-65.
84. V.R.R. Dikshitar, "Southern India and China", in *SIS*, Vol. II, Part I, Calcutta, 1946, pp. 160-61.
85. S.K. Maity, *op.cit.*, p. 124, M.S. Shukia, *A History of Gem Industry in Ancient and Medieval India*, Varanasi, 1972, p. 44.
86. James Leg (Tr.), Fa-Hien's *Travels in Indian and Ceylon*, 1886, p.101.
87. Pariplus, 36. *Xinra Liu, Silk and Religion, op.cit.*, pp. 26-30.
88. Xinru Liu, *Ancient India and Ancient China, op.cit.*, pp. 57-58. R.S. Aggarwal, *Trade Centres and Routes in Northern India*, Delhi, 1982, pp. 120-35.
89. Xinru Liu, *Ancient India and Ancient China, op.cit.*, pp. 25-85. Xinru Liu, *Silk and Religion, op.cit.*, pp. 26-27. Xinru Liu, *Ancient India and Ancient China, op.cit.*, pp. 175-76. R.S. Sharma, *Indian Feudalism, op.cit.*, 202-03.

Bibliography

Epigraphical Inscriptions

Barua, B.M., *Aśoka and His Inscriptions,* Calcutta, 1946.

Basak, R.G., *Aśokan Inscriptions*, Calcutta, 1959.

Basu, B.N., *Aśhoka and His Inscriptions*, parts I and II, Calcutta, 1946.

Bhandarkar, D.R., *Corpus Inscriptionum Indicarum*, Vol. III, revised and edited by B.C. Chhabra and G.S. Gai, Delhi, 1981.

Chaudhary, R.K. (ed.), *Selected Inscriptions of Bihar*, Patna, 1958.

Dikshit, M.G., *Selected Inscriptions from Maharashtra*, fifth to tenth century A.D., Poona, 1949.

Epigraphia Indica, Government of India, Calcutta and Delhi, several volumes.

Fleet, J.F., *Corpus Inscriptionum Indicarum*, Vol. III, *Inscription of the Early Guptas Kings and Their Successors*, reprint, Varanasi, 1963.

Hultzsch, E., *Corpus lnscriptionum lndicarum*, Vol. I, *Inscriptions of Aśoka*, reprint, Varanasi, 1969.

Karamabelkar, V.W., *Select Inscriptions of Sanskrit*, Nagpur, 1959.

Konow, Sten, *Corpus Inscriptionum Indicarum*, Vol. II, part I, *Kharōshti Inscriptions*, reprint, Varanasi, 1969.

Lūders, Heinrich., *A List of Brahmi Inscriptions from the Earliest Exception of Those of Aśoka*, reprint, Varanasi: 1973.

Majumdar, N.G., *Inscriptions of Bengal*, Vol. III, Rajshahi, 1929.

Mirashi, V.V., ed., *Corpus Inscriptionum Indicarum*, Vol. IV, 2 pts., *Inscription of the Kalachudichedi Era, Ootacamund*, 1955-63.

——, *The Ghatotkacha Cave Inscriptions*, Hyderabad, 1952.

——, *Vākaṭaka Inscription in Cave XVI at Ajanta*, Calcutta, 1941.

Pandey, R.B. (ed.), *Historical and Literary Inscriptions*, Varanasi, 1962.

Phogat, S.R. (ed.), *Inscriptions of Haryana*, Kurukshetra, 1978.

Ramesh, K.V., *Inscriptions of Western Gangas*, New Delhi, 1984.

Rana, S.S., *Bhāratiya Abhilekha*, Delhi, 1975.

Rice, L., *Mysore Inscriptions*, Delhi, 1983.

Shahi, B., *The Inscriptions of Bihar*, Delhi, 1983.

Sircar, D.C., *Select Inscriptions*, Vol. I, Calcutta, 1942, 1965.

——, Select Inscriptions, Vol. II, Delhi, 1983.

Thapliyal, K.K., *Inscriptions of the Maukharis, Later Guptas, Puśpabhutis and Yalśovariman of Kanauj*, New Delhi, 1985.

Upadhyaya, V., *A Study of Ancient Indian Inscriptions*, Patna, 1970.

Numismatics

Allan, John, *Catalogue of the Coins of the Gupta Dynasties and Sasanka, King of Gauda*, London, 1914, reprint, New Delhi, 1975.

Altekar, A.S., *The Coinage of Gupta Empire*, Varanasi, 1951.

——, *Gūptakalina Mudrayen*, (in Hindi), second edn., Patna, 1972.

——, *Catalogue of the Gupta Gold Coins in Bayana Hoard*, Bombay, 1954.

Badher, D., *Second Supplementary Catalogue of Coins*, Vol. I, Calcutta, 1977.

——, *South Indian Coins*, Delhi, 1984.

Chakraberty, S., *Socio-Religious and Cultural Study of the Ancient Indian Coins*, Delhi, 1986.

Chattopadhyaya, B., *The Age of the Kushaṇas: A Numismatic Study*, Calcutta, 1975.

——, *Coins and Icons: A Study of Indian Myth and Symbols in Indian Numismatic Art*, Calcutta, 1977.

Chattopadhyaya, B.D., *Coins and Currency System in South India (c. AD 225-1300)*, New Delhi, 1977.

Cunningham, A., *Coins of the Indo-Scythians*, reprint, Varanasi.

Gardner, P., *A History of Ancient Coinage (700-300 B.C.)*, reprint, New Delhi, 1975.

Gopal, L., *Early Medieval Coins-Types of Northern India*, Delhi, 1975.

Hanola, D., *Studies in Indian Coins and Seals*, Delhi, 1985.

Jenkins, G.R., *Coin-Types of Saka-Pahlava King of India*, Varanasi, 1957.

Kosambi, D.D., *On the Study and Metrology of Silver Punchmarked Coins*, Vol. IV, Nos. I and II, Delhi, 1966.

Maity, S.K., *Early Indian Coins and Currency System*, New Delhi, 1970.

Murthy, A.V.N., *The Coins of Karnataka*, Mysore, 1975.

Mohan, M., *The Indo-Greek Coins*, Ludhiana, 1967.

Narain, A.K. (ed.), *Local Coins of Northern India (c. 300 BC to AD 300)*, Varanasi, 1968.

Parkash, S., *Coinage in Ancient India*, Delhi, 1968.

Ray, P.C., *Coinage of Northern India*, Delhi, 1980.

Rocker, T.H.E., *Coins of Greek and Indo-Scythian Kings and their Coins*, Delhi, 1972.

Sharan, M.K., *Tribal Coins: A Study*, New Delhi, 1944.

Singh, J.P. (ed.), *Tribal Coins of Ancient India (c.200 BC to AD 400)*, Varanasi, 1977.

Singh, O.P., *Religion and Iconography on Early Indian Coins*, Varanasi, 1978.

Singh, R.U., *Coins of India*, Chandigarh, 1978.

Sircar, D.C., *Studies in Indian Coins*, Delhi, 1960.

Smith, V.A., *Catalogue of the Coins in Indian Museum, at Calcutta*, Vol. 1, *Coins of Ancient India*, Calcutta, 1906.

Literary

Vedas

Atharvaveda, with Sayaoa Bhasya (ed.), Vishva Bandhu, 4 parts, Hoshiarpur, 1960-64.

The Atharvaveda, (trans.) Devi Chand, New Delhi, 1982.

Rigveda with commentaries, (ed.) Vishva Bandhu, 7 parts, Hoshiarpur, 1963-65; trans-Hymns of the *Ṛgveda*, R.T.H. Griffith, 2 vols., New Delhi, 1999.

The Ṛgveda, (trans.) H.H. Wilson, 7 Vols., Delhi, 1977.

Ṛgveda Saṁhita, (trans.) Svami Satya Parkash Sarsvati and Ṣatyakam Vidyalankar, 13 Vols., Delhi, 1977.

Sāmaveda Saṁhita, (trans.) Acharya Dharma Deva, Jwalapur, 1967.

Samhitas

Māitrayani Saṁhita, (ed.) S.D. Satavalekar, Bombay, vs 1998.

Tāiṭṭiriya Saṁhita, with Sayana's commentaries, (ed.) Kashinath Sattar, Poona, 1905.

Tāiṭṭiriya Saṁhita, N.S. Sontakke and T.N. Dharmadhikari, Vol. I, Poona, 1970.

Brāhmaṇas

Āitareya Brāhmaṇa, R. Anantakrishna Sastri, Trivandrum, 1942.

The Āitareya-Brāhmaṇas, (ed.) A.B. Keith, rep., Delhi, 1981.

Chāndogya Brāhmaṇas, (ed.) Durga Mohan Bhattacharya, Calcutta, 1958.

Jaiminiya Brāhmaṇa of Samaveda, (ed.) Raghuvira, Nagpur, 1945.

Pancavimsa Brāhmaṇa, (trans.) W. Caland, Calcutta, 1931.

Śatapatha Brāhmaṇa, (trans.) Julius Eggeling, *SBE*, Vols. 12, 26, 41, 43-44, reprint, Delhi, 1972-78.

Śatapatha Brāhmaṇa, G.D. Upadhaya, 3 Vols., Delhi, 1967-69.

Tāiṭṭiriya Brāhmaṇa, (ed.) A.M. Sastri, 4 Vols., Delhi, 1985.

Tāiṭṭiriya Brāhmaṇa, with commentaries of Brattabhaskara, Mistri, (ed.) A. Mahadeva Sastri, Parts 1-3, Mysore, 1908.

Upanisad

The Chāndoyga Upaniṣad, (trans.) F. Max Muller, *SBE*, Vol., 1, reprint, Delhi, 1975.

The Principal Upaniṣads, edited and translated by S. Radhakrishnan, London, 1953.

Śrauta and Dharmasutras

Āpastamba Dharamsūtra, (ed.) Narasinghachar and Srinivasagopala, (trans.) G. Buhler, *SBE*, Vol. 2, reprint, Delhi, 1975.

Boudhayāna Dharmasūtra, (ed.) A. Chinnaswami Sastri, Banaras, 1934, (trans.) G. Buhler, *SBE*, Vol. 2, Vol. 14, reprint, Delhi, 1984.

Baudhayāna Śrautaśatra, (ed.) W. Caland, 3 vols., Calcutta, 1904, reprint, Delhi, 1982.

Gautam Dharmasūtra, (ed.) Stenzter, V.G. Apte, Poona, 1931; (trans.) G. Bohier, *SBE*, Vol. 2, reprint, Delhi, 1975.

Buddhist

The Buddhacariṭa, (ed.) E.H. Johnston, New Delhi, 1995.

Dialogues of the Buddha, (trans.) T.W. Rhys Davids and C.A.F. Rhys Davids, 3 Vols., *SBB*, London, 1923-51.

Jātaka Stories, (ed.) E.B. Cowell, (trans.) Robert Chalmers, 6 vols., reprint, Cambridge, 1973.

Mahāvastū, (ed.) E. Senart, 3 Vols., Paris, 1881-97.

The Mahāvastū, (trans.) J.J. Jones, 3 Vols., London, 1949-56.

Milindapañha, (trans.) T.W. Rhys David, *SBE*, Vol. 35, reprint, Delhi, 1956.

Question of King Milinda, T.W. Rhys Davids, (trans.) *SBE*, Vol. 35, reprint, Delhi, 1969.

Epics

The Rāmāyaṇa of Valmiki, R.T.H. Griffith, Banaras, 1915.

Valmiki Rāmāyaṇa (in Hindi), (trans.) Dwarka Parsad Sharma Chaturvedi, 20 Vols., Allahabad, 1949-50.

Mahābhārata (in Hindi), (trans.) D. Satwalekar Pardi, 1952; Gita Press, Gorakhpur, various Vols. and critical edition, various Vols., BORI, Poona, 1971-74, (trans.) M.N. Datta, Calcutta, 1908.

The Mahābhārata, (trans.) K.M. Ganguli, Vols. I-XII, third edition, New Delhi, 1975.

The Valmiki Rāmāyaṇa, critical edition, ed. by U.P. Shah, 7 Vols., Oriental Institute, Baroda, 1962-75.

Smrtis

Brahspaṭismṛti, (trans.) J. Jolley, *SBE*, Vol. 33, reprint, Delhi, 1977.

Manusmṛti, Jwala Prasad, Bombay, 1963, (trans.) by George Buhler, The Law of Manu, *SBE*, Vol. 25, reprint, Delhi, 1975, (trans.) Ganganath Jha with the Bhasya of Medhatithi, several Vols., Calcutta, 1965, (trans.) H.B. Sastry, Varanasi, 1970.

Kātyayānasmṛti on Saroddhara, (ed.) with reconstituted text, (trans.) P.V. Kane, Bombay, 1933.

Nāradasmṛti, (ed.) J. Jolly, *SBE*, Vol. 33, reprint, Delhi, 1977.

Visṇūsmṛti, (ed.) 3. Jolly, Calcutta, 1888; trans. J. Jolly, *SBE*, Vol. 7, reprint, Delhi, 1977.

Yajñavalkasmṛti, with Viramitrodaya of Mitaksara, (ed.) Nargana Sastri, Varanasi, 1930.

Pūrāṇas

Brāhmanda Pūrāṇa, Sri Venkateswara Press, Bombay, 1966.

Matsya Pūrāṇa, (ed.) Raghuvira Singh Sastri, Calcutta, vs 1812.

Markaṇḍeya Pūrāṇa, (ed.) M.M. Banerjee, Calcutta, n.d.

Skanda Pūrāṇa, (ed.) Panchanan Tarakaratna, Calcutta, 1918.

Vāyū Pūrāṇa, Sri Venkateswara Press, Bombay, 1890.

Visṇū Pūraṇa, Gita Press, Gorakhpur, vs 2024.

Historical and Semi-historical Works

Harṣacarita of Bāṇabhatta with the commentary, (ed.) K.B. Parab, Bombay, 1937.

Harṣacarita of Bāṇa, (trans.) E.B. Cowell and F.W. Thomas, London, 1897.

Kādambari of Bāṇa, with a commentary by M.R. Kale, Bombay, 1928.

Kādambri of Bāṇa, (trans.) C.M. Riddling, reprint, New Delhi, 1974.

Kāmasūtra of Vātsyayana, with the commentary Jayamangala of Yasodhara, (ed.) Goswami Damodar Sastri, Banaras, 1920.

Kauṭilya Arthaśāstra, (ed.) and (trans.) R. Shamasastry, Mysore, 1960-61.

Kangle, R.P., *The Kauṭilya Arthaśāstra*, Parts I-III, Delhi, rep. 1986.

Rangarajan, L.N., *Kauṭilya, the Arthaśāstra*, Delhi, 1992. T. Ganapati Sastri, *The Arthaśāstra of Kauṭilya*, Pts 3, Trivandrum, 1924-25. Devadatta Sastri, *Kauṭilya Arthaśāstra*, (Hindi) Allahabad, 1957.

Rājatarangiṇi of Kalhana, (trans.) M.A. Stein, Westminster, 1900.

Rājatarangiṇi of Kalhana (Hindi), (trans.) Raghunath Singh, 3 Vols., Varanasi, 1976.

Abhijnāna Sakuntala of Kālidāsa ed. and (trans.) C.M. Acharya, Varanasi, 1963.

Meghadūtam of Kālidāsa, (trans.) M.R. Kale, Bombay, 1930.

Mālavikagnimitra of Kālidāsa, (trans.) P.B. Sane, Bombay, 1950.

Raghūvaṁṣa of Kālidāsa, (ed.) H.R. Hranik, Bombay, 1953. *Raghūvaṁṣa of Kālidāsa*, R.D. Karmarkar, Poona, 1954.

Foreign Sources

Chinese

Beal, S. (trans.), *Travels of Fa-Hien and Sung un*, London, 1869.

——, *The Tavels of Hiuen-Tsiang*, Calcutta, 1957-58.

Giles, H.A. (trans.), *The Travels of Fa-Hien or Records of Buddhist Kingdoms*, Cambridge, p. 1933.

Legge, James, *The Travels of Fa-Hien*, second (ed.), Bombay, 1973.

Watters, T., *On Yuan Chwangs Travels in India (629-45)*, 2 Vols., reprint, New Delhi, 1973.

Greek

McCrindle, J.W., *Ancient India as Described by Megasthenes and Arrian*, Calcutta, 1926 reprint, New Delhi, 2000.

——, *Ancient India as Described in Classical Literature*, Westminster, 1901; reprint, New Delhi, 1979.

Koltas, N.S., *India as Described by Megasthenes*, Delhi, 1976.

Modern Works

Aiyer, R.A.K., *Agriculture and Allied Arts in Vedic India*, Bengalore, 1947.

Allchin, B. and R. Allchin, *Origin of a Civilization of the Prehistoric and Early Archaeology of South Asia*, Delhi, 1997.

Aiyangar, K.V.R., *Aspects of Ancient Indian Economic Thought*, Varanasi, 1934.

Alleber, B. (ed.), *South Asian Archaeology*, Cambridge, 1984.

Anderson, P., *Lineage of the Absolutist State*, London, 1974.

——, *Passage from Antiquity to Feudalism*, London, 1974-75.

Appadorai, A., *Economic Condition of Southern India*, Vol. 2, Madras, 1936.

Arora, U.P., "Plagriarism and Prejudices in Megasthenes Indica," *IHC*, Kurukshetra, 1982.

Aveneri, S., *Karl Marx on Colonialism and Modernization*, New York, 1969.

Daily, A.M., and R. Joseph (eds.), *The Asiatic Mode of Production Science and Politics*, London, 1981.

Baber, Zaher, *The Science Empire, Scientific Knowledge, Civilization and Colonial Rule to India*, Calcutta, 1962.

Bagchi, P.C., *India and China*, 2nd (edn.), Calcutta, 1981.

Basham, A.L., *The Wonder that was India*, reprint, London, 1954.

Bandyopadhyaya, M.C., *Economic Life and Progress in Ancient India*, Allahabad, 1980.

Bloch, M., *Feudal Society*, (trans.) C.A. Morgan, London.

——, *Land and Work in Medieval Europe*, London, 1967.

——, *Slavery and Serfdom in the Middle Age*, (trans.) W.R. Beer, London, 1975.

Bois, G., *The Crises of Feudalism*, Cambridge, 1981.

Bose, AN., *Social and Rural Economy of Northern India*, Vol. II, Calcutta, 1967.

Buch, M.A., *Economic Life in Ancient India,* Allahabad, 1979.

Burns, J.F., *Middle Ages*, New York, 1946.

Byres, T.J. (eds.), *Feudalism and Non-European Societies*, London, 1985.

Chakrabarti, D.K., "Distribution of Iron Ores and the Archaeological Evidence of Early Iron in India," *JESHO*, Vol. XX, part II, Leiden, 1977.

Chanana, D.R., "Ideological Aspects of Slavery in Ancient India", *JOI*, VIII, Delhi, 1959.

——, *Slavery in Ancient India*, New Delhi, 1960.

Chandra, B., *Karl Marx, His Theories of Asian Society and Colonial Rule*, Delhi, 1981.

Chaudhary, R.K., "Feudalism in Ancient India", *JIH*, Vols. 37-38.

——, *Kauṭilya's Ideas and Institutions*, Varanasi, 1971.

Chaudhary, R.K., "Problem and Methods of Socio-Economic History of Ancient India in a New Perspective", *JBRS*, Vol. 54, Patna, 1968.

——, "Some Aspects of Feudalism in Cambodia", *JBRS*, Vol. 47.

——, "Visti (Forced Labour) in Ancient India", *IHO*, 1962.

Chattopadhyaya, B.D. (ed.), *Essays in Ancient Indian Economic History*, New Delhi, 1987.

Chandra, Moti, *Trade and Trade Routes in Ancient India*, Delhi, 1977.

Champaklakshmi, R., *Trade and Urbanization in South India*, 300 B.C. to 1300 A.D., Delhi, 1996.

Chauhan, G.C., "The Nature of Chauhan Land-Grants as Gleaned from their Epigraphical Traditions" in *RJSS*, P.U. Chandigarh, Vol. 17, No. 2, 2009, pp. 60-70.

——, "The Kauṭilyan Theory Rate Interest: An Ingredient of Welfare State", in *ABORI*, LXXXIX, Poona, 2009, pp. 33-39.

——, "Defining Peasant: Understanding His Relation with Donees in Early Medieval Northern India", in *JAS*, Vol. 81, Mumbai, 2008, pp. 19-33.

——, "The Economic Implications of Land Grants in Early Medieval Northern India", *IHS*, Vol. III, No. 2. Tiruchirappalli, 2007, pp. 35-50.

——, "A Rational Understanding of Some Copper-Plate Inscription of Western Himalayas (Himachal Pradesh)" in *Indica*, Vol. 44, No. 1, Mumbai, 2007, pp. 67-80.

——, The Visti in Ancient Indian Traditions: Its Transformation to Forced Labour", in *ABORI*, Vol. LXXXVI, Poona, 2006, pp. 121-25.

——, *Origin and Growth of Feudalism in Early India (From The Mauryas to 650 A.D.)*, Delhi, 2004.

——, "Agricultural Formation as Depicted in Early Medieval Indian Traditions" in *SHC*, Vol. 9, No. 1, Berhampur, 2004, pp. 30-44.

Chauhan, G.C., *Economic History of Early Medieval Northern India*, Delhi, 2003.

——, "Slave Mode of Production in Early India", in *QRHS*, Vol. XXXVIII, Nos. 1-2, Calcutta, 1998, pp. 15-19.

——, "The Artisan—A Question of Socio-Economic Contrast", in *JOI*, Vol. XLVI, Nos. 3-4, Vadodara, 1997, pp. 201-06.

——, "Sāmanta as a Feudal Lord in Early India", in *JOI*, Vol. XXXIX, Nos. 1-2, 1989, Vadodara, 1989.

——, *Some Aspects of Early Indian Society*, Pittsburgh, USA, 2012.

Cox, T., "Awkward Class or Awkward Classes, Class Relation in the Russian Peasantry before Collectivisation," *JPS*, Vol. XXII, London, 1979.

Coulbourn, R. (ed.), *Feudalism in History*, London, 1956.

Critichleg, J., *Feudalism*, London, 1978.

Dange, S.A., *India from Primitive Communism to Slavery*, New Delhi, 1949.

Dass, A.C., *Ṛgvedic Culture*, Calcutta, 1925.

Dasgupta, Ajit, *A History of Economic Thought*, London, 1993.

Datta, B.N., *Dialectives of Land Economics in India*, Part I, Calcutta, 1950.

Desai, D., "Art Under the Feudalism", *IHC*, 1, No. 1, 1974.

Deyell, Johns, *Living without Sliver*, Delhi, 1990.

Dew, S.M., *Economic Conception of Ancient India*, Delhi, 1987.

Dhar, S.N., *Kauṭilya and Arthaśāstra*, Delhi, 1981.

Duby, Georges, *The Early Growth of the European Economy*, London, 1974.

Deepak, B.R., *India-China Relations in the First Half of the 20th Century*, Delhi, 2001.

Farquin, Gulg, *Lordship and Feudalism in the Middle Ages*, London, 1976.

Fick, R., *The Social Organisation in North-East India in Buddha's Times*, (trans.) S.K. Maitra, reprint, Delhi, 1972.

Frykenberg, R.E. (ed.), *Land Control and Social Structure in Indian History*, Delhi, 1969, Second rev. edn., Delhi, 1979.

Gangopadhyaya, Radharaman, *Some Material for the Study of Agriculture and Agriculturists in Ancient India*, Serampore, 1932.

Ghosh, A., *The City in Early Historical India*, Shimla, 1973.

Ghoshal, U.N., *The Agrarian System in Ancient India*, Calcutta, 1929-30.

——, *Contribution to the History of Hindu Revenue System*, Calcutta, 1940.

Gopal, L., *Aspects of the History of Agriculture in Ancient India*, Varanasi, 1980.

——, *Economic Life on Northern India (700-1200 A.D.)*, Varanasi, 1965.

——, Srivastava (ed.), *History of Agriculture in India*, Vol. I, Part 1, Delhi, 2009.

——, "On Feudal Polity in Ancient India", *JIH*, 1963.

——, "Sāmanta—Its Varying Significance in Ancient India", *JRAS*, London, 1963.

——, "Slavery in Ancient India", *JRAS*, XXVII, 1961.

——, Gopal, M.H., *Mauryan Public Finance*, London, 1935.

Gurakhal, R., "The Agrarian system and Socio-Political Organisation under the Early Pandyas (600-1000 A.D.)", Ph.D. Thesis, Jawaharlal Nehru University, New Delhi, 1989.

Gupta, A.K., "Origin of Agriculture and Domestication of Plants and Animals Linked to early Holocene Climate Amelioration" in *Current Science*, Vol. 87, No. 1, 2004.

Habib, Irfan, "The Peasant in Indian History," *IHC*, 43rd Session, Kurukshetra University, 1982.

Haidar, Mansura, *Central Asian Relation from Early Times to Medieval Period*, Delhi, 2004.

Herlipy, D., *The History of Feudalism*, New York, 1970.

Hilton, R. (ed.), *Transition from Feudalism to Capitalism*, London, 1975.

Hopkino, K., *Conquerors and Slaves*, Cambridge, 1978.

Hussani, S.H.O., *The Economic History of India*, I, Calcutta, 1962.

Jayaswal, K.P., *Hindu Polity*, Bangalore, 1943.

Jha, D.N., *Ancient India: an Introductory Outline*, Delhi, 1977.

——, "Early Indian Feudalism: A Historiographical Critique, *IHC*, 40th Session, Andhra University, 1979.

——, "The Economic History of India upto 1200 A.D., Trends and Prospects," *JESHO*, Vol. XVIII, 1974.

—— (ed.), *Feudal Social Formation in Early India*, Delhi, 1987.

——, *Revenue System in Post-Mauryan and Gupta Times*, Calcutta, 1987.

——, *Studies in Early Indian Economic History*, Delhi.

Jha, K.N. and L.K. Jha, *Chanakya the Pioneer Economist*, Delhi, 1997.

Jones, B. (trans.), *Feudal Society and Its Culture*, Moscow, 1988.

Kane, P.V., *History of Dharmasastra*, Vol. II, Parts I-II, Poona, 1941.

Kansara, N.M., *Agriculture and Animals Husbandry in Vedas*, Delhi, 1995.

Kher, N.N., *Agrarian and Fiscal Economy* (324 B.C.-A.D. 320), Delhi, 1973.

Kosambi, D.D., *An Introduction to the Study of Indian History*, Bombay, 1956.

——, "Early Stages of the Caste System in Northern India", *IBRAS*, New Series, XXII, 1946.

——, "Indian Feudal Trade Character", *JESHO*, Vol. II, Leiden, 1960.

Kosambi, D.D., *The Culture and Civilization of Ancient India in Historical Outline*, London, 1965.

Krader, Lawrence, *The Asiatic Mode of Production*, Assen, 1975.

Kula, W., *An Economic Theory of the Feudal System*, London, 1976.

Ahiri, Latika (tr.), *Chinese Monks in India*, Delhi, 1996.

Liu, Xinru, *Ancient India and Ancient China*, Delhi, 2nd (ed.), 1989.

Mabbett, I.W., *Truth, Myth and Politics in India*, reprint, Delhi, 1971.

Maity, S.K., *The Economic Life of Northern India in Gupta Period* (300-500 A.D.), Calcutta, 1957.

Majumdar, R.C. (ed.), *History and Culture of Indian People*, Vol. II, *The Age of Imperial Unity*, Bombay, 1968.

——, Vol. III, *The Classical Age*, third edn., Bombay, 1970.

——, Vol. I, *The Vedic Age*, Bombay, 1988.

Marshall, J., *Taxila*, 3 Vols., reprint, Varanasi, 1975.

Marx, Karl and Friedrich Engels, *Pre-Capitalist Socio-Economic Formation*, Moscow, 1979.

Majumdar, B.P., *Socio-Economic History of Northern India*, Calcutta, 1960.

Mishra, B.B., *Policy in the Agni Purana*, Calcutta, 1965.

Monier-Williams, M., *Sanskrit-English Dictionary*, New Delhi, 1999.

Mukhia, H., "Was there Feudalism in Indian History", *JPS*, VIII, No. 3, 1981; and *IHCAPU*, 1979.

Nagarajan, *Foundation of Hindu Economic States*, Nagpur, 1997.

Nandi, R.N., "*Growth of Rural Economy in Early India*", Presidential Address, *IHC*, 45th Session, Annamalainagar, 1984.

——, *Social Roots of Religion in Ancient India*, Calcutta, 1986.

Nath, Pran, *Economic Condition of Ancient India*, London, 1929.

——, and Niyogi, P., *Contributions to the Economic History of Northern India*, Calcutta, 1967.

North, D.C., "The Rise and Fall of Manorial System—A Theoretical Model", *IES*, XXXI, 1971.

Pandey, G.C., *Foundation of Indian Culture*, Vol. II, Delhi, rep. 1995.

Parkash, B., "The Genesis and Character of Landed Aristocracy in Ancient India", *JESHO*, Vol. XIV, Leiden, 1971.

Parkash, Om, *Early Indian Land Grants and State Economy*, Allahabad, 1988.

Parsad, P.C., *Foreign Trade and Commerce in Ancient India*, Delhi, 1977.

Pirenee, H., *Economic and Social History of Medieval Europe*, London, 1961.

Price, B.B. (ed.), *Ancient Economic Thoughts*, Vol. I, New York, 1997.

Raghavan, D. (ed.), *Agriculture in Ancient India*, Delhi, 1964.

Rai, G.K., "Forced Labour in Ancient and Early Medieval India, *IHR*, II, 1976.

——, *Involuntary Labour in Ancient India*, Allahabad, 1981.

Randhawa, M.S., *A History of Agriculture in India*, Vol. I, Delhi, 1980.

Roy, S.N., *Historical and Cultural Studies in the Puranas*, Allahabad, 1978.

Sahu, B.P. (ed.), *Land System and Rural Society in Early India*, Delhi, 1997.

Schafer, E.H., *Great Ages of Man, Ancient China*, Netherland, Rep. 1995.

Saletore, R.N. *Early Indian Economy*, 2nd edn., Bombay, 1993.

Selin, Helaine (ed.), *Encyclopedia of the History of Science Technology*, Springular, 2008.

Sharma, Mahesh, *Western Himalayan Temples Records: State, Pilgrimage, Ritual and Legality in Chambā*, Leiden, 2009.

Sharma, R.R., "Slavery in Mauryan Period," *JESHO*, Vol. XXI, Leiden, 1978.

Sharma, R.S., *Aspects of Political Ideas and Institutions in Ancient India*, Delhi, 1968.

——, "Decay of Gangetic Towns in Gupta and Post-Gupta Times," *JIH*, 1973.

——, "How Feudal was Indian Feudalism," *JPS*, XII, No. 2, 1984.

——, *Indian Feudalism*, Delhi, 1981.

——, "Indian Feudalism Retouched," *IHR*, Nos. 1-2, 1974.

——, "Kusana Polity", *JBRS*, Vol. 43, Patria, 1967.

——, *Land Revenue in India, Historical Studies*, Delhi, 1971.

——, *Light on Early Indian Society and Economy*, Bombay, 1966.

——, *Material Culture and Social Formation in Ancient India*, New Delhi, 1963.

——, *Some Economic Aspects of the Caste System in Ancient India*, Patna, 1969.

——, *Perspectives in Social and Economic History of Early India*, 2nd Ed., Rep. Delhi, 2003.

——, *Sudras in Ancient India*, Delhi, 1980.

——, "The Kali Age: A Period of Social Crisis," in S.N. Mukherjee (ed.), *India, History and Thought*. Essays in Honour of A.L. Basham, Calcutta, 1982.

——, "The Origin of Feudalism in India", *JESHO*, Leiden, 1958.

——, *Urban Decay in India* (A.D. 300-1000), New Delhi, 1987.

Singh, S.D., "Iron in Ancient India", *JESHO*, Vol. 5, Leiden, 1962.

Sircar, D.C., *Indian Epigraphical Glossary*, Delhi, 1966.

——, Landlordism and Tenancy in Ancient and Medieval India as Revealed by Epigraphical Records, Lucknow, 1959.

Sircar, D.C. (ed.), *The Land System and Feudalism in Ancient India*, Calcutta, 1966.

——, *Early Indian Trade and Industry*, Calcutta, 1972.

Stein, Burton, *Essays on South India*, Delhi, 1975.

——, *Peasant State and Society in Medieval South India*, Delhi, 1980.

Steven, G.D., "The Economic History of the Ganges to the End of Gupta Time," *JESHO*, Vol. XIII, Leiden, 1970.

Swami, Subramanian, *India's China Perspective*, Delhi, 2001.

Taylor, J.G., "Underdevelopment and Modes of Production, a Reply to Nicos Mouzelis", *JPS*, Vol. 8, London, 1981.

Thakur, Upendra, "A Study in Barter Exchange in Ancient India", *JESHO*, Vol. XV, Leiden, 1972.

Thakur, V.K., *Historiography of Indian Feudalism Trends a Model of Early Medieval India*, Patna, 1989.

Thakur, V.K., *Urbanisation in Ancient India*, Delhi, 1981.

——, *Peasant in India History*, Patna, 1996.

Thapar, Romila (ed.), *Recent Perspective of Early Indian History*, 2nd edn. Bombay, 1988.

White Law, Ian, *A Measure of all things: The Story of Man and Measurement*, London, 2007.

Wolff, B.C., *A History of Civilization*, Vol. 1, New Jersey, 1967.

Yadava, B.N.S., *Society and Culture in Northern India in the Twelfth Century A.D.*, Allahabad, 1973.

——, "The Problems of the Emergence of the Feudal Relation in Early India", Presidential Address, IHC, 41st Session Bombay, 1980.

Yadava, Seema, *The Myth of Indian Feudalism*, Delhi, 2005.

Journals

Journal of American Oriental Society.

Journal of the Andhra Historical Research Society.

Journal of Asiatic Society of Mumbai.

Journal of the School of Oriental and African Studies, London,

Journal of Bihar and Orissa Research Society, Patna.

Journal of Bihar Research Society, Patna.

Journal of the Economic and Social History of the Orient, Leiden.

Journal of the Economic History, Wilmington.

Indian Economic and Social History Review, Delhi.

The Indian Historical Review, Delhi.

Indian Historical Quarterly, Calcutta.

Journal of Indian History.

Journal of the Numismatic Society of India, Varanasi.

Journal of the Oriental Research, Poona.

Journal of Oriental Institute, Vadodara.

Journal of the UP Historical Society, Lucknow.

Journal of Peasant Study, London.

Journal of Royal Asiatic Society of Great Britain in Ireland.

Journal of Royal Central Asian Society.

Journal of the World History (UNESCO).

Proceeding of Indian History Congress.

Index